New Swan Shakespeare ADVANCED SERIES

GENERAL EDITOR Bernard Lott M.A., Ph.D.

Othello

WILLIAM SHAKESPEARE

Othello

Edited by Gāmini Salgādo B.A., Ph.D.

Longman

Longman Group Limited
London
Associated companies, branches and representatives throughout the world

First published 1976
New impression 1978

ISBN 0 582 52748 1

Filmset by Keyspools Ltd, Golborne, Lancs.
Printed in Hong Kong by Yu Luen Offset Printing Factory Ltd.

Contents

Acknowledgements

The editor acknowledges the invaluable help he has received in the preparation of this edition from Dr Bernard Lott, the General Editor of this series, and Mr Dickie Swan of Longman Group Ltd. They have saved him from many blunders; any that remain are of course his own. He would also like to thank Anna Johnston who typed the manuscript and helped with the proof reading.

WE ARE grateful to the following for permission to reproduce copyright material:

Associated Book Publishers Ltd. for an extract from *The Wheel of Fire* by G. Wilson Knight. Published by Methuen & Co. Ltd; Chatto and Windus Ltd. and New York University Press for an extract from *The Common Pursuit* by F. R. Leavis. Reprinted by permission of New York University Press © 1952 by F. R. Leavis; Constable Publishers and Oxford University Press Inc. for an extract from *The Characters of Love* by John Bayley; Faber and Faber Ltd. for an extract from *The Unfinished Hero* by Ronald Bryden. Reprinted by permission of Faber and Faber Ltd; Longman Group Ltd. for an extract from *Angel With Horns* by A. P. Rossiter; Macmillan Publishers Ltd. and St. Martin's Press Inc. for an extract from *Shakespearean Tragedy* by A. C. Bradley.

WE ARE also grateful to the Harvard Theatre Collection for permission to reproduce copyright photographs on pages lviii and lix (photographs by Angus McBean).

Foreword

THE AIM of this edition of *Othello* is to ensure that the reader fully understands and appreciates the play. It explains the text in detail. Points of difficulty often taken for granted or touched on inconclusively are here treated at length. And besides dealing with such matters as archaic language and allusions to bygone custom, the notes explain briefly certain rare words still current in English which happen to occur in the play (e.g. *sequent, wheeling*). Help is also given with complicated syntactical constructions and with patterns of imagery which may not be obvious at first sight. The content of the play, its historical, social and philosophical bases, and the conventions implied in the ways the characters react to one another may be strange to many readers and are therefore dealt with in full. Although the subjects treated are sometimes difficult, the explanations are simple in language, and avoid the long expositions to be found in some editions. Again, much space in other editions is sometimes given to alternative readings of the text and to various conjectural explanations of difficult passages. Almost all speculation of this kind is omitted here. Where the meaning of the text is doubtful, the editor has chosen the interpretation which seems to fit the context most satisfactorily, and has avoided giving many alternative suggestions. If there is a possible alternative which genuinely serves to illuminate the text, this is added, but no more than two possible explanations are ever given. Specific reference is made here and there to variant readings of the original text (the Folios, the Quartos), but only where a more helpful explanation of the passage will result than if no cross references were made.

A certain amount of background knowledge is essential to a full under-standing of the play. Some passages can be understood only in the light of aspects of the 'world view' of Shakespeare's day, or of some piece of information about the region of the world and the period of history in which the action of the play supposedly takes place. A sufficient amount of information is given to clarify the meaning of the passage in question, although no attempt is made to give a far-reaching account of the whole subject.

At the end of the book there is an index which glosses and gives the location in the text of all the difficult or unusual words in the play. By reference to the location in the text the student will find a note which will in most instances expand the brief equivalent given in the index. The index will also help him in tracking down particular passages in the play, since if he remembers a key word likely to be indexed he can look it up and find a line reference to the text of the play. In this way the glossarial index is also an index to the notes.

Full enjoyment of the play comes with full understanding of what it means. All the help offered, in the form of notes, glosses, and the introduction, has only this end in view. No attempt has been made to give an elaborate critical account of the play, but sources of useful criticism are indicated in the bibliography. A study of these sources however can wait until the play is thoroughly known and appreciated for its own sake.

Part One of the Introduction which follows is a general essay on *Othello*. Part Two contains a series of articles which give more detailed information on certain subjects, as listed on page v. These articles are not essential to an understanding of the play, but include matter which the student of the play may like to have in order to widen his knowledge. The section contains also some extracts from the great critics of *Othello* and some extracts from accounts of performances of *Othello*.

Introduction

PART ONE

Othello and ourselves

Of all Shakespeare's tragedies, the appeal of *Othello* seems to be the simplest and most direct. The story is powerful and straightforward, the characters clearly defined and strongly contrasted, and the dramatic development rapid and full of excitement. Above all, the language of the play moves us by its sheer passion, grandeur and amplitude. To enter the world of *Othello*, we need less in the way of background knowledge than is the case with any of the other major tragedies. In some ways this is of course a great advantage, but it can be an obstacle too; there is a danger that because we can respond to the play so immediately and intimately, we shall assume that we need not pay patient attention to it in order fully to understand it. An even greater danger is that we shall easily and lazily assume that our response to *Othello* is necessarily that of Shakespeare's original audience.

The simplicity of *Othello* is misleading. This is not to say that it is not really there, but rather that it is a simplicity that lies on the surface. Story, character and theme all appear to lend themselves to easy summary as they do not in, for instance, *Hamlet* or *Antony and Cleopatra*. The story tells us how a noble black general secretly married a beautiful and well-born white girl and how their marriage was destroyed through the wicked intrigues of the general's standard bearer who poisoned Othello's mind with doubts about his new bride's faithfulness and eventually drove the Moor to murder her and kill himself. The principal characters are Othello himself, the very type of the gallant soldier, valiant, virtuous and totally without guile, his bride Desdemona, beautiful and faithful unto death, the deceitful Iago whom all Venice is wrong about, his good-natured but uncomprehending wife Emilia, the broken-hearted father Brabantio, and the loyal lieutenant Cassio. And the theme seems to be something like tragic waste or, in Othello's own words, 'the pity of it'.

But these simplicities, though they are genuine enough as far as they go, do not really take us to the heart of the drama. They tend to obscure many of the most interesting questions about character, theme and situation. Why, for instance, if Othello is so completely straightforward and guileless, does he make a secret marriage with Desdemona, instead of openly asking for her hand? How far is Othello's nobility a self-conscious and acquired quality, and how far does he believe his own protestation about being 'rude' in his speech?

How does such a manifestly devious character as Iago manage to deceive practically everyone he meets, including his own wife? Why does Othello abandon his faith in Desdemona with such alacrity? These and many other questions begin to arise in our minds when we reflect on the gap between a bald summary of the play and its tremendous impact on our imagination and feelings.

The truth is that *Othello* is not a simple play, though, like all Shakespeare's plays, part of its appeal lies at a very simple level. Its simplicity seems to be more closely related to its total effect than is the case with other Shakespearian tragedies but, as I have suggested, this impression is deceptive. From one point of view, *Othello* is narrower in scope than the other tragedies; it does not have the wide political, philosophical and religious implications of *King Lear*, *Macbeth* or *Hamlet*. Its emphasis is more personal and psychological, though not exclusively so. But whatever the play may lack in range of reference it more than makes up for in depth, power and subtlety.

Othello is a tragedy of faith enkindled, destroyed and renewed; of radical misunderstanding and incomprehension between father and daughter, husband and wife, general and lieutenant, and of a love so intense and sublime that it could only breathe the air of absolute trust and certainty, so pure that when it is tainted by mistrust it degenerates into the most hideous and deforming hatred, as 'lilies that fester smell far worse than weeds' (Shakespeare, Sonnet 99). It is a play about a heroic larger-than-life individual who comes from across the sea with something of the myth and mystery of the sea still clinging to him, an individual who seems to inhabit, in his imagination and ours, a freer and ampler world than that of the sober, matter-of-fact commercial republic of Venice to which he has pledged his loyalty and his soldierly skill. The blackness of his skin marks him off as an outsider 'an extravagant and wheeling stranger of here and everywhere' (I.i.133), though the republic treats him with courtesy and respect and he is a welcome visitor in the homes of the Venetian magnificos. But beneath the outward show of honour this stranger stirs deeper feelings of doubt and resentment and these are brought to the surface when he marries the daughter of one of the most important men in Venetian society.

These latent feelings are deliberately aroused and heightened by the very man to whom Othello, the outsider in Venetian society, turns for reassurance and guidance. Iago is in some ways the typical insider, trusted by everyone in Venice, from well-meaning dupes like Roderigo to the most eminent senators in the Signiory. Who better to help the noble Othello, unused to the ways of this sophisticated city-state and its society, to find his way about than honest Iago? Ironically, Iago is far more of an alien than Othello himself, for while Othello is merely a stranger in Venice, Iago has cut himself off from the entire human world. To him people are no more and no less than puppets or machines, to be pushed and pulled about to produce this or that result. Love, nobility, honour, self-sacrifice – to Iago these are only catch-words, traps to catch the gullible and the unwary. To trap a Roderigo may be profitable, and to trap a Cassio profitable as well as agreeable. But the real prize is Othello himself and Desdemona, for their very existence in mutual love and trust is a living refutation of the values Iago lives by – expediency, deviousness and ruthless self-assertion.

In contrast to these qualities, the love of Othello and Desdemona stands as the central positive value of the play, triumphant even in its destruction. Othello's blackness is a vivid and constant reminder of the absoluteness and integrity of Desdemona's commitment. It is a commitment totally divorced from everything in her background and upbringing, and one in which the ordinary commonsense prudence and calculation represented by Emilia plays not the slightest part. That is to say, her love and devotion to Othello spring not out of Desdemona's 'social' self but out of her inner nature (if we can sidestep for the moment the difficult question of the relationship between these two). And as long as Othello accepts this absolute commitment with an equally wholehearted commitment of his own, their relationship cannot be sundered or even shaken, for it has that inner fortitude in it which 'looks on tempests and is never shaken' (Sonnet 116). As long as Othello can respond to Desdemona's impassioned words 'I saw Othello's visage in his mind' (I.iii.248) with his own fervent realization that 'she had eyes, and chose me' (III.iii.189), nothing, not even death, can destroy their absolute content.

But because calculation and prudential considerations have nothing to do with the nature and quality of their love, the one thing that love cannot survive, at least where Othello is concerned, is doubt and suspicion based on calculation and prudence. Calculation, prudence, reasonableness – these are of course necessary qualities in our day-to-day transactions, but they are based on the average and the general, not the individual and the particular. What we call common sense is usually the sum total of our ideas about how people *generally* behave in this or that situation, and Iago is a past master in the art of convincing everyone that he has ample stocks of this kind of 'gained knowledge' (I.iii.369). He tells Roderigo confidently of the inevitable outcome of the marriage between Othello and Desdemona by generalizing about the behaviour of *any* well-brought up young white girl after a few weeks of marriage with *any* hot-blooded but ageing black man. And he is quick to point out to Othello that he, Iago, knows a lot more about Venetian women and their ways than Othello does. And the heart of the tragedy is that Othello renounces the deep and intuitive truth he knows about the *individual* who is Desdemona in favour of Iago's paltry and yet deadly generalizations about the *average* Venetian woman, and soon begins himself to talk about Desdemona as one of 'these delicate creatures' (III.iii.268) and of being cuckolded as the general 'plague of great ones' (III.iii.272). For the 'knowledge' that Othello and Desdemona have about each other is not the kind of knowledge Iago offers, which is the knowledge that arrives at a reasonable conclusion by the gradual accumulation of relevant facts. This is the way in which scientific inquiry is conducted, and in its own sphere it can yield valuable results. But it is not the way human beings usually acquire knowledge about each other, and it certainly does not apply to a relationship such as that of Othello and Desdemona, in which, as the poetry convinces us, loyalty and love are instinctive and instantaneous. Before we condemn this view as immature and romantic, we would do well to reflect that Desdemona and Othello are indeed *right* about each other, and Iago the 'realist' completely and disastrously wrong. It is that realization which lights up the tragedy at the very end, when Othello recovers his sense of a world as radiant as 'one entire and perfect chrysolite' (V.ii.142) in his knowledge that Desdemona was what he had believed her to be. That knowledge, of course, comes too late for anything but a heroic death. Othello's tragedy is not that he did not adopt the right means to find the answer to an agonizing question, but that he asked the question in the first place.

Elizabethans and Moors

Othello was first performed in 1604, in the first year of James I's reign. At this time there would have been few citizens of Shakespeare's London who would have had first-hand acquaintance with 'Moors', but that did not prevent Shakespeare's audience having a good many preconceptions and prejudices about them. These are of more than documentary interest, because it is probable that Shakespeare so constructed the drama that it first accepted and then subverted many of the ordinary assumptions about black men current in his day.

In one sense it is dangerous to talk of the assumptions and prejudices of a bygone age. In the first place, the 'telescoping' effect of time tends to make us think that a past society was more homogeneous than our own instead of consisting, as ours does, of myriads of individuals with different prejudices held with differing intensity. Secondly, it is always difficult to be confident about how people *felt*, as opposed to what they believed, or said they believed. The evidence, documentary and pictorial, is never quite conclusive, and needs to be interpreted. And finally, as the problem of marriage between black and white was not a particularly pressing one in 17th century society, there is not a great deal of explicit comment on it at this period, one way or the other.

Nevertheless there is enough for us to be able to go beyond the region of random guesswork, and in any case the play *Othello* compels us to make some sort of judgment about contemporary racial attitudes. The first point that needs making is that to Shakespeare's original audience a 'Moor' meant a black man, a negro, not a bronzed or tawny semitic type. The word 'Moor' was not associated with any specific country but certainly carried the twin associations of blackness and heathen idolatry. Again, while, as I have said, there was not much first-hand experience of Moors, they were certainly regarded as inferior beings, much as Englishmen tended to regard all foreigners as inferior. The information which travellers brought from voyages of discovery did not greatly alter the racial stereotype of the black man, except that it was used in the contemporary debate about whether the 'savages' in the newly discovered countries were nearer to unfallen man than civilized Europeans. The affirmative line of argument tended to produce the image of a 'noble savage' (Red Indian or Negro) which ran counter to the popular idea of the black man as barbarous and barely human. But the latter stereotype was probably the more widespread.

The association between the colour black and evil and death is pre-Christian and almost universal. Medieval Christianity always painted the devil black and many paintings and sculptures show at least one of the tormentors of Christ as a black man, though from the fourteenth century onwards one of the three kings who visited Christ's birthplace is also portrayed as a black man. It is likely that in medieval drama the faces of evil persons were blackened. Conversely white was associated with virtue, and innocence. This symbolism was very much alive in Shakespeare's day.

'Moors' were among the participants in several Lord Mayors' shows in London during the sixteenth and early seventeenth centuries. In English drama the first important representation of a Moor is in the character of Muley Hamet in Peele's *The Battle of Alcazar* (1589). Muley Hamet was a historical figure with whom Elizabeth I had a treaty, but the play makes the conventional association between him and the devils of hell. In another play, *Lust's Dominion* (1600), we have a black man called Eleazar who is explicitly associated with sexual excess. And finally, in Shakespeare's own early play *Titus Andronicus* (1592), we have the fearsome figure of Aaron the Moor, a very monster of cruelty and lust.

Even from this bare outline we can see that ignorance and unfamiliarity as usual created a stereotype of the black man. According to Reginald Scot, a contemporary whom Shakespeare read, the Devil's favourite human form was that of a Negro or Moor. To the Elizabethan, the Moor or Negro was black, ugly, cruel, evil, pagan, sexually rampant and barely human. It is necessary to set forth this catalogue in its barest form so that we can fully appreciate what a remarkable innovation Othello would have represented to Shakespeare's first audience. To begin with, Iago and Roderigo, and later Brabantio express an attitude to Othello which embodies nearly all the features that have just been noted. Their language, especially that of the first two, would bring before the audience's mind the figure of a black man which would exactly coincide with their stereotype – ugly, cruel and bestial in his appetite. Shakespeare allows this image to grow and assume clarity and depth, and it is no accident that Iago is one of the most eloquent delineators of this horrible vision; Iago, the 'realist', the man who isn't taken in by anything or anyone, is made the custodian of the popular stereotype of the black man. The effect is to intensify the audience's shocked surprise when Othello himself eventually makes his first splendid entrance with the marvellously self-assured terseness which contrasts with Iago's empty volubility: "Tis better as it is' (I.ii.6). For Shakespeare has changed everything about the stereotyped black man except his blackness. He is not a pagan but a Christian, and a Christian leader at that, defending the faith in the remote island of Cyprus, which indeed fell into Turkish hands during the period in which the action of the play is set. He is not a barbarian (though the world of magic and witchcraft with which he is associated in the mind of Brabantio and others is never far away) but a truly civilized and noble figure. And there is a suggestion that his sexual appetite, far from being excessive is, if anything, in decline. Shakespeare exploits to the full the many paradoxes which the symbolism of black and white would have suggested to his audience. The chief of these, from which the others derive, is that of a 'black' man whose soul is truly 'fair'. (We must accept the fact that the notion 'black is beautiful' had no currency whatever in the England of Shakespeare's day. Even if the idea had occurred to Shakespeare, he could hardly have exploited it as he exploited the dramatic ironies generated by the 'black skin – white soul' paradox.) Closely related to this is the general idea of the contrast between 'outside' and 'inside', surface appearance and inner reality. And, since in Shakespeare's day the soul, the invisible inner essence, was considered the true reality while the body was transient and insubstantial, we can see that the play asks us to affirm the nobility of Othello's nature as the 'essential vesture of creation' (II.i.63), the true reality. Given the historical situation of the audience and its prejudices, it would be too much to expect Shakespeare to offer us an Othello who is beautiful *because* he is black; but he achieves the equally difficult task of working on the audience's own preconceptions to extort from it the realization that Othello the Moor is in every way exalted enough for his tragic role. (One interpretation of Aristotle's theory of tragedy required that the tragic hero should be noble.) We may object that, towards the end of the play, Shakespeare himself seems to surrender to the popular contemporary idea of the black man as a savage and vengeful beast when he shows us an Othello demented with jealous rage murdering his innocent wife. But our objections will disappear as we realize, first, that Othello is brought to this pass against everything in his own nature by the poisonous malice of a super-subtle white villain, and secondly that, in his final exit, as at his first entrance, Othello assumes the nobility and heroic stature with which Shakespeare has invested him.

Venice and Cyprus

The action of *Othello* illustrates a pattern which is common to many of Shakespeare's plays, that of movement from a comparatively sheltered place to a wilder one, ending with the beginning of the journey back. *Othello* begins in Venice, and though it soon moves out to Cyprus and never returns, the closing moments of the play look back from the tragic chaos to the orderly processes of the city state, and the powerful impact of the opening scenes remains with us throughout. Venice is very far from being a mere background to the action of the play; rather, its presence is felt almost like that of another character. To the Englishman of the seventeenth century, Italy generally and Venice in particular had many associations, favourable and unfavourable. It was a republic, with a reputation for religious and political tolerance. It was also dazzlingly successful as a commercial centre. Venetians, like all Italians, were held to be extremely cunning, and the women were believed to be sensual and sophisticated. At the time during which the events of the play are supposed to take place (in 1571, some thirty-five years before the first performance), Venice was involved in a struggle with the Turks, and was in some sense regarded as the champion of Christendom against the barbarian infidel. All these associations are developed by Shakespeare in the course of the action. Within minutes of the play's opening in the murky darkness, we hear Brabantio's assertion

> This is Venice;
> My house is not a grange

(I.i.102)

with its implication that the kind of lawlessness Iago is talking about cannot take place within the boundaries of the civilized and well-ordered republic. This sense of Venice as a society where order, reason and justice are operative is enhanced when we see the great scene in which Othello and Brabantio each state their case before the assembled council. At this point the wider national and political significance of Venice meshes in with Othello's personal situation. This meeting of public and private worlds is embodied in the action by the two separate search parties which converge on Othello's lodging, one bent on state affairs, the other seeking redress for a private grievance. The news of the Turkish threat to Cyprus puts us in mind of Venetian responsibility for safeguarding the Christian heritage. But we cannot wholly forget the commercial aspect of this responsibility, for we are reminded of it by the presence of Othello, the alien who is employed by his 'very noble and approved good masters' (i.iii.78) to defend the republic and its possessions. For all its dignity and courtesy, the relationship between Othello and the signiory is that of employee and employed; the bond that links them is wages. This scene shows us, then, an ordered state committed to reason and justice, but it also contains hints that the reason and the justice are too summary and short-sighted, the tolerance not based on full understanding of the issues and passions involved. There is something off-hand about the Duke's appeal to Brabantio to 'take up this mangled matter at the best' (i.iii.172) and something more than a little facile about the series of platitudes with which he tries to console the grieving father.

But Venice contains not only sober and law-abiding magnates; Iago the wily schemer and Roderigo the foolish sensualist are also its representative inhabitants, as is Emilia, who typifies commercial calculation applied to private life as well as a somewhat permissive sexual morality. Above all, Venice contains Desdemona. Just as Shakespeare takes the stereotype of the black man and creates Othello by playing on that stereotype, so he creates in Desdemona a character who upsets the Elizabethan image of a typical Venetian woman by departing from conventional expectation while seeming to satisfy it. Desdemona is cultivated, warm-blooded and capable of mild flirtation, as is shown by the scene with Cassio when she first arrives in Cyprus. There is just enough in her behaviour, superficially considered, to enable Iago to convince a fool like Roderigo (and later, the tragic fool that Othello becomes) that she is a typical Venetian woman. But in one quite crucial respect Desdemona is totally unlike the stereotype – she is utterly constant in her love for her husband. Thus, while in certain respects she is a product of Venetian society, ultimately she transcends her place of origin, as Othello transcends his.

The physical movement of the principal characters from Venice to Cyprus corresponds to a psychological movement from the calm and security of rational order, where individual energy is shaped and supported by social forms, to the chaos of emotional turbulence, of individuals thrown on their own inner resources. The storm which comes as a prelude to the arrival of Desdemona and Othello in Cyprus is a compact metaphor for this passage from security to disorder. The sea itself, as it appears in the language of the play, embodies those ideas of richness and strangeness, power and danger, fruitfulness and bereavement which typify the new world which the characters have come into. And it is neither accidental nor unimportant that we should associate Othello with the sea, even though he is a soldier. The sea has something of the quality of Othello's world, with its 'antres vast and deserts idle' (i.iii.140).

At the time *Othello* was written, Cyprus had been in Turkish hands for more than thirty years. But the action of the play takes place at just the time (1570–1) when the Turks were beginning to attack the island, which had then belonged to Venice for a century. It was this Turkish invasion of Cyprus which led to the famous sea battle of Lepanto in the following year, when the united Christian states of Europe under Don John of Austria inflicted a heavy defeat on the Turkish fleet. Thirty years is a long time for an audience to remember a single victory, but Lepanto was a memorable event for all Europe, and an English audience may have been freshly reminded of it because a poem on the subject written by the new king, James I, had been published not long before *Othello* was performed. In any case, Shakespeare certainly shows us Cyprus as a precarious outpost of the Christian world, hemmed by the perilous seas and constantly under threat of attack from 'the general enemy Ottoman' (I.iii.50). In such a place the security and rationality of Venice are no longer at hand, or if they are, they are embodied in one man, Othello. The tension we feel in the early Cyprus scenes is not merely that of a place which has only just been freed from the threat of an attack, but also that of Venetian Christians who feel themselves cut off from their native community. And the nocturnal brawl, in which normal social relationships are all upset, is an external representation of the chaos and destruction whose inner workings we see in the torment which Othello undergoes and the destruction he wreaks.

Venice, Cyprus and the sea are therefore more than geographical features of the play; they are part of its dramatic symbolism, and an understanding of what they meant in Shakespeare's day will give us a livelier sense of the relationship between character, action and setting in the tragedy.

The passage of time in the play

A picture in perspective to be seen from a certain angle (HOB)

One hundred and twenty-five years ago, a brilliant scholar named Wilson, writing in *Blackwood's Magazine* (November 1849, April and May 1850) under the pseudonym of 'Christopher North' pointed out a number of discrepancies in Shakespeare's handling of time in *Othello*. Since then many scholars and critics, such as Bradley, Granville Barker and Dover Wilson have considered this problem in great detail. There is no need to go into all the minute particulars involved, but a brief outline of the so-called 'double time' in *Othello* may help us to understand better Shakespeare's marvellous dramatic artistry.

If we ask ourselves the question 'How much time is supposed to pass between the beginning of *Othello* and the end?' we seem to get two different and mutually exclusive answers, each of which seems, on the evidence of the play itself, to be the only possible answer. The play opens in Venice at night-time and the events of the first act, up to the departure of Othello for Cyprus, seem to flow without interruption and to take almost the same amount of time to present on the stage as they would in real life. So, on the very day that Othello has secretly married Desdemona, he is summoned before the council of state and instructed to set sail for Cyprus immediately.

We now have a time during which the principal characters travel by sea to Cyprus. They arrive on the island on the same day but in three separate ships, Othello in one, Cassio in another, and Desdemona, with Iago and Emilia, in a third. From their landing till the death of Desdemona and Othello, the time which elapses is not much more than thirty-three hours, and this period too seems to flow without a break. The arrival takes place on Saturday afternoon (the herald refers to 'this present hour of five' in II.ii.9) and Cassio is dismissed later that evening. The scene lasts till Sunday morning, which is the time when Cassio meets Desdemona to ask her to plead his case. The third act opens with two short scenes, one between the musician, the clown, Cassio, Emilia and Iago, and the other between Othello and Iago, which make it quite clear that it is still Sunday morning. The great temptation scene obviously comes without a break in time because Othello, on his way back from the fortifications he had visited in the previous scene, comes upon Desdemona and Cassio. There may just possibly be a break between scenes iii and iv of Act Three, but it is very unlikely, as Othello's line 'O hardness to dissemble!' (III.iv.30) suggests that this is the first time he has to dissemble and therefore the first time he has seen Desdemona since Iago made his venomous insinuations in the earlier scene.

Again, there is the faint possibility that some time may have passed between the end of Act Three and the beginning of Act Four, but there is a strong feeling that the action is continuous, as well as the fact that Bianca speaks of the handkerchief Cassio gave her 'even now' (IV.i.146) which seems to suggest that not much time has passed since he gave her the handkerchief in the previous scene. From the beginning of Act Four events move swiftly and uninterruptedly. The party from Venice are invited to supper in the first scene, the meal ends at the beginning of the third scene, and later the same evening Iago kills Roderigo after the latter has attacked Cassio, and Othello kills Desdemona and then himself.

Thus the events of the play move rapidly and, except for the sea journey, without interruption. This sense of swiftly flowing time heightens the suspense and excitement of the drama, but it is also essential for the plot, because Iago's diabolical scheme can only succeed if neither Othello nor anyone else has the time and the opportunity to expose him. As it is, he only just manages to keep Othello and Cassio apart at crucial moments. But if the events on the island of Cyprus take place within some thirty odd hours, how can Cassio possibly have committed adultery with Desdemona, in Cyprus or anywhere else? There clearly was no opportunity in Venice, nor could adultery have taken place during the voyage, as Desdemona and Cassio travelled separately. And all Cassio's (and Desdemona's) time in Cyprus can be accounted for.

Shakespeare has to make Iago's story possible and plausible to Othello and to ourselves as we watch it unfolding. He does this by scattering throughout the play suggestions of another, longer period of time during which Desdemona and Cassio may at least have had the opportunity of committing adultery. There are many such suggestions throughout the play, and their effect is to give us the illusion that Othello and Desdemona had been married for a fairly long time (as indeed the Moor in Shakespeare's original source-story was). Examples of this 'long time' are the reference to Roderigo having almost spent all his money, Iago's reference to Cassio talking in his sleep (which could not have taken place in Cyprus, since Cassio only spent one night there, during which he hardly slept at all), Bianca's talk of not seeing Cassio for a week and so on.

When we have leisure to look into all the details of the plot, we notice this discrepancy in the time-scheme of the play, but in the theatre we are completely convinced both of the swift passage of time and of the fact that Othello has been married to Desdemona for some time. It has been suggested that Shakespeare wrote the second part of the play first and the rest some time later, and did not bother to straighten out the discrepancies in time. This may be so, but the important point to realize is that both time-schemes are necessary for the play and that Shakespeare has made what would be an obvious contradiction and therefore an 'impossibility' in real life triumphantly successful in the theatre.

The source of the play

Shakespeare found the story of *Othello* in a collection of Italian stories called the *Hecatommithi* by Giraldi Cinthio, an aristocrat and philosophy professor of Ferrara. This book was published in Venice in 1566 and translated into French by Gabriel Chappuys in 1584. Shakespeare could have known the work either in the original Italian or in the French translation, but no English version is known before 1753.

Cinthio's collection is divided into ten 'decades' or groups of ten tales. Each group deals with a single topic, and the story on which *Othello* is based comes from the third decade, which is devoted to 'The Unfaithfulness of Husbands and Wives'.

While the plots of Shakespeare's play and Cinthio's story are recognizably similar, there are many important differences in character, atmosphere, emphasis and tempo. Some of these differences are an inevitable result of converting a narrative into the more compressed and direct medium of drama, but others show Shakespeare enriching his theme by expanding hints in Cinthio and giving a greater depth to Cinthio's rather wooden and conventional characters. Where Cinthio gives us one somewhat sordid world of sexual intrigue and jealousy to which both Iago *and* Othello belong, Shakespeare put them in different worlds and made a tragedy out of their collision.

The simplest and most obvious of Shakespeare's additions concerns the matter of names. In Cinthio, only Desdemona, or Disdemona as he calls her (the name is derived from two Greek words together meaning 'ill-fated soul') is given a name. All the other characters are identified by their role (e.g. 'the captain') or their relationship (e.g. 'the ensign's wife'). Othello is simply 'the Moor'. Obviously in a play the characters would need to have proper names.

Brabantio does not appear in the original tale, except in the phrase 'the parents of the lady' and the character of Roderigo is entirely Shakespeare's creation. Apart from his part in the plot, Roderigo serves several important purposes, such as enabling Iago to reveal his true nature to him and through him to us, and heightening the poignancy of the situation as we become aware that only Roderigo knows what Iago is really like.

The character of Iago is given immense depth and complexity in Shakespeare's play. In Cinthio, he is simply a handsome villain who is in love with Disdemona, and, finding that his love is not returned, resolves to destroy her. He does not engineer the captain's (Cassio's) dismissal, which happens quite independently. Furthermore, Othello tells him of Disdemona's pleas on Cassio's behalf. All this makes the Iago-character a straightforward, rather melodramatic villain, very different from the fascinating and mysterious figure we find in Shakespeare.

Emilia's character and role undergo a similar transformation, though not such an extensive one. In Cinthio, she knows about her husband's plot but is afraid to speak out. In Shakespeare, her shocked horror at finding out what her husband is really like is not only deeply moving, it also suggests that if Iago's own wife was unaware of his villainy, Othello cannot be considered too credulous for being taken in by him.

As can be expected in a play, the action moves to its climax much more rapidly than in the original story. The crucial incident of the handkerchief is handled by Shakespeare with far greater deftness and subtlety (in Cinthio, Iago steals the handkerchief himself, while Disdemona is holding his three-year-old daughter). But as far as the plot is concerned, Shakespeare's most striking improvement on Cinthio is in the death scene. In the Italian tale, Othello and Iago murder Disdemona by beating her with a sand-filled stocking and then pulling the roof down on her bed. This is not only crude – and impracticable in a theatre – but, as Cinthio handles it, puts a good deal of emphasis on Othello's desire not to get caught for the murder. In altering the manner of Desdemona's death, Shakespeare has at the same time transformed the scene from melodrama into high tragedy.

If we come to Shakespeare's play from reading Cinthio's tale, we soon realize that we are in a different world. Shakespeare creates the world of *Othello* principally by the language he uses. We may briefly note three areas in which Shakespeare developed the linguistic richness of the play. The first is in the account of Othello's courtship, which takes up a bare sentence in Cinthio, the second is in the storm scene, and the imagery associated with it, which does not occur in Cinthio at all, and the last is in the strand of imagery connected with magic and witchcraft which finds its visual focus in the fatal handkerchief. Together they go a long way to create the distinctive atmosphere of Shakespeare's *Othello*, an atmsophere wholly absent from the original source.

The theatre of Shakespeare's day

Othello was written for a theatre very different from most modern theatres, both in its physical appearance and in its conventions of acting and stage presentation. While we can appreciate the power and pathos of the tragedy without knowing anything about Shakespeare's theatre, some knowledge of that theatre will add vividness and sharpness of detail to our appreciation and enjoyment.

Shakespeare wrote many of his plays for the Globe theatre in which the company to which he belonged, the Lord Chamberlain's Men (later the King's Men) regularly acted. We do not have much direct knowledge of the Globe itself, but there is a famous drawing of the Swan, a public playhouse like the Globe, and there is also a contract for the building of yet another theatre, the Fortune, dated four years before *Othello* was first performed. This drawing and the contract, together with the stage directions found in printed play-texts of the time, provide the only solid evidence we have of what the theatre of Shakespeare's day looked like. It is not therefore surprising that imaginative guesswork has had a share in building up our current ideas. There is a good deal of agreement on the general shape and structure of the Shakespearian playhouse, though scholars naturally differ in matters of detail. We need not assume that every theatre was identical in Shakespeare's day any more than in ours (though there is good reason to believe that all were of the same basic design), nor is it an area in which absolute certainty is possible or likely. In the remainder of this section I shall state briefly what is generally agreed about the Shakespearian theatre together with a few suggestions about how that theatre and its conventions may have affected *Othello*.

Shakespeare was twelve years old when the first building expressly designed as a public theatre (called, simply, the Theatre) was put up in London. Before that, dramatic entertainments had been presented in the halls of great houses, in the courtyards or (more probably) public rooms of inns, at court, and, earlier, in the open air on makeshift platforms or 'scaffolds'. All these helped to shape the design of the purpose-built theatres, of which the Globe was one of the most celebrated. Viewed from outside, the theatre building was circular or octagonal, as we can see from many panoramic views of sixteenth and seventeenth century London. The Swan drawing also shows us that the seating is in three tiers which surround a projecting stage. At the back of this stage are two doors, through which the actors made their entrances and exits, and above these is an upper gallery which was also regularly used as an acting area. Part of the stage was covered by a projecting roof supported by pillars. This roof was sometimes painted to represent the sky and various celestial bodies, and was called 'the heavens'. Above 'the heavens' was a room with a thatched roof, called the 'hut', where a trumpeter played to signal the start of a performance and also, where necessary, to give emphasis to the action (for instance, to give Iago the cue for his line, 'The Moor! I know his trumpet' just before Othello lands in Cyprus). Though the Swan drawing does not show one, some theatres probably had an 'inner stage' just below the balcony which could be used for scenes separated in some way from the main action, or those which revealed some kind of tableau or set-piece. From the Fortune contract, we learn that the inside dimension of the auditorium was 55 feet square, and that the stage projected halfway into it and was 43 feet wide, leaving a narrow space on either side where the 'groundlings' could stand. There was also standing room in the 'pit' directly in front of the stage.

Performances were given in daylight, in a theatre most of which was open to the sky. There was no artificial lighting used on stage, except for special effects (torches to indicate night-time, for instance). This, together with the 'thrust' of the stage and the fact that the audience surrounded it on three sides (with no one more than about 25 yards from the back of the stage) created a feeling of intimacy which we can hardly experience today unless we see a so-called 'theatre-in-the-round' performance.

There was no painted perspective scenery in this theatre, but we should not imagine that it was a drab and barn-like place. In the first place, the permanent structure, the pillars, 'the heavens' and the balcony were richly ornamented. For a tragedy, this structure was draped in black, so that the audience knew what *kind* of play it was going to see even before the play began. Secondly, costumes were elaborate and expensive. Acting companies often paid much more for a costume than they did for a new play. A scene such as that in which the assembled senate listen to Othello and Brabantio, for example, would probably have given an impression of lavish spectacle, with the contrast between the assembled senators in their full regalia, Brabantio with his dressing-gown hastily thrown over his night attire, Othello in whatever strange and splendid garb he wore as a private citizen, and the various members of the two search parties. Finally, though painted scenery was lacking, there were plenty of *properties* (movable objects used in plays). These could be quite elaborate, and often the language of the play would concentrate the audience's attention on them, as is done with the handkerchief and Othello's sword in the last scene. In general, these properties were not used realistically, but rather as a kind of visual shorthand, as a candle might signify a chamber at night time. Together, the painted permanent structure, the lavish costumes and the properties would give a stage presentation plenty of colour and spectacle.

Because there was no permanent painted scenery to 'fix' the place of action, the stage could be any place which the action demanded it should be. The playwright was free either to draw attention to features of the permanent structure, or to ignore them. And since the audience was used to this structure, it probably simply dismissed it *unless* its attention was focused on it by the words. This happens in *Othello* when, in the great 'temptation' scene (III.iii), Othello kneels down to swear 'by yond marble heaven' (III.iii.458) which is the painted roof of the theatre. Iago refers to the same feature when he speaks a few lines later of 'yon ever-burning lights above' and the easy way in which he moves immediately to the 'elements that clip us round about' reminds us that 'the heavens' of the playhouse opened out to the real 'elements' of sun, rain and sky. This flexibility with regard to place gave the playwright great freedom and contributed to the swift and free-flowing movement which is characteristic of so many plays of the time; it is an especially prominent feature of *Othello*.

The balcony stage offered visual variety by providing two levels of action which could be used either separately or together. In the scene where Brabantio is harangued by Iago and Roderigo and again in the 'storm' scene at Cyprus, we see two quite different ways in which it could be used.

The opening of this scene (II.i) also illustrates another important feature of this stage, one which shows the playwright making a virtue out of a necessity. Because the stage lacked painted scenery and artificial lighting to create atmosphere, most of the work which would today fall to the scenic artist and the lighting technician had to be undertaken by the playwright, and his chief instrument for doing this would, of course, be language. We see in this scene how the atmosphere of the storm is created almost entirely by the dialogue between Montano and the three gentlemen, aided perhaps by a few sound effects. Much of the richness of language in Shakespeare's plays comes from the fact that in the theatre for which he wrote, language had to perform so many tasks which in our theatre have been taken over by other media. This is not to deny Shakespeare's genius but to suggest that it was directly and constantly stimulated by the conditions of his theatre.

Among the conventions of Shakespeare's theatre, those of soliloquy and direct address to the audience, and the playing of women's roles by men are worth noting. While Shakespeare is marvellously adept at creating the atmosphere of the particular place where the action happens at a given moment if this is dramatically important, he is never afraid to make a character address the audience directly, as Iago often does. The theatre he wrote for did not have to pretend that it was anything but a theatre. The audience were used to a kind of 'double focus', one part of their imagination taking them to Venice or Cyprus or whatever, the other remaining in the theatre. Of course, we all have this double focus in any theatre, but in the Shakespearian theatre it is recognized and made use of rather than ignored as it is in the realistic 'picture-frame' theatre which keeps the audience in darkness and usually pretends that it is not there at all. Sometimes a character on the stage, when he is soliloquizing, is not addressing the audience directly so much as speaking his thoughts out aloud, but there are numerous occasions when the audience is quite explicitly spoken to. One example occurs just after the drunken brawl (II.iii) when Cassio, on Iago's advice, has left to seek Desdemona 'betimes in the morning'. Iago, alone on the stage, has a soliloquy which begins with a question to the audience –

> And what's he then that says I play the villain,
> When this advice is free I give, and honest,
> Probal to thinking, and indeed the course
> To win the Moor again?

(II.iii.315)

He asks the question again a little later on –

> How am I then a villain
> To counsel Cassio to this parallel course,
> Directly to his good?

(II.iii.327)

– and concludes by telling the audience what the next stage of his devilish plan is going to be. Both soliloquy and direct address are important ways in which the playwright can shape our responses to the unfolding drama by heightening suspense or irony, giving us a view of a character which we can compare with the view which other characters have of him.

As for the convention of boys taking the parts of women, we should not too readily dismiss this as nothing but a disadvantage in Shakespeare's theatre, and one which we have happily overcome. From the latter part of the seventeenth century onwards, actresses have appeared regularly on the English stage, and today we would probably find it strange and disconcerting if female roles were once again to be played by boys (though this happens quite often in plays put on by boys' schools). But to the audiences of

Shakespeare's day there was nothing unusual about boy actors playing the parts of female characters. What is worth noting is that once again Shakespeare turns a necessary limitation of his stage to an advantage. In broad daylight, with fairly crude make-up, it would not have been easy to make young boys *look* very much like women. So once again, language had to be used to persuade the audience not only of the beauty but of the femininity of the women. Too much physical contact between men and 'women' had to be avoided, or relegated to fairly unimportant areas of the stage. There is not much kissing or embracing in Shakespeare's plays, but we get the overwhelming impression, in the case of characters such as Cleopatra, Juliet and Desdemona, that they are not only beautiful, but endowed with a tremendous sensuous power. This impression is almost entirely due to Shakespeare's verbal artistry. For instance, much of our idea of Desdemona is derived from what Othello, Brabantio, Cassio and others say of her. Not having beautiful and sensuous women to act in his plays, Shakespeare had to create them through language. By all accounts the boy actors in his company rose triumphantly to the challenge of playing female roles, for we learn that when *Othello* was performed at Oxford in 1610, the boy who played Desdemona moved the audience to tears in the death scene.

The language of the play

The Elizabethans, like the rest of us, spoke to each other in prose, not verse. But when they went to the theatre, especially to see a tragedy or a historical play, they expected most of the characters to speak in blank or unrhymed verse. The reason for this is partly historical. The roots of English drama are in certain Latin rituals of the medieval church, which are metrical in form, and the earliest English drama, which is derived from them, is almost entirely in verse (as indeed is most literature till well after Shakespeare's time). Metrical form also helps to make lines memorable, and to give added emotional power to the words by playing off the natural pause of the speaking voice according to the sense of the words against the pause demanded by the metrical pattern. The basic pattern of the Shakespearian line is the iambic pentameter, or five groups of two syllables each, with the second syllable more strongly stressed than the first:

> If she | be in | her cham | ber or | your house,
> Let loose | on me | the jus | tice of | your state
>
> (I.i.134)

Here the vertical strokes mark the division into feet and the signs ˘ and ´ denote the weak and the strong stress respectively in each foot. But if the lines were spoken only with regard to the metrical pattern, they would sound strange and even comical. On the other hand, it would be awkward and wasteful to speak them as if they were ordinary prose: it is the tension between the two patterns of metre and sense which quickens the lines into dramatic life.

The two lines quoted above are in quite straightforward iambic pentameter. But it would be monotonous if every line were as regular as this. So Shakespeare uses many variations on the basic metrical pattern; sometimes he adds weakly stressed syllables which are gathered into the general rhythm of the lines by being spoken without special emphasis:

And throwing | but shows | of ser | vice on | their lords

(i.i.49)

where the second syllable of 'throwing' is almost literally thrown away. Sometimes the metrical pattern of the line is made up by the sounding of the final -ed in verbs, not sounded in normal speech:

The wealthy curlèd darlings of our nation

(i.ii.67)

This usually draws attention to the word affected. Then again, especially in his later plays, Shakespeare distorts the metrical pattern so violently that it is barely recognizable:

Nakĕd | in bed, | Iagŏ |, and not | mean harm |!

(iv.i.5)

Here the inversion of the stresses in the first word gives it a fierce emphasis, while the extra weak syllable of Iago's name seems to heighten the desperate entreaty in Othello's tone of voice. Occasionally the distortion of the pattern goes so far that we ought really to speak of the pattern being destroyed rather than distorted. But it is useful to remember that it is the existence of the metrical norm of five iambic feet to the line that enables Shakespeare to achieve many striking effects by variation of pause, stress and number of syllables. It is not necessary to be able to give a detailed metrical analysis of Shakespeare's verse to appreciate it, and, in any case, where the pattern is severely distorted, it is possible to analyse it in different ways. What is important is that we should be aware that the pattern of the verse is not an extra ornament to Shakespeare's language but one of the essential sources of its power.

Shakespeare came to use prose more and more for serious dramatic ends in his later plays, so that in a play like *Othello* we have not only the variations within the verse pattern, but a broader contrast between verse and prose. Most of the prose in the play belongs to Iago, and this is not accidental, for Iago's prose is the antithesis of Othello's poetry. These two kinds of language stand for two different attitudes to life and love. Iago's prose is almost scientific in its readiness to talk about *general* laws, *average* behaviour, *typical* reactions, and so on The general, the average, the typical – these are the concern of science, and Iago is always applying them to human aspirations and relationships (see page xii). As far as he is concerned, Desdemona is a typical sophisticated Venetian girl seeking forbidden sexual thrills, and Othello a typical barbarian:

> It cannot be long that Desdemona should continue her love
> to the Moor . . . it was a violent commencement in her and
> thou shalt see an answerable sequestration . . . These Moors
> are changeable in their wills . . . If sanctimony and a frail
> vow betwixt an erring barbarian and a supersubtle Venetian
> be not too hard for my wits, and all the tribe of hell, thou
> shalt enjoy her.

(1.iii.336)

Prose is the natural idiom for this habit of generalization and abstraction, but it is noteworthy that even when Iago speaks verse, his language never quite sheds these features, although it gains a certain intensity:

> Thus do I ever make my fool my purse;
> For I mine own gained knowledge should profane
> If I would time expend with such a snipe
> But for my sport and profit.

(I.iii.368)

By contrast, Othello's poetry is the language which expresses Othello's sense of the uniqueness of his good fortune, and the absoluteness of his devotion to Desdemona. It draws its imagery from the sea, from precious stones, from magic and from his own fabulous past, as Iago draws his from poison and the behaviour of animals. The poetry of Othello, with its resonant music and its sweeping imaginative power, enables us to share his own matchless vision of his love and high destiny:

> It gives me wonder great as my content
> To see you here before me. O my soul's joy,
> If after every tempest come such calms,
> May the winds blow till they have wakened death.
> And let the labouring bark climb hills of seas
> Olympus-high, and duck again as low
> As hell's from heaven. If it were now to die,
> 'Twere now to be most happy; for I fear

My soul hath her content so absolute
That not another comfort like to this
Succeeds in unknown fate.

(II.i.177)

One way of describing Othello's tragedy would be to say that it begins when Othello is persuaded to discard his own idiom, the poetry of uniqueness and faith, for Iago's alien prose of dry and apparently objective measurement and description. For of course Iago's language is not really objective and impersonal, as science aspires to be. Rather it is reductive, it insists on bringing human beings to the level of mere objects or animals out of a deep and obsessive malice against humanity itself. And when Othello begins to speak this language, he is doomed, because this language stands for, or rather is, a form of self-destruction. 'It is not words that shakes me thus' (IV.i.42) Othello cries out just before he falls down in a trance; the tragedy is that to a great extent it *is* words, Iago's words and the way of looking at people which they embody, that shake him from his absolute faith.

PART TWO

Language difficulties

Considering that *Othello* was written over 370 years ago, it is amazing how much of it can be understood and enjoyed without difficulty by anyone reasonably competent in modern English. But there are of course certain uses of language which will not be immediately clear. The most obvious of these is perhaps the occurrence of words which have dropped out of use. Such words as *callet, grise* and *gastness* draw attention by their unfamiliarity, and the notes and glossary will help to make their meaning clear. This also applies to a few words, such as *exsufflicate* which occur only in Shakespeare. There are also in this play a number of words which have been made by adding the prefix *en-* to an adjective or verb – *ensteeped, enchafed, englut* and so on. These words help to strengthen the impression of rapid and urgent activity.

Words whose meanings have undergone quite considerable changes while the spelling has remained unchanged present a special difficulty because it is not always clear from the context that the meaning has changed. Sometimes, as when Emilia says she would not commit adultery for 'any petty exhibition' (IV.iii.75) it is fairly clear that the word *exhibition* cannot bear its modern sense, and reference to the notes will be indicated. But elsewhere, as in 'an *extravagant* and wheeling stranger' (I.i.132), it may not be immediately clear that the meaning of the word in italics is different from the modern meaning. If a word sounds in the slightest degree odd, the safest plan is to see if the notes say anything about it. It should be remembered that the glossary usually gives only the meaning of a given word in the context in which it occurs; other possible senses of the word are ignored, but if they have some bearing on the context, the notes will usually clarify it.

So much for difficulties regarding individual words. There are also certain grammatical forms which are frequent in Shakespeare but which are no longer used in modern English, or have a slightly different implication. For instance, when *do* is used as an auxiliary verb in modern English, it gives a special emphasis to the verb. 'I did pay you back' implies that the speaker is quite definite on the point. But in the English of Shakespeare's time, the auxiliary *do* carries no such special stress:

> For I do know the state
>
> (I.i.143)

Here *do know* = 'know'. Conversely, *do* and its derived forms are sometimes missing where, in modern English, we would expect to find them:

> We lose it not so long as we can smile
>
> (I.iii.209)

where *lose it not* = 'do not lose it'.

Othello also contains a number of oaths such as *Zounds!, By the Mass!* and *God bless the mark!* These are all explained as they occur.

In addition to 'you, your, yours', Elizabethan English also uses the forms *thou, thee, thy* and *thine* for the second person singular. Usually, but not always, the latter forms are used to indicate friendship or kinship or to give commands to a social inferior or in order to be deliberately insulting. We can learn a good deal about the social and emotional relationships between characters by paying attention to this *you/thou* distinction. The interchange between Iago, Roderigo and Brabantio at the end of I.i. offers a good example of the different uses and their implications. The verb forms associated with *thou* end in *-st* or *-est*, though for the commoner verbs there are other forms, e.g. 'Thou art a villain' (I.i.114).

The present tense ending *-eth* or *-th* is sometimes used with third person singular subjects, where modern English would have the *-s* ending. In particular the verb *has* occurs in the form *hath*:

> Your daughter, if you have not given her leave
> I say again, hath made a gross revolt,
>
> (I.i.129)

Very infrequently, a plural subject is used with what would be, in modern English, a singular verb form, e.g.:

> It is not words that shakes me thus
>
> (IV.i.42)

Finally, the metre sometimes demands that words such as *it* should be abbreviated to *'t*; these abbreviations are usually easily recognizable.

The provenance of *Othello*: the extant texts

Shakespeare wrote his plays to be performed by the theatrical company of which he was a member and a shareholder. There is nothing to suggest that he was particularly interested in their printed form. For many of his plays, the only text we have is that found in the great Folio edition of his works edited by two of his fellow actors, John Heminges and Henry Condell in 1623, seven years after Shakespeare's death. Othello exists in two separate versions, the Folio of 1623 and the first quarto (Q1) printed a year earlier. (Both versions appeared several years after the play's first performance in 1604.) There is also a quarto edition of 1630, but this was printed from the Folio (F).

Briefly, the chief differences between F and Q1 are these: F includes about 160 lines not found in Q1, while Q1 contains many oaths omitted from F as well as fuller stage directions. It seems as if someone went through the Quarto version systematically expurgating the oaths and often reducing the dramatic effect. There also are differences in certain individual words and phrases, e.g. 'togéd' (Q1) and 'tonguéd' (F) (I.i.22).

There were many ways in which a play could find its way from the playhouse to the printing house in Shakespeare's day. A printer could acquire the author's original draft (or 'foul papers') or, better still, the copy used by the company during rehearsals and performance (the 'prompt-book'). Someone could be induced to transcribe a play during rehearsal or performance, or an actor might, for a few shillings, set down the play for the printer as well as he could remember it. (We should remember that Elizabethan education laid a great emphasis on the training of memory.) How near to the author's finished work we should consider a given version of a play to be will depend on our judgment as to the source of the printed version. In this respect Othello is one of the most difficult of Shakespeare's plays and scholars are by no means agreed as to whether F or Q1 is the more accurate text. One theory which has a good deal of support is that Q1 was printed from a copy made from Shakespeare's 'foul papers', but several years later, while F uses as its basis a copy of Q1 corrected by the original 'prompt-book' (made from 'foul papers' tidied up and transcribed for production) of about 1604. This would make F the more reliable text.

This edition is based on F, but includes oaths and stage-directions from Q1 as the latter are often more vivid, being designed for the reader, rather than the more practical stage-directions of F; occasionally a later emendation has been adopted. In general, discussion of textual 'cruces' or variant readings is deliberately avoided, but I ought to mention that I have adopted an interpretation of one of the most famous and difficult lines in the play which is not that of most editors. The line is

in my defunct and proper satisfaction

(I.iii.260)

and I have accepted Hilda Hulme's suggestion (in *Explorations in Shakespeare's Language*) that the word *defunct* may be related to the Latin 'defungor' and means, in the context, something like 'free from penalty or punishment'. Wherever scholars and critics have disagreed about a reading, I have used what seems to me the most likely reading and have not drawn attention to possible variations.

The principal characters

OTHELLO commands our interest and attention before we ever see him. At the very beginning of the play, we hear of him only as someone whom Iago hates, and who, according to the latter, is one given to 'loving his own pride and purposes'. Soon we learn that he is a Moor and Roderigo refers to him viciously as 'the thick-lips'. Throughout this first scene a picture is built up of Othello as boastful, sensual and generally hateful. It is when we see him, and above all, when we hear him that we realize how very different he is from the monstrous figure conjured up by Iago and Roderigo; and this realization in turn affects our view of these two characters.

Shakespeare has given us a character far more fascinating than the conventionally 'noble' warrior and vengeful husband whom he found in Cinthio's story. He uses Othello's colour as a visual symbol of the principle on which the character is built. This principle, as I have already suggested, is that he is the outsider. Just as his colour sets him visually apart from all the other characters on the stage, many of his other attributes serve to define him as a stranger within the community. In addition to being a Negro, he is a soldier in a commercial republic. This gives a certain ambivalence to his separateness from the city state. He is not Venetian and not typical of the activity by which Venice lives and thrives, but Venice needs him and his services for its continued prosperity. Iago himself bears grudging witness to this when he tells Roderigo that

> for their souls
> Another of his fathom they have none
> To lead their business.

(I.i.147)

Because they need him the Venetians accept him, but there is more to it than this, because the Duke, on listening to the tale of Othello's wooing, murmurs

> I think this tale would win my daughter too.

(I.iii.171)

Brabantio, Iago and Roderigo are perhaps more representative of Venetian attitudes to black Othello, but we should not forget the more human voice of the Duke who in his own way represents the Venetian state itself.

In addition to his colour and his profession, there are two other ways in which Othello is set apart from the community which he has lately entered. One is the scale on which Shakespeare has portrayed him. Othello is drawn much larger and grander than life. He towers above the other characters in the play, and his history and background assume the proportions of myth. He bestrides the narrow world of Venice like a Colossus. The other factor that sets him apart is his being a convert to Christianity rather than a Christian by birth, as the rest of the Venetians are. Thus, although Othello's Christian faith is fervent and sincere, Shakespeare suggests that underlying it is a fiercer and more primitive paganism. When Sir Laurence Olivier played the title role in a celebrated production some years ago, he appeared with a large golden cross hung on a chain round his neck. When Othello, swayed by Iago, swore vengeance against Cassio and Desdemona he broke the chain off violently and flung the cross away; this gesture identified the upsurge of the primitive passion of revenge in Othello with the pagan element which is still an important part of his character. This element is also associated with the numerous references to magic and witchcraft in the play, notably Brabantio's accusations against the Moor and Othello's own account of the handkerchief and its history. In the final scene, as Othello stabs himself while recounting the story of how he once killed 'a malignant and a turbaned Turk' for abusing a Venetian, he becomes in his own imagination, and perhaps in ours, both Christian and pagan, tragic hero and murderer together.

This emphasis on Othello as an outsider helps us to appreciate the unique value of what he stands for. But it also suggests that to some extent the seeds of the final tragic outcome are already present in the tragic hero and his situation. Othello's world is the spacious, heroic, masculine world of combat and high adventure. 'The flinty and steel couch of war' is to him 'My thrice-driven bed of down' (I.iii.228). As he himself recognizes, he is not at home in the sophisticated society of Venice, and he feels particularly insecure in his new domestic role of husband. Othello's love for Desdemona is thus a precious passion, but also a precarious one. As a recent critic has remarked, Othello is the tragedy of a man who went into a house.

IAGO is in almost every respect the very antithesis of Othello. Where the Moor is open and straightforward, Iago is not only crooked in all his dealings but actually revels in his crookedness. Where Othello judges men by his own high motives and standards, to Iago men are no more than animals erect. Above all, while love is the soul and centre of Othello's world, without which 'chaos is come again' (III.iii.92), Iago lives, moves and has his being in a world of pure hatred.

Iago's attitude to life has been described by the poet and critic Samuel Coleridge in a famous phrase as 'the motive-hunting of motiveless malignity'.

The last two words are often quoted by themselves as if they gave an adequate account of Iago's character, but we should note that Iago, far from not having any motives for what he does, has too many. In the first place, he has been deprived of the lieutenancy which he coveted. Secondly he is clearly prejudiced against Othello's race and colour. Further, there is his suspicion that Othello, and perhaps Cassio, too, have cuckolded him. Finally, there is the merest hint in Shakespeare's play of Iago's thwarted love for Desdemona, which is the primary motive in Cinthio's original story.

But the trouble with these motives is that we are not convinced that they really are the mainsprings of Iago's villainy. At times he tosses a motive so casually at us that we feel he is not even interested in convincing us, let alone himself. He tells us of his hate first and offers a motive for it afterwards:

> I hate the Moor,
> And it is thought abroad that 'twixt my sheets
> H'as done my office. I know not if 't be true,
> But I, for mere suspicion in that kind,
> Will do, as if for surety.
>
> (I.iii.371)

At others he expresses the same motive with such virulence that we feel he is trying to convince himself, to key himself up for action:

> For that I do suspect the lusty Moor
> Hath leaped into my seat; the thought whereof
> Doth, like a poisonous mineral, gnaw my inwards;
> And nothing can or shall content my soul
> Till I am evened with him, wife for wife.
>
> (II.i.286)

Either way, what we are always aware of is a gap between what Iago does and the reasons he offers for what he does; the two seem to spring from different levels of his being. This is the point of Coleridge's remark about 'motive-hunting'. Perhaps there is a clue to a different, more general, kind of explanation for Iago's wickedness in what he says about Cassio:

> He hath a daily beauty in his life
> That makes me ugly.
>
> (v.i.19)

In other words, Iago is committed to a valuation of life which sees it as governed by the basest of motives and therefore mean and sordid, so there is an instinctive antipathy between him and all the human values of love, loyalty, self-sacrifice and so on. But this kind of explanation leaves Iago's motivation as mysterious as ever; when we look into Iago's heart we find, at the end, that we are looking into the heart of darkness.

But if Iago's true motivation is mysterious, there is no real mystery about how he contrived to impose himself on all Venetian society as an honest and straightforward character. The word *honest* is a key word in the play and it is often, though by no means always, associated with Iago. William Empson, in his book called *The Structure of Complex Words* has a chapter in which the wide range of implication of *honest* and *honesty* in *Othello* are discussed in illuminating detail. He notes that there are different uses of this key word for all the main characters and that 'everybody calls Iago honest once or twice, but with Othello it becomes an obsession'. Iago's 'honesty' is, however, entirely on the surface; it amounts to nothing more than a bluff and open manner which seems to go well with the style of life of the soldier unused to nice distinctions and refinements of language. But Iago works very hard at cultivating and developing this manner; so hard that even his wife appears to be taken in by it. This aspect of Iago's character can be related to the influence on English drama of the ideas of the Italian political thinker Niccolo Machiavelli. Machiavelli claims that he is concerned not with what men, particularly rulers of states, ought to be or were supposed to be, but with what they actually are, that is, with the rules that actually govern political behaviour. In England, and particularly in the drama, this 'political realism' led to the creation of 'Machiavellian characters' whose only real criterion of action was expediency and self-interest, but who, to achieve their aims, had to dissemble their real motives and appear to be open, honest and virtuous. Such a 'doubleness' makes a character intensely dramatic and there are many examples of the Machiavellian character in Elizabethan drama; in Shakespeare we find that characters like Edmund in *King Lear* and Richard III have a strong family resemblance to Iago. The Machiavel is also associated with new methods of scientific inquiry and experiment which occupied men's minds in the sixteenth and seventeenth centuries, and it is plain that there is a kind of cold-blooded 'scientific' curiosity behind Iago's 'experiments'. There is also an artist's delight in the exercise of his own creative skills. Iago is a superb actor but also a skilled director of little 'plays' in which he makes other people follow his intentions, as when he manipulates Cassio and Roderigo in the brawl scene. This is why the character of Iago is endlessly fascinating, for while our moral being is repelled by the scope and intensity of his villainy, we are drawn, in spite of ourselves, to admire his sheer virtuosity and power of improvization.

DESDEMONA is more than the passive victim of Othello's tragic error. As with Othello, we hear about her before we see her, and once again, there is a contrast between the picture we form before and after her first appearance. The first time her name is mentioned it is by Othello:

> For know, Iago,
> But that I love the gentle Desdemona,
> I would not my unhouséd free condition
> Put into circumscription and confine
> For the seas' worth.

(I.ii.23)

Before this, we have heard of her only in general terms as Brabantio's daughter who has eloped with a Moor. To the father this action seems to go so much against everything he believes his daughter to be that in his view only black magic could account for it, though the thought that he might be mistaken about his daughter flickers momentarily into his distraught consciousness:

> Fathers, from hence trust not your daughters' minds
> By what you see them act.

(I.i.166)

But it is the idea that witchcraft has been used against her that obsesses him, and impels him to give the first extended description of her character that we hear:

> A maiden never bold,
> Of spirit so still and quiet that her motion
> Blushed at herself; and she, in spite of nature,
> Of years, of country, credit, everything –
> To fall in love with what she feared to look on!

(I.iii.95)

Othello's account of his courtship offers us a glimpse of a Desdemona who seems to have more spirit and initiative than this, for she it is who invited him and questioned him about his history. We also see a young woman who, her mother being dead, is now mistress of the household, for 'the house affairs' (I.iii.147) kept demanding her attention when she wanted to listen to Othello. And her oblique hints to Othello about 'a friend that loved her' (I.iii.164) suggest that she is not entirely free from feminine wiles, though an infinite distance from anything approaching the 'supersubtle Venetian' (I.iii.349) of Iago's twisted imagination. When we do see her we realize that there is a side to her that her father has apparently never even suspected, for she is a woman of great independence, determination and courage. She also has something of the skill in presenting a case that Portia shows in *The Merchant of Venice*

> You are the lord of duty,
> I am hitherto your daughter. But here's my husband,
> And so much duty as my mother showed

> To you, preferring you before her father,
> So much I challenge that I may profess
> Due to the Moor my lord.
>
> (i.iii.183)

This independence is allied in Desdemona to a tremendous and unshakeable devotion which ultimately leads to her tragic death. Her love, though pure and untarnished, is not only spiritual, for she is quite outspoken in her claim that if she were separated from her husband she would be deprived of her conjugal rights. She even indulges in a certain amount of badinage with sexual overtones in her exchanges with Iago while awaiting Othello's arrival, and converses affectionately with Cassio. All this is a far cry from her father's description of 'a maiden never bold' (i.iii.95). But for all her boldness, there is a shining innocence, even perhaps a quality of naivety in Desdemona. We can see this best in her question to Emilia as to whether there really are women who are unfaithful to their husbands, and her belief that there is no capacity for jealousy in Othello's nature. Thus Desdemona's character is compounded of many contrasting but not contradictory qualities. All Venice, only Iago excepted, seems to endorse Cassio's commendation of her as 'the divine Desdemona' (ii.i.72); even Roderigo, fool though he may be, cannot bring himself to believe Iago's lies about her. As some of the darkest and most devilish elements in human nature are embodied in Iago, so Desdemona stands for the radiant faith and fortitude of which humanity is also capable; and she is all the more convincing because Shakespeare has not made her woodenly perfect but touchingly fallible and human.

EMILIA, like her husband, is a realist. But the crucial difference between them, far more important than any similarity, is that Emilia's realism leads her to a loving acceptance of human beings for what they are, whereas Iago's is only a justification of his desire to exploit them. Emilia is a little like a typical heroine of Shakespearian comedy such as Rosalind in *As You Like It* who can say that love is only a madness and deserves whipping and yet admit that she herself is madly in love. Emilia is a shrewd, practical woman of the world who knows that one should not expect too much from people, especially men. Her outburst against husbands who provoke their wives into being unfaithful by their own conduct shows that her idea of marriage is something much more like a social contract than a sacrament. We do not, of course, believe Iago's insinuations that she has committed adultery with either Othello or Cassio, but this is because of what we know of these two men, not because we feel that Emilia has any strong theoretical objections. In this respect then, Emilia's hard-headed practicality contrasts with Desdemona's starry-eyed idealism. One of her functions is to rescue 'common sense' from the taint of inhumanity with which Iago has corrupted it. But at the end of the play we realize that

Emilia too is capable, in her own way, of the courage, loyalty and self-sacrifice shown by her mistress. Like everyone else, she has been taken in by Iago, but when she realizes this (and she is the first to do so) she is not afraid to speak out, though she knows that to do so will be to risk death. Thus we see that there is something more to her character than mere shrewdness or expediency. While she has her husband's habit of generalizing from ordinary experience, she is also able to recognize the unique exception when she meets it. She is enough of a woman of the world to know what most women are like, but she knows enough of Desdemona to recognize that she is not like most women; and, like Desdemona, she dies for her faith.

CASSIO is perfectly adapted to his part in the dramatic action, though this makes him sound somewhat mechanical, which he is not. He is a good soldier, but also a man of charm and civility, a typical product of Italian sophistication (he is a Florentine, not a native Venetian). He offers us independent testimony both to Othello's nobility and to Desdemona's beauty of person and character. He is also something of a ladies' man, which, together with his elegant manners, makes Iago's insinuations about him and Desdemona sound plausible to Othello. In spite of Iago's calumnies, we know that he is a responsible officer, for the Venetian state has no hesitation in appointing him deputy when Othello is to leave (according to Lodovico, this is the news contained in the letter he has brought), but he also has a bad head for drinking, which enables Iago to arrange the incident which leads to Cassio's dismissal. Finally, his weakness for women leads to his liaison with Bianca which Iago puts to such diabolical use. There are some inconsistencies in Shakespeare's portrayal of Cassio (for instance, it seems odd that Cassio has to ask Iago whom Othello has married, if he 'came awooing' with Othello as Desdemona says), but these do not seriously impair our impression of his character.

RODERIGO exists in the play almost wholly in terms of his relationship with Iago. He is almost always the dupe pure and simple. But he provides important evidence of Desdemona's virtue, for he holds her in high esteem even though he is attempting, through Iago, to seduce her. There is something forlorn in Roderigo's attempts to win Desdemona's favours; we have the impression that he himself does not believe in his eventual success. The fact that Roderigo is a fool for whom Iago has nothing but contempt is dramatically important because it enables Iago to speak freely to him (and so to us) about his real motives. The way Iago fools Roderigo prepares us for the far greater deception which he practises on Othello, but also perhaps prompts in our minds the question whether Othello himself is not, in some ways, a fool, as Roderigo is.

Though characters have been sometimes considered in isolation in this section, it is very important to remember that their real existence is in terms of their relationship with one another and above all in terms of the theme of the play. In real life, we may be aware of ourselves or those around us as acting out a role, as characters in a play do; but the important difference is that in a drama we have some idea, which grows with the unfolding action, of what the play is 'about'; that is, we become aware of a theme or themes which the characters exist to serve, not as mere puppets of course, but as figures with a life of their own.

The central theme of *Othello* is the conflict between two worlds, that of Iago and that of Othello. This antithesis informs not only the larger structure of the play (so that a scene which shows the 'Iago world-view' in action is typically followed by one embodying that which Othello stands for), but is very often the structural principle within each scene, as well as being the basis of the distinction of style between the 'prose' of Iago and the 'Othello music'. It is within these two worlds that the characters of the tragedy are most vividly and most meaningfully alive.

A few passages of literary criticism relating to *Othello*

Like all Shakespeare's plays, *Othello* has been endlessly discussed. The following brief extracts represent some of the main points of critical discussion.

(a) The great Romantic poet and critic Samuel Taylor Coleridge gave several public lectures on Shakespeare, from one of which the following notes are taken. They include the famous phrase 'the motive-hunting of a motiveless malignity' which has had so much influence on subsequent views of Iago's character.

> Admirable is the preparation, so truly and peculiarly Shakespearian, in the introduction of Roderigo, as the dupe on whom Iago shall first exercise his art, and in so doing display his own character. Roderigo, without any fixed principle, but not without the moral notions and sympathies with honour, which his rank and connections had hung upon him, is already well fitted and predisposed for the purpose; for very want of character and strength of passion, like wind loudest in an empty house, constitute his character. The first three lines happily state the nature and foundation of the friendship between him and Iago, – the purse, – as also the contrast of Roderigo's intemperance of mind with Iago's coolness, – the coolness of a preconceiving experimenter. The mere language of protestation, –
>
> > If ever I did dream of such a matter, abhor me, –

which, falling in with the associative link, determines Roderigo's continuation of complaint, –

Thou told'st me, thou didst hold him in thy hate, –

elicits at length a true feeling of Iago's mind, the dread of contempt habitual to those who encourage in themselves, and have their keenest pleasure in, the expression of contempt for others. Observe Iago's high self-opinion, and the moral, that a wicked man will employ real feelings, as well as assume those most alien from his own as instruments of his purposes : —

And, by the faith of man,
I know my price, I am worth no worse a place.

*   *   *

Iago's speech : —

Virtue? a fig! 'tis in ourselves, that we are thus, or thus, etc.

This speech comprises the passionless character of Iago. It is all will in intellect; and therefore he is here a bold partizan of a truth, but yet of a truth converted into a falsehood by the absence of all the necessary modifications caused by the frail nature of man. And then comes the last sentiment : —

Our raging motions, our carnal stings, our unbitted lusts,
whereof I take this, that you call – love, to be a sect or scion!

Here is the true Iagoism of, alas! how many! Note Iago's pride of mastery in the repetition of 'Go, make money!' to his anticipated dupe, even stronger than his love of lucre: and when Roderigo is completely won, –

I am chang'd. I'll go sell all my land, –

when the effect has been fully produced, the repetition of triumph : —

Go to; farewell; put money enough in your purse!

The remainder – Iago's soliloquy – the motive-hunting of a motiveless malignity – how awful it is! Yea, whilst he is still allowed to bear the divine image, it is too fiendish for his own steady view, – for the lonely gaze of a being next to devil, and only not quite devil, – and yet a character which Shakespeare has attempted and executed, without disgust and without scandal!

S. T. Coleridge: *Shakespeare: Notes and Lectures*, 1877.

(b) A. C. Bradley saw Othello as a noble romantic figure surrounded by the glamour of an exotic background.

> Othello is, in one sense of the word, by far the most romantic figure among Shakespeare's heroes, and he is so partly from the strange life of war and adventure which he has lived from childhood. He does not belong to our world, and he seems to enter it we know not whence – almost as if from wonderland. There is something mysterious in his descent from men of royal siege; in his wanderings in vast deserts and among marvellous peoples; in his tales of magic handkerchiefs and prophetic Sibyls; in the sudden vague glimpses we get of numberless battles and sieges in which he has played the hero and has borne a charmed life; even in chance references to his baptism, his being sold to slavery, his sojourn in Aleppo.
>
> And he is not merely a romantic figure; his own nature is romantic. He has not, indeed, the meditative or speculative imagination of Hamlet; but in the strictest sense of the word he is more poetic than Hamlet. Indeed, if one recalls Othello's most famous speeches – those that begin, 'Her father loved me', 'O now for ever', 'Never, Iago', 'Had it pleased Heaven', 'It is the cause', 'Behold, I have a weapon', 'Soft you, a word or two before you go' – and if one places side by side with these speeches an equal number by any other hero, one will not doubt that Othello is the greatest poet of them all. There is the same poetry in his casual phrases – like 'These nine moons wasted', 'Keep up your bright swords, for the dew will rust them', 'You chaste stars', 'It is a sword of Spain, the ice-brook's temper', 'It is the very error of the moon' – and in those brief expressions of intense feeling which ever since have been taken as the absolute expression, like
>
> > If it were now to die,
> > 'Twere now to be most happy; for, I fear,
> > My soul hath her content so absolute
> > That not another comfort like to this
> > Succeeds in unknown fate,
>
> or
>
> > If she be false, O then Heaven mocks itself,
> > I'll not believe it;
>
> or
>
> > No, my heart is turned to stone; I strike it, and it hurts my hand,
>
> or
>
> > But yet the pity of it, Iago! O Iago, the pity of it, Iago!
>
> or
>
> > O thou weed,

> Who are so lovely fair and smell'st so sweet
> That the sense aches at thee, would thou hadst ne'er been born.

And this imagination, we feel, has accompanied his whole life. He has watched with a poet's eye the Arabian trees dropping their med'cinable gum, and the Indian throwing away his chance-found pearl; and has gazed in a fascinated dream at the Pontic sea rushing, never to return, to the Propontic and the Hellespont; and has felt as no other man ever felt (for he speaks of it as none other ever did) the poetry of the pride, pomp, and circumstance of glorious war.

So he comes before us, dark and grand, with a light upon him from the sun where he was born; no longer young, and now grave, self-controlled, steeled by the experience of countless perils, hardships and vicissitudes, at once simple and stately in bearing and in speech, a great man naturally modest but fully conscious of his worth, proud of his services to the state, unawed by dignitaries and unelated by honours, secure, it would seem, against all dangers from without and all rebellion from within. And he comes to have his life crowned with the final glory of love, a love as strange, adventurous and romantic as any passage of his eventful history, filling his heart with tenderness and his imagination with ecstasy. For there is no love, not that of Romeo in his youth, more steeped in imagination than Othello's.

The sources of danger in this character are revealed but too clearly by the story. In the first place, Othello's mind, for all its poetry, is very simple. He is not observant. His nature tends outward. He is quite free from introspection, and is not given to reflection. Emotion excites his imagination, but it confuses and dulls his intellect. On this side he is the very opposite of Hamlet, with whom, however, he shares a great openness and trustfulness of nature. In addition, he has little experience of the corrupt products of civilised life, and is ignorant of European women.

In the second place, for all his dignity and massive calm (and he has greater dignity than any other of Shakespeare's men), he is by nature full of the most vehement passion. Shakespeare emphasises his self-control, not only by the wonderful pictures of the First Act, but by references to the past. Lodovico, amazed at his violence, exclaims:

> Is this the noble Moor whom our full Senate
> Call all in all sufficient? Is this the nature
> Whom passion could not shake? whose solid virtue
> The shot of accident nor dart of chance
> Could neither graze nor pierce?

Iago, who has here no motive for lying, asks:

> Can he be angry? I have seen the cannon
> When it hath blown his ranks into the air,
> And, like the devil, from his very arm
> Puffed his own brother – and can he be angry?[1]

This, and other aspects of his character, are best exhibited by a single line – one of Shakespeare's miracles – the words by which Othello silences in a moment the night-brawl between his attendants and those of Brabantio:

> Keep up your bright swords, for the dew will rust them.

And the same self-control is strikingly shown where Othello endeavours to elicit some explanation of the fight between Cassio and Montano. Here, however, there occur ominous words, which make us feel how necessary was this self-control, and make us admire it the more:

> Now, by heaven,
> My blood begins my safer guides to rule,
> And passion, having my best judgment collied,
> Assays to lead the way.

We remember these words later, when the sun of reason is 'collied', blackened and blotted out in total eclipse.

Lastly, Othello's nature is all of one piece. His trust, where he trusts, is absolute. Hesitation is almost impossible to him. He is extremely self-reliant, and decides and acts instantaneously. If stirred to indignation, as 'in Aleppo once', he answers with one lightning stroke. Love, if he loves, must be to him the heaven where either he must live or bear no life. If such a passion as jealousy seizes him, it will swell into a well-nigh incontrollable flood. He will press for immediate conviction or immediate relief. Convinced, he will act with the authority of a judge and the swiftness of a man in mortal pain. Undeceived, he will do like execution on himself.

A. C. Bradley: Shakespearean Tragedy, 1904.

(c) G. Wilson Knight drew attention to the nobility and resonance of the play's rhythm and imagery in an essay entitled 'The Othello Music'.

In *Othello* we are faced with the vividly particular rather than the vague and universal. The play as a whole has a distinct formal beauty: within it

---

[1] For the actor, then, to represent him as violently angry when he cashiers Cassio is an utter mistake.

we are ever confronted with beautiful and solid forms. The persons tend to appear as warmly human, concrete. They are neither vaguely universalized, as in *King Lear* or *Macbeth*, nor deliberately mechanized and vitalized by the poet's philosophic plan as in *Measure for Measure* and *Timon of Athens*, wherein the significance of the dramatic person is dependent almost wholly on our understanding of the allegorical or symbolical meaning. It is true that Iago is here a mysterious, inhuman creature of unlimited cynicism: but the very presence of the concrete creations around, in differentiating him sharply from the rest, limits and defines him. *Othello* is a story of intrigue rather than a visionary statement. If, however, we tend to regard Othello, Desdemona, and Iago as suggestive symbols rather than human beings, we may, from a level view of their interaction, find a clear relation existing between *Othello* and other plays of the hate-theme. Such an analysis will be here only in part satisfactory. It exposes certain underlying ideas, abstracts them from the original: it is less able to interpret the whole positive beauty of the play. With this important reservation, I shall push the interpretative method as far as possible.

Othello is dominated by its protagonist. Its supremely beautiful effects of style are all expressions of Othello's personal passion. Thus, in first analysing Othello's poetry, we shall lay the basis for an understanding of the play's symbolism: this matter of style is, indeed, crucial, and I shall now indicate those qualities which clearly distinguish it from other Shakespearian poetry. It holds a rich music all of its own, and possesses a unique solidity and precision of picturesque phrase or image, a peculiar chastity and serenity of thought. It is, as a rule, barren of direct metaphysical content. Its thought does not mesh with the reader's: rather it is always outside us, aloof. This aloofness is the resultant of an inward aloofness of image from image, word from word. The dominant quality is separation, not, as is more usual in Shakespeare, cohesion. Consider these exquisite poetic movements:

> O heavy hour!
> Methinks it should be now a huge eclipse
> Of sun and moon, and that the affrighted globe
> Should yawn at alteration.

(v.ii.98)

Or,

> It is the very error of the moon;
> She comes more near the earth than she was wont,
> And makes men mad.

(v.ii.109)

These are solid gems of poetry which lose little by divorce from their context: wherein they differ from the finest passages of *King Lear* or *Macbeth*, which are as wild flowers not to be uptorn from their rooted soil if they are to live. In these two quotations we should note how the human drama is thrown into sudden contrast and vivid, unexpected relation with the tremendous concrete machinery of the universe, which is thought of in terms of individual heavenly bodies: 'sun' and 'moon'. The same effect is apparent in:

> Nay, had she been true,
> If Heaven would make me such another world
> Of one entire and perfect chrysolite,
> I'd not have sold her for it.

(v.ii.141)

Notice the single word 'chrysolite' with its outstanding and remote beauty: this is typical of *Othello*.

The effect in such passages is primarily one of contrast. The vastness of the night sky, and its moving planets, or the earth itself – here conceived objectively as a solid, round, visualized object – these things, though thrown momentarily into sensible relation with the passions of man, yet remain vast, distant, separate, seen but not apprehended; something against which the dramatic movement may be silhouetted, but with which it cannot be merged. This poetic use of heavenly bodies serves to elevate the theme, to raise issues infinite and unknowable.

G. Wilson Knight: The Wheel of Fire, 1930.

(d) F. R. Leavis made an influential attack on Bradley's view of the romantic Othello, elaborating on a remark made by the poet and critic T. S. Eliot about Othello 'cheering himself up' in his last speech.

> The tragedy is inherent in the Othello-Desdemona relation, and Iago is a mechanism necessary for precipitating tragedy in a dramatic action. Explaining how it should be that Othello, who is so noble and trustful ('Othello, we have seen, was trustful, and thorough in his trust'), can so immediately doubt his wife, Bradley says:

> > But he was newly married; in the circumstances he cannot have known much of Desdemona before his marriage. (p. 192.)

> Again we read:

> > But it is not surprising that his utter powerlessness to repel it [Iago's insinuation] on the ground of knowledge of his wife . . . should complete his misery . . . (p. 193.)

Bradley, that is, in his comically innocent way, takes it as part of the datum that Othello really knows nothing about his wife. Ah, but he was in love with her. And so poetically. 'For', says Bradley, 'there is no love, not that of Romeo in his youth, more steeped in imagination than Othello's'. Othello, however, we are obliged to remark (Bradley doesn't make the point in this connection) is not in his youth; he is represented as middle-aged – as having attained at any rate to maturity in that sense. There might seem to be dangers in such a situation, quite apart from any intervention by an Iago. But then, we are told Othello is 'of a great openness and trustfulness of nature'. – It would be putting it more to the point to say that he has great consciousness of worth and confidence of respect.

The worth is really and solidly there; he is truly impressive, a noble product of the life of action – of

> The big wars
> That make ambition virtue.

'That make ambition virtue' – this phrase of his is a key one: his virtues are, in general, of that kind; they have, characteristically, something of the quality suggested. Othello, in his magnanimous way, is egotistic. He really is, beyond any question, the nobly massive man of action, the captain of men, he sees himself as being, but he does very much see himself:

> Keep up your bright swords, for the dew will rust them.

In short, a habit of self-approving self-dramatization is an essential element in Othello's make-up, and remains so at the very end.

It is, at the best, the impressive manifestation of a noble egotism. But, in the new marital situation, this egotism isn't going to be the less dangerous for its nobility. This self-centredness doesn't mean self-knowledge: that is a virtue which Othello, as soldier of fortune, hasn't had much need of. He has been well provided by nature to meet all the trials a life of action has exposed him to. The trials facing him now that he has married this Venetian girl with whom he's 'in love' so imaginatively (we're told) as to outdo Romeo and who is so many years younger than himself (his colour, whether or not 'colour-feeling' existed among the Elizabethans, we are certainly to take as emphasizing the disparity of the match) – the trials facing him now are of a different order.

F. R. Leavis: 'Diabolic Intellect and the Noble Hero' in *The Common Pursuit*, 1952.

(e) 'Othello: A Moral Essay' is the full title of the essay by A. P. Rossiter from which the following extract is taken. He points to an important ambiguity in one of the play's key words.

What we say about *Othello* will necessarily depend greatly on our attitudes towards jealousy; and those will depend in turn on (1) what reflection we have given the subject – one it would be fantastic to describe as only of literary, critical importance; and on (2) whether we do or do not suppose that in the 1950s we are in a position to see deeper into the matter than people were in the psychological past. I do not mean Shakespeare; I mean those who have written on his play, or on the psychology or pathology of love. Popularly, conventionally, there is no love without jealousy; and jealousy is a measure of intense love. Its opposite is indifference, I suppose. A modern psychologist, however, ends his study with 'In short, jealousy is a sign of weakness in love, not of strength; it takes its source in fear, guilt and hate, rather than in love.' I say no more than that there is no possibility of compromise between those two positions (although *Sonnet 130* may suggest that Shakespeare found one). And outside Shakespearian criticism, your life may hang on which you take. I suggest that the whole meaning of *Othello* can be said to hang on how you interpret the half line 'of one not easily jealous' – or the one and a half lines that surround it: 'Of one that lov'd not wisely, but too well', and 'but, being wrought. . . .'

Now only a concordance is required, and reflection, to show that *jealous* in Shakespearian usage *cannot* always mean 'sexually jealous'. Cassius, for example, 'And be not jealous on me, gentle Brutùs' (I.ii.71), and Brutus, 'That you do love me, I am nothing jealous' (I.ii.162), both plainly mean 'suspicious'; 'I have no suspicion of the genuineness of your apparent friendship: I think you sincere.' In *Hamlet* the Queen says,

> So full of artless jealousy is guilt
> It spills itself in fearing to be spilt (IV.v.19–20)

'Guilty minds are so uncontrolled in their suspiciousness that they betray themselves by their very precautions.' Polonius 'beshrews his jealousy' in the same sense: he suspected that Hamlet was only trifling with Ophelia; whereas it was serious, he now thinks. Lear speaks of the neglect he has received in his daughter's castle: 'I have perceived a most faint neglect of late, which I have rather blamed as mine own jealous curiosity than as a very pretence and purpose of unkindness. (I.iv.67–9): i.e., he has dismissed it from his mind, telling himself that it is *finnicking suspicion* on his part; but now he sees that it is more than that.

The word in Elizabethan usage has two clear meanings; and for the most part today we neglect the non-sexual one (although 'jealous' *is* used to mean 'envious', especially by girls). There is a good example of both senses together, yet distinct, in *King Lear*:

> *Edmund:* To both these sisters have I sworn my love;
>   Each jealous of the other, as the stung
>   Are of the adder. (v.i.55–7)

We can assume (although the action has not yet shown it) that Goneril and Regan *know* of the rival attachment: hence *jealous* must mean 'sexually jealous'. But the comparison, trope, can only apply to a 'suspicious' situation, where *jealous* also means 'anxiously watchful, seeing dangers in every appearance': for, in a sane world, there is no competition for adders' favours; and, alternatively, if the adder is the rival, the fear lest it bite *me* does not fit the sexual situation. The double-meaninged word enables Shakespeare to say two distinct things at once: but the sense 'suspicious' is still the predominant one. *Henry V* (IV.i.281–2) –

> My lord, your nobles, jealous of your absence,
> Seek through your camp to find you –

shows a sense one further removed from 'sexual' than this. They are 'anxiously apprehensive', not 'suspicious'. It should be noted how the dates of these citations are closely contiguous: 1599 (two), 1601, 1603, 1605. Confirmatory evidence is given by usages in *As You Like It*, *Twelfth Night*, *2 Henry IV*.

If it be agreed that Othello's lines (v.ii.350ff.) contain an ambiguous term, 'jealous', then we can estimate what is being said, and, with that, its bearing on the whole Othello and on the whole play. If 'jealous' means *suspicious*, the lines can be taken at face value. Othello is 'not *given* to suspicion': he is trusting (Iago agrees there), and all his dealings with Iago demonstrate it. But a man who denies an ambiguous term may be denying either of its distinct senses. If he is simultaneously aware that he can truthfully deny the one, but not the other, then he is an equivocator. If he could, perhaps should, be aware of what he is falsely denying even in making a true denial of its equivoke, he is a self-deceiver, or is self-deceived. 'The fiend', we can say, if we like, 'equivocates with him (or within him).' The fault in him is not hypocrisy, but lack of insight, self-knowledge: i.e., of sincerity in its deepest sense of integrity. If 'jealous' means capable of or subject to extreme *sexual jealousy*, then Othello is, to say the least, deceived; for III.iii. has been a long revelation of just that: proneness to sexual jealousy. While Iago's game has been made the easier by Othello's *not* being jealous in the sense he still prefers to insist on (in v.ii).

The integrity of the *'noble Othello'* depends enormously on taking without adulteration:

> Of one not easily jealous, but, being wrought,
> Perplex'd in the extreme. . . .

His defence as not sexually jealous will hinge on when he can be said to have been 'wrought'. For that, there is nothing to do but to go back to III.iii.34, and from there follow the character-deployment in detail. But I will anticipate by suggesting that in 'not easily jealous' Othello is right and wrong at once; and add that with his own continual behaviour behind him – and its consequence beside him – he has no good *reason* to be wrong ('excuse' is another matter).

A. P. Rossiter: Angel with Horns, 1961.

(f) The final extract is taken from a chapter entitled 'Love and Identity' in a book by John Bayley and puts the stress on *Othello* as a tragedy of mutual incomprehension.

In claiming for the play a far greater degree of complexity than is generally assumed, I am not saying that it closely resembles Shakespeare's other great plays, or that it works in the same way as they do. *Othello* is a tragedy of incomprehension, not at the level of intrigue but at the very deepest level of human dealings. And one would expect that the effect of such a tragedy would be significantly different from those in which a kind of understanding links the actors ever more closely as they suffer or inflict suffering; that it would be, in fact, more like that of a great novel. No one in *Othello* comes to understand himself or anyone else. None of them realize their situation. At the centre, between the poles of the play, Desdemona, Cassio, and Emilia show common sense and humanity, but it is more a matter of good instinct than illumination. Iago maintains to the end the dreadful integrity of his own ignorance, and in spite of – or perhaps because of – the revelation of Desdemona's innocence, Othello retains to the end his agonized incomprehension – the incomprehension which is so moving an aspect of tragedy in sexual love. His love for Desdemona was to him a marvellous revelation of himself rather than a real knowledge of her. And the proof of her innocence is no substitute for such an awareness. This is the final tragic separation, intensified by the conviction that she is going to heaven and he is going to hell. But although the characters never achieve understanding, and although our response to them – as theirs to each other – shifts with the successive and conflicting pulls of emotion and analysis, so that we see Othello through his own eyes and Iago's as well as with our own, yet if we wait for the fullness of what the play has to offer we do reach a state of tragic comprehension; we are left with a greater insight into the passions and the will, and how they operate to cut us off from each other and from ourselves.

The way this happens is however, as I have suggested, unique in Shakespeare. The tragic atmosphere offers none of that harmonious and formal communion in sorrow which plays at the end of *King Lear*, or the participation in *Macbeth* at the re-establishment of spiritual order. Othello's tragedy is personal, ending in a total loneliness of spirit, and our recognition of it can only be correspondingly solitary. A parallel with the essentially private revelation of the novel form is always making itself felt.

John Bayley: The Characters of Love, 1960.

Some extracts from accounts of *Othello* in performance

Othello has always been a popular stage play ever since the first recorded performance given at Whitehall before King James I in November 1604. Here are some accounts of memorable performances of the tragedy. The first is by William Hazlitt, and describes the great actor Edmund Kean (1787–1833) in the role of Othello. This is followed by a brief account by Charles Lamb of Richard Bensley (1742–1817) as Iago. Finally, there is an account of one of the most famous twentieth century Othellos; that of Sir Laurence Olivier, in 1964, as seen by the critic Ronald Bryden.

(1) *Mr Kean's Othello* –

Mr Kean's Othello is, we suppose, the finest piece of acting in the world. It is impossible either to describe or praise it adequately. We have never seen any actor so wrought upon, so 'perplexed in the extreme.' The energy of passion, as it expresses itself in action, is not the most terrific part; it is the agony of his soul, showing itself in looks and tones of voice. In one part, where he listens in dumb despair to the fiend-like insinuations of Iago, he presented the very face, the marble aspect of Dante's Count Ugolino. On his fixed eyelids 'Horror sat plumed.' In another part, where a gleam of hope or of tenderness returns to subdue the tumult of his passions, his voice broke in faltering accents from his over-charged breast. His lips might be said less to utter words, than to bleed drops of blood gushing from his heart. An instance of this was in his pronunciation of the line 'Of one that loved not wisely but too well.' The whole of this last speech was indeed given with exquisite force and beauty. We only object to the virulence with which he delivers the last line, and with which he stabs himself – a virulence which Othello would neither feel against himself at that moment, nor against the turbaned Turk (whom he had slain) at such a distance of time. His exclamation on seeing his wife, 'I cannot think but Desdemona's honest,' was 'the glorious triumph of exceeding love;' a thought flashing conviction on his mind, and irradiating his countenance with joy, like sudden sunshine. In fact, almost every scene or sentence in this extraordinary exhibition is a masterpiece of natural passion. The convulsed motion of the hands, and the involuntary swellings of the veins of the forehead in some of the most painful situations, should not only suggest topics of critical panegyric, but might furnish studies to the painter or anatomist.

The Times   Drury Lane Oct. 27, 1817.

(2) Bensley's Iago

He let the passion or the sentiment do its own work without prop or bolstering. He would have scorned to mountebank it; and betrayed none of that *cleverness* which is the bane of serious acting. For this reason, his Iago was the only endurable one which I remember to have seen. No spectator from his action could divine more of his artifice than Othello was supposed to do. His confessions in soliloquy alone put you in possession of the mystery. There were no by-intimations to make the audience fancy their own discernment so much greater than that of the Moor – who commonly stands like a great helpless mark set up for mine Ancient, and a quantity of barren spectators, to shoot their bolts at. The Iago of Bensley did not go to work so grossly. There was a triumphant tone about the character, natural to a general consciousness of power; but none of that petty vanity which chuckles and cannot contain itself upon any little successful stroke of its knavery – as is common with your small villains, and green probationers in mischief. It did not clap or crow before its time. It was not a man setting his wits at a child, and winking all the while at other children who are mightily pleased at being let into the secret; but a consummate villain entrapping a noble nature into toils, against which no discernment was available, where the manner was as fathomless as the purpose seemed dark, and without motive.

Charles Lamb: *Essays of Elia,* 1823.

(3) Olivier's Moor

All posterity will want to know is how he played. John Dexter's National Theatre *Othello* is efficient and clear, if slow, and contains some intelligent minor novelties. But in the long run all that matters is that it

left the stage as bare as possible for its athlete. What requires record is
how he, tackling Burbage's role for the first time at 57, created the Moor.
He came on smelling a rose, laughing softly with a private delight;
barefooted, ankleted, black. He had chosen to play a Negro. The story
fits a true Moor better: one of those striding hawks, fierce in a narrow
range of medieval passions, whose women still veil themselves like
Henry Moore sleepers against the blowing sand of Nouakchott's
surrealistically modern streets. But Shakespeare muddled, giving him
the excuse to turn himself into a coastal African from below the Senegal:
dark, thick-lipped, open, laughing.

He sauntered downstage, with a loose, bare-heeled roll of the
buttocks; came to rest feet splayed apart, hip lounging outward. For
him, the great *Richard III* of his day, the part was too simple. He had
made it difficult and interesting for himself by studying, as scrupulously
as he studied the flat vowels, dead grin and hunched time-steps of
Archie Rice, how an African looks, moves, sounds. The make-up, exact
in pigment, covered his body almost wholly: an hour's job at least. The
hands hung big and graceful. The whole voice was characterised, the o's
and a's deepened, the consonants thickened with faint, guttural
deliberation. 'Put up your bright swords, or de dew will rus' dem': not
quite so crude, but in that direction.

It could have been caricature, an embarrassment. Instead, after the
second performance, a well-known Negro actor rose in the stalls
bravoing. For obviously it was done with love; with the main purpose of
substituting for the dead grandeur of the Moorish empire one modern
audiences could respond to: the grandeur of Africa. He was the
continent, like a figure of Rubens allegory. In Cyprus, he strode ashore
in a cloak and spiked helmet which brought to mind the medieval
emirates of Ethiopia and Niger. Facing Doge and senators, he hooded his
eyes in a pouting ebony mask: an old chief listening watchfully in tribal
conclave. When he named them 'my masters' it was proudly edged: he
had been a slave, their inquisition recalled his slavery, he reminded
them in turn of his service and generalship.

He described Desdemona's encouragement smiling down at them,
easy with sexual confidence. This was the other key to the choice of a
Negro: Finlay's Iago, bony, crop-haired, staring with the fanatic mule-
grin of a Mississippi redneck, was to be goaded by a small white man's
sexual jealousy of the black, a jealousy sliding into ambiguous
fascination. Like Yeats's crowd staring, sweating, at Don Juan's mighty
thigh, this Iago gazed, licking dry lips, on a black one. All he had to do
was teach his own disease.

Mannerisms established, they were lifted into the older, broader imagery of the part. Leading Desdemona to bed, he pretended to snap at her with playful teeth. At Iago's first hints, he made a chuckling mock of twisting truth out of him by the ear. Then, during the temptation, he began to pace, turning his head sharply like a lion listening. The climax was his farewell to his occupation: bellowing the words as pure, wounded outcry, he hurled back his head until the ululating tongue showed pink against the roof of his mouth like a trumpeting elephant's. As he grew into a great beast, Finlay shrank beside him, clinging to his shoulder like an ape, hugging his heels like a jackal.

He used every clue in the part, its most strenuous difficulties. Reassured by Desdemona's innocence, he bent to kiss her – and paused looking, sickened, at her lips. Long before his raging return, you knew he had found Cassio's kisses there. Faced with the lung-torturing hurdle of 'Like to the Pontic sea', he found a brilliant device for breaking the period: at 'Shall ne'er look back', he let the memories he was forswearing rush in and stop him, gasping with pain, until he caught breath. Then, at 'By yond marble heaven', he tore the crucifix from his neck (Iago, you recall, says casually Othello'd renounce his baptism for Desdemona) and, crouching forehead to ground, made his 'sacred vow' in the religion which caked Benin's altars with blood.

Possibly it was too early a climax, built to make a curtain of Iago's 'I am your own for ever.' In Act Four he could only repeat himself with increased volume, adding a humming animal moan as he fell into his fit, a strangler's look to the dangling hands, a sharper danger to the turns of his head as he questioned Emilia. But it gave him time to wind down to a superb returned dignity and tenderness for the murder. This became an act of love – at 'I would not have thee linger in thy pain' he threw aside the pillow and, stopping her lips with a kiss, strangled her. The last speech was spoken kneeling on the bed, her body clutched upright to him as a shield for the dagger he turns on himself.

As he slumped beside her in the sheets, the current stopped. A couple of wigged actors stood awkwardly about. You could only pity them: we had seen history, and it was over. Perhaps it's as well to have seen the performance while still unripe, constructed in fragments, still knitting itself. Now you can see how it's done; later, it will be a torrent. But before it exhausts him, a film should be made. It couldn't tell the whole truth, but it might save something the unborn should know.

Othello: National Theatre 1st May, 1964.

Ronald Bryden: *The Unfinished Hero*, 1969.

Select Bibliography

(1)   Books and Articles dealing mainly or at length with *Othello*

Bradley, A. C.: *Shakespearean Tragedy*, Macmillan 1904. Contains a fine psychological discussion of the chief characters.

Gardner, Helen: *The Noble Moor*, Proceedings of the British Academy XLI (1955).

Heilman, R. B.: *Magic in the Web: Action and Language in 'Othello'*, University of Kentucky Press, 1956. A detailed and often illuminating discussion of many aspects of the play, including language, theme and character.

Hunter, G. K.: *'Othello' and Colour Prejudice*, Proceedings of the British Academy LIII (1967). A survey of Elizabethan attitudes towards coloured people.

Jones, Eldred: *Othello's Countrymen: the African in English Renaissance Drama*, Oxford University Press for Fourah Bay College 1965. A more extended treatment of the theme of colour in English drama.

Knight, G. Wilson: 'The Othello Music', in *The Wheel of Fire*, Methuen 1930. A famous and illuminating account of Othello's language and its significance.

Leavis, F. R.: 'Diabolic Intellect and the Noble Hero', in *The Common Pursuit*, Chatto & Windus 1952. An attempt to argue that Othello's tragedy is largely the result of his own egotism and ignorant possessiveness.

Mack, Maynard: *The Jacobean Shakespeare* in Stratford-upon-Avon Studies, Vol. I ed. J. R. Brown and B. Harris, Edward Arnold 1960. Contains a brilliant discussion of the nature of the tragic hero and of the language of Shakespearian tragedy.

Rosenberg, Marvin: *The Masks of Othello*, University of California Press 1961. An attempt to arrive at an understanding of the play through the interpretations of the principal characters by great actors from the seventeenth to the twentieth century.

Shakespeare Survey 21 ed. K. Muir, Cambridge University Press 1968. Most of the articles in this issue are devoted to *Othello*, and includes one by Ned B. Allen suggesting that the play was written in two parts at different times, thus accounting for some of its inconsistencies.

(2)   Shakespeare's Language and Imagery

Clemen, Wolfgang H.: *The Development of Shakespeare's Imagery*, Methuen 1951.

Hulme, H. M.: *Explorations in Shakespeare's Language*, Longman 1962.

Spurgeon, C. F. E.: *Shakespeare's Imagery and what it tells us*, Cambridge University Press 1935.

(3)   Sources

Bullough, G.: *Narrative and Dramatic Sources of Shakespeare*, Vol. VII, Routledge 1973. The sources of *Othello* are reprinted at pp 239ff, and discussed at pp. 193ff.

(4)   The Texts of the play

Schröer, M.: (editor) *Paralleldruck der ersten Quarto und der ersten Folio*, Heidelberg 1949. Reprints the texts of the first Quarto alongside that of the first Folio.

(5)   The Age of Shakespeare

Craig, H.: *The Enchanted Glass: The Elizabethan Mind in Literature*, Oxford 1950.
Lee, S. and Onions, C. T. (editors): *Shakespeare's England: An Account of the Life and Manners of his Age*, Oxford, 2 vols. 1916.
Wilson, J. Dover: *Life in Shakespeare's England*, Cambridge 1915.

(6)   The Theatre of Shakespeare's day

Bradbrook, M. C.: *Elizabethan Stage Conditions: a Study of their Place in the Interpretation of Shakespeare's Plays*, Cambridge 1932.
Gurr, A.: *The Shakespearean Stage, 1574–1642*, Cambridge 1970
Hodges, C. W.: *The Globe Restored: A Study of the Elizabethan Theatre*, London 1968.
Nagler, A. M.: *Shakespeare's Stage*, New Haven, Conn. 1958.

(7)   Shakespeare's Life

Alexander, P.: *Shakespeare*, London 1964.
Williams, C.: *A Short Life of Shakespeare with the Sources*, Oxford 1933.

John Bayley Domestic – the subject
matter of novel – JA, Prout, HJ. So it's
relevant to ask what kind of love etc

Remarkable how much criticism ignores
its main theme of sex. Not an 'impersonal'
tragedy because sex not an impersonal emotion.
O's love was a revelation of himself
rather than a real knowledge of her.

W Knight Solidity & precision of
Dickensque phrase & image – no
fixed metaphysical content. Fine
jungle words characteristic – Anthropophagi,
Sagittary

This beauty changes to extreme
ugliness (compare O's & Lear's mad
speeches)

Not part of a universe – separate people
Othello loves emotion for its own
sake (like R II)

H Gardner Duties not of status, but
of profession.
tragedy of lost faith

[handwritten annotations at top:]

Kerman in Signet. Symbolic geography
Venice "the city" – not a grange
Turks + infidels Cyprus + O between
Passions controlled, Iago excites
them + disrupts order.

Venice – Brabantio's complaint examined
Cyprus – Turks' intentions unveiled
The threatening outpost (storm?)

Othello

[handwritten:] Aaron in TA uses
'coal-black' of ...

Dramatis personae

OTHELLO, *a noble* Moor *in the service of the Venetian state*
BRABANTIO, *a Senator of Venice, Desdemona's father*
CASSIO, *Othello's lieutenant*
IAGO, *Othello's ensign*
RODERIGO, *a Venetian gentleman*
DUKE OF VENICE
MONTANO, *Governor of Cyprus*
GRATIANO, *Brabantio's brother*
LODOVICO, *Brabantio's kinsman*
DESDEMONA, *Brabantio's daughter, Othello's wife*
EMILIA, *Iago's wife, Desdemona's waiting woman*
BIANCA, *a courtesan*
SENATORS, CLOWN, SAILOR, MESSENGER, HERALD, OFFICERS, GENTLEMEN,
MUSICIANS, ATTENDANTS

SCENE: ACT I, *Venice*; ACTS II–V, *Cyprus*.

[handwritten notes at bottom:]

Ridley in Arden Prefans
Plot simple
Few characters (? 7 vs ? 12 in Ham KL AC
Unities (time + tone – no comedy)
Domestic. Senator senior.
Whenever Othello trusts his instinct, he
is right – when reason, wrong.
He falls because of credulity, not
jealousy. He thinks men honest. Jealousy
is an unfamiliar emotion which he cannot
handle

The illustrations below are taken from the 1964 Laurence Olivier production at the National Theatre, London.

Brabantio confronting the Senate, accusing Othello of having bewitched Desdemona (Act I, Scene iii)

Othello being asked by the Duke of Venice to take charge of the situation in Cyprus (Act I, Scene iii)

Othello, now convinced by Iago of Desdemona's unfaithfulness, is determined to kill her (Act III, Scene iii)

Othello embracing Desdemona, after having strangled her (Act V, Scene ii)

I.i.   Iago, an ensign, expresses to Roderigo, a young Venetian, his hatred of his superior officer Othello. Apparently he, Iago, has been passed over for promotion in favour of a Florentine, Michael Cassio.

Roderigo, who is infatuated with Desdemona, is angry because Iago has not told him of Othello's elopement with her. Iago denies prior knowledge of the elopement and urges Roderigo to rouse Desdemona's father Brabantio, and tell him of his daughter's conduct. On hearing the news Brabantio with his servants and officers of the night watch goes in search of Othello.

The action begins in a street in Venice, in Shakespeare's time the great commerical republic of the western world. These opening lines convey very vividly not only the situation at the beginning of the story, but also the different characters of the speakers, the relationship between them, and the atmosphere of mystery and intrigue surrounding their conversation. Roderigo's phrase, *Never tell me* suggests his impatience, while the reference to his *purse* tells us exactly what the link is between him and Iago. Roderigo is complaining that Iago has spent a good deal of his (Roderigo's) money with no apparent results. Iago's rejoinder, *'Sblood, but you'll not hear me,* in spite of the oath with which it begins (and which would, after all, come fairly easily to a professional soldier), has the tone of a grown-up waiting for a quick-tempered child to calm down, and is in sharp contrast to Roderigo's petulance. But there is also an element of real menace in Iago's constant emphatic assertions and oaths. He is trying to weaken Roderigo's attack before it gathers strength by taking the offensive himself.

The sense of mystery and intrigue is suggested in several ways. Though Iago is named in the second line, the audience is not told who the other speaker is for over fifty lines of dialogue. The central character, after whom the play is named, is referred to indirectly to begin with, and we have to wait a long time before we understand what the *matter* is that Iago says he never *did dream of*.

The fact that these opening scenes take place at night also adds to the air of suspense and urgency. In the open-air theatre for which Shakespeare wrote, plays were presented in daylight, but the actors would probably suggest night and darkness not only by their words but also by their gestures and movements.

1	*Tush! Never tell me:* Nonsense, don't try to make me believe that. – Roderigo's expression of impatient disbelief indicates that the action opens in the middle of a conversation. Roderigo refuses to believe Iago's protestations of ignorance.
2	*thou* – see p. xxx of the Introduction for a discussion of 'thou' forms.
3	*strings:* cord used to fasten money-purses. – Roderigo is implying that Iago had a free hand with his (Roderigo's) funds. We have as yet no knowledge of what *this* (*shoulds't know of this*) may be, but Roderigo has just had news of it, presumably from Iago.
4	*'Sblood:* By God's blood – an oath.
8	*In personal suit:* personally bearing a petition.
8	*Lieutenant:* second-in-command.
9	*Off-capped:* took off their caps. – A sign of respect in Othello's presence.
10	*I know my price:* I know my value. – Iago has a high opinion of himself, and now that he has quietened Roderigo, is not shy about asserting it. His sense of unrewarded merit is an important key to his attitude and actions.
12	*a bombast circumstance:* an exaggerated and long-winded expression. – Bombast was originally a kind of cotton used for padding clothes. From this it came to refer to pompous and inflated language. (*Stuffed* in line 13 continues the metaphor.)
13	*epithets of war:* military terms. – We shall remember the picture Iago gives here of Othello as a pompous, conceited and arbitrary man when we actually see the Moor and especially when he appears before the Signiory in I.iii.
14	*Nonsuits:* rejects. – Originally a legal term meaning that a court action is judged to be wholly unjustified and therefore rejected. Iago is not, of course, saying that an actual court action was involved, merely that Othello rejected him out of hand.
14	*mediators:* supporters – i.e. those who spoke on Iago's behalf.
14	*Certes:* Certainly.
15	*chose:* chosen.
15	*what* – i.e. what kind of man.
16	*Forsooth:* In truth. – An expression of sarcastic contempt.
16	*arithmetician:* (i) one who knows only the theory (of soldiership) not its practice; (ii) a mere clerk or book-keeper. – As Florence was known throughout Europe for its great banking activities, this second gibe was just what a Venetian might level at a Florentine such as Cassio.

Othello ACT I scene i

Venice. A street.

Enter RODERIGO *and* IAGO.

RODERIGO Tush! Never tell me.* I take it much unkindly
That thou,* Iago, who hast had my purse
As if the strings* were thine, shouldst know of this.

IAGO 'Sblood,* but you'll not hear me! If ever I did dream
Of such a matter, abhor me.

RODERIGO   Thou told'st me   5
Thou didst hold him in thy hate.

IAGO   Despise me
If I do not. Three great ones of the city,
In personal suit* to make me his lieutenant,*
Off-capped* to him; and by the faith of man,
I know my price;* I am worth no worse a place.   10
But he, as loving his own pride and purposes,
Evades them with a bombast circumstance,*
Horribly stuffed with epithets of war,*
Nonsuits* my mediators.* For, 'Certes,'* says he,
'I have already chose* my officer.' And what* was he?   15
Forsooth,* a great arithmetician,*
One Michael Cassio, a Florentine,
(A fellow almost damned in a fair wife)*
That never set a squadron in the field,
Nor the division of a battle* knows   20
More than a spinster,* unless* the bookish theoric,*
Wherein the togéd* consuls can propose*
As masterly* as he. Mere prattle without practice

----

18   *A fellow almost damned in a fair wife* – The sense is obscure, as Cassio does not appear to be
           married. If *fair wife* is taken to mean 'pretty woman' then Iago may simply be
           saying that Cassio is the sort of man whose fondness for women could be his ruin.
20   *division of a battle:* line of battle, front line.
21   *More than a spinster* – i.e. who knows no more than a spinster about it.
21   *unless:* except for.
21   *bookish theoric:* abstract book-knowledge. – Iago is elaborating on his accusation that
           Cassio has no first-hand experience of battle.
22   *togéd:* wearing togas (like the ancient Romans).
22   *propose:* make suggestions.
23   *masterly:* skilfully.

1

24	*had th'election:* was chosen (for the appointment). The 'he' referred to in this line is Cassio, who is also the 'he' of line 29. 'His' in line 25 and 29 refers to Othello.
25	*proof:* trial, practical ability.
26	*grounds:* battlefields.
27	*belee'd and calmed:* cut off from the wind. – Iago means that Cassio has come between him and the possibility of advancement.
28	*debitor and creditor:* a book-keeper.
28	*counter-caster:* one who reckons by adding counters (discs of metal). – In using both this expression and *debitor and creditor*, Iago is enlarging on his notion of Cassio as a contemptible theorist.
30	*God bless the mark!:* God help us! – a mild oath.
30	*his Moorship's ancient:* his Moorish lordship's standard-bearer (i.e. aide-de-camp). – Iago of course uses *his Moorship* contemptuously.
33	*Preferment . . . affection:* promotion depends on theoretical knowledge (*letter*) and favouritism.
34	*by old gradation:* according to seniority. – Iago is carefully building himself up as a traditionalist injured by a rash intruder with no regard for ancient custom.
36	*in any just term:* on any reasonable ground.
36	*affined:* bound.
38	*content you:* rest assured.
39	*to serve . . . him:* to use him to my own advantage.
40–41	*nor . . . cannot:* neither can all masters be.
42	*knee-crooking:* bending and bowing.
43	*doting . . . bondage:* completely preoccupied by his own servile behaviour.
45	*provender:* food and drink.
45	*cashiered:* dismissed.
46	*Whip me* – an obsolete form equivalent to 'let (them) be whipped'.
47	*trimmed . . . duty:* putting on an outward appearance of respectful obedience. – The contrast is with *hearts* in the next line.
48	*Keep . . . themselves:* inwardly seek only their own advantage.
50	*well thrive:* greatly prosper.
50	*lined their coats:* feathered their nests, benefited themselves. – Iago has no hesitation in telling Roderigo the exact truth, confident that the latter is too stupid and gullible to understand how it applies to himself and Iago.
51	*Do themselves homage:* Respect themselves. – Iago is saying that those who pay respect to others for their own advancement, once they have gained their ends can follow their own inclinations openly.
51	*soul:* spirit.
54	*Were I . . . be Iago* – like many of Iago's remarks, this seems clearer at first sight than on reflection. 'If I were Othello, I would not want such a man as myself near me' seems to be the meaning.
57	*peculiar:* own individual.
59	*native act and figure:* true action and nature.
60	*complement extern:* outward aspect. – Iago scorns to make his outward behaviour a true guide to his inner feelings.
60	*'tis not long after/But:* it will not be long before I . . .
61	*upon my sleeve:* – where serving men usually wore their badges. The phrase 'to wear one's heart upon one's sleeve' has passed into the language and means 'to show one's feelings openly'.
62	*daws:* jackdaws. – Figuratively, fools.
62	*I am not what I am:* My true nature is not what I portray outwardly. – Very early on in the drama, we are offered this important clue to Iago's true nature, but what exactly Iago is remains elusive, a constantly changing mystery.

Is all his soldiership. But he, sir, had th'election;*
And I, of whom his eyes had seen the proof*   25
At Rhodes, at Cyprus, and on other grounds*
Christian and heathen, must be belee'd and calmed*
By debitor and creditor.* This counter-caster,'
He, in good time, must his lieutenant be,
And I – God bless the mark!* – his Moorship's ancient.*   30

RODERIGO By heaven, I rather would have been his hangman.

IAGO Why, there's no remedy. 'Tis the curse of service:
Preferment* goes by letter and affection,
And not by old gradation,* where each second
Stood heir to th'first. Now, sir, be judge yourself,   35
Whether I in any just term* am affined*
To love the Moor.

RODERIGO   I would not follow him then.

IAGO O sir, content you.*
I follow him to serve* my turn upon him.
We cannot all be masters, nor* all masters   40
Cannot be truly followed. You shall mark
Many a duteous and knee-crooking* knave
That, doting* on his own obsequious bondage,
Wears out his time, much like his master's ass,
For naught but provender;* and when he's old,
                              cashiered.*   45
Whip me* such honest knaves! Others there are
Who, trimmed* in forms and visages of duty,
Keep* yet their hearts attending on themselves,
And, throwing but shows of service on their lords,
Do well thrive* by them, and when they have lined their
                              coats*   50
Do themselves homage.* These fellows have some soul,*
And such a one do I profess myself. For, sir,
It is as sure as you are Roderigo,
Were I* the Moor, I would not be Iago.
In following him, I follow but myself.   55
Heaven is my judge, not I for love and duty,
But seeming so, for my peculiar* end;
For when my outward action doth demonstrate
The native act and figure* of my heart
In complement extern,* 'tis not long after   60
But* I will wear my heart upon my sleeve*
For daws* to peck at; I am not what I am.*

63   *What . . . thick-lips owe:* How fortunate the negro is. *(owe:* own). – The Elizabethans made no distinction between Moor and Negro, but Roderigo is being deliberately offensive here.

64   *carry't thus:* bring it off in this manner, get away with this.

64   Iago's speech beginning *Call up her father* introduces a quicker and more urgent tempo into the action. The succession of short, jerky phrases is in strong contrast to the slower and more argumentative rhythm of the dialogue up to this point, reaching one climax with the cry of *Thieves, thieves!* (I.i.78).

65   *him* – i.e. Othello.

67   *though he . . . dwell:* though he has found good fortune and favour.

68   *Plague him with flies:* Torment him, as the Egyptians were tormented by the plague described in the Old Testament, *Exodus* 8:20.

68   *though that:* though.

69   *chances of vexation:* possibilities of misfortune.

70   *lose some colour:* be somewhat faded and spoilt.

71   *Here is her father's house* – The freedom and flexibility of the Elizabethan stage made this kind of localization seem entirely natural.

72–73 *like . . . As . . . :* with the same frightening tone and desperate shouting as . . .

73   *by night and negligence:* at night and due to negligence.

S.D.78 *Brabantio above* – Brabantio appears on the rear balcony, a permanent feature of the Elizabethan stage, here used to represent the upper storey of Brabantio's house.

79   *terrible:* terrifying.

83   *Zounds:* (By) God's wounds!

86   *tupping:* sexually enjoying. – These lines contain the most striking of many animal images into which Iago's speech habitually falls, and indicate his view of human relationships and desires. Though he appears to loathe the thought of the union between the Moor and Brabantio's daughter, there is something like lip-smacking relish mixed with the loathing.

87   *snorting:* snoring.

87   *bell:* the church bells – rung in case of fire or other emergency.

88   *the devil . . . of you ·* the devil will make you a grandfather. – To the Elizabethans black was the colour of the devil.

92   *worser:* worse, less.

93   *charged:* ordered.

95   *not for thee:* not intended for you (to marry).

96   *distemp'ring draughts:* intoxicating drinks.

97   *Upon malicious knavery:* with the deliberate intention of doing mischief.

98   *start my quiet:* disturb my rest.

RODERIGO What* a full fortune does the thick-lips owe
          If he can carry't thus!*
    IAGO   Call up her father,*
          Rouse him,* make after him, poison his delight,   65
          Proclaim him in the streets. Incense her kinsmen,
          And though he* in a fertile climate dwell,
          Plague him with flies;* though that* his joy be joy,
          Yet throw such chances of vexation* on't
          As it may lose some colour.*   70
RODERIGO Here is her father's house.* I'll call aloud.
    IAGO Do, with like* timorous accent and dire yell
          As when, by night and negligence,* the fire
          Is spied in populous cities.
RODERIGO What, ho, Brabantio! Signior Brabantio, ho!   75
    IAGO Awake! What ho, Brabantio! Thieves, thieves!
          Look to your house, your daughter, and your bags!
          Thieves, thieves!

          BRABANTIO *above,* at a window.*

BRABANTIO What is the reason of this terrible* summons?
           What is the matter there?   80
RODERIGO Signior, is all your family within?
    IAGO Are your doors locked?
BRABANTIO   Why, wherefore ask you this?
    IAGO Zounds,* sir, y'are robbed! For shame, put on your gown!
          Your heart is burst, you have lost half your soul.
          Even now, now, very now, an old black ram   85
          Is tupping* your white ewe. Arise, arise!
          Awake the snorting* citizens with the bell,*
          Or else the devil* will make a grandsire of you.
          Arise I say!
BRABANTIO   What, have you lost your wits?
RODERIGO Most reverend signior, do you know my voice?   90
BRABANTIO Not I; what are you?
RODERIGO My name is Roderigo.
BRABANTIO   The worser* welcome!
          I have charged* thee not to haunt about my doors.
          In honest plainness thou hast heard me say
          My daughter is not for thee;* and now, in madness,   95
          Being full of supper and distemp'ring draughts,*
          Upon malicious knavery* dost thou come
          To start my quiet.*

99   *must needs be sure:* must be assured.
100   *my spirits and my place:* my feelings and my authority.
101   *bitter:* extremely unpleasant.
102–3   *This is Venice . . . grange:* This is Venice (a crowded and busy city), not a lonely farmhouse. – A *grange* was originally a monastic farm, hence any isolated dwelling.
104   *In simple and pure soul:* honestly and straightforwardly. – Roderigo is denying Brabantio's earlier charge of *malicious knavery.* (I.i.97).
105   *Will not . . . bid you:* will not even serve God if it is the devil who commands you to do it. – Iago means that Brabantio refuses to hear good counsel (or the truth) just because it comes from someone whom he believes to be evil.
106   *to do you service:* to help you. – But *service* could also carry the sexual sense of copulation, particularly between animals.
108   *covered with:* sexually enjoyed by. Iago is now thoroughly enjoying his bestial humour. The headlong succession of variations on the central metaphor suggests that his fevered imagination is out of control.
108   *Barbary:* from the north African coast.
109   *nephews:* grandsons or any lineal descendants. – Like *cousins* in the next line, the term was used far more loosely than it is today. In speaking the word, Iago would probably bring out the similarity of sound to *neigh.* There are many examples in this speech and elsewhere of Iago's taste for alliteration.
109   *coursers:* swift horses.
110   *gennets:* small-sized Spanish horses. – The name derives from the Zeneta tribesmen who originally supplied these horses to the Moorish sultans.
110   *germans:* blood relations.
111   *profane* – literally 'irreverent or blasphemous', but here meaning 'foul-mouthed'.
113   *making . . . backs:* having sexual intercourse. – The phrase is typical of Iago's tendency to see human activity in animal terms.
114   *You are – a senator* – Iago probably pauses before uttering Brabantio's title, thus making it sound like an insult. The implication is that he could have called the *senator* by a name as bad as *villain* which Brabantio has just applied to him. The interplay between the 'thou' form of address which Brabantio habitually uses and the 'you' of Iago and Roderigo serves to indicate not only the social rank of the different characters but their frame of mind.
119   *odd-even* – The *even* of night is midnight; the *odd-even* is probably the period between midnight and one o'clock.
119   *dull:* sleepy.
119   *watch:* one of the periods into which the night was divided in former times. – It still survives in naval usage, referring to a period of duty.
120   *Transported with:* should be transported by.
121   *But:* than.
121   *knave:* servant.
121   *common hire:* available for hire by anyone – i.e. not attached to a single private household.
122   *clasps:* embraces.
123   *your allowance:* (done with) your consent.
124   *saucy:* outrageous – a sense stronger than its modern meaning, 'cheeky'.
125   *manners tell:* moral sense tells.
126   *have your wrong rebuke:* are unjustly censured by you.
127   *from . . . civility:* far removed from the boundaries of decent behaviour. – Considering the unwelcome news he brings, the apparently reasonable tone of Roderigo's speech is calculated to upset Brabantio all the more.
128   *your reverence:* your honourable self.
132   *Tying . . . in an extravagant and wheeling stranger:* Placing all her future in the hands of a wandering and unsteady alien. – Shakespeare always uses the word *extravagant* in its classical sense of 'wandering' or 'vagrant'. The contrast between the restless and unreliable foreigner and the long-established citizenry of Venice is one which we shall be offered several times in the play.
133   *Straight:* Immediately.

RODERIGO Sir, sir, sir —

BRABANTIO   But thou must needs be sure*
My spirits and my place* have in their power   100
To make this bitter* to thee.

RODERIGO   Patience, good sir.

BRABANTIO What tell'st thou me of robbing? This is Venice;*
My house is not a grange.

RODERIGO   Most grave Brabantio,
In simple and pure soul* I come to you.

IAGO Zounds, sir, you are one of those that will not* serve God   105
if the devil bid you. Because we come to do you service*
and you think we are ruffians, you'll have your daughter
covered with* a Barbary* horse, you'll have your
nephews* neigh to you, you'll have coursers* for cousins,
and gennets* for germans.*   110

BRABANTIO What profane* wretch art thou?

IAGO I am one, sir, that comes to tell you your daughter and the
Moor are making* the beast with two backs.

BRABANTIO Thou art a villain.

IAGO   You are — a senator.*

BRABANTIO This thou shalt answer. I know thee, Roderigo.   115

RODERIGO Sir, I will answer anything. But I beseech you,
If't be your pleasure and most wise consent,
As partly I find it is, that your fair daughter,
At this odd-even* and dull* watch* o'th'night,
Transported with* no worse nor better guard   120
But* with a knave* of common hire,* a gondolier,
To the gross clasps* of a lascivious Moor —
If this be known to you, and your allowance,*
We then have done you bold and saucy* wrongs;
But if you know not this, my manners tell* me   125
We have your wrong rebuke.* Do not believe
That from* the sense of all civility
I thus would play and trifle with your reverence.*
Your daughter, if you have not given her leave,
I say again, hath made a gross revolt,   130
Tying her duty, beauty, wit, and fortunes
In an extravagant and wheeling stranger*
Of here and everywhere. Straight* satisfy yourself.
If she be in her chamber, or your house,
Let loose on me the justice of the state   135
For thus deluding you.

136   *strike on the tinder* – the ancient method of producing fire for a light.
137   *taper:* large candle, thinner at the end to be lighted than at the other.
138   *This accident . . . my dream* – The fact that Brabantio has had a dream concerning his daughter's elopement partly accounts for the readiness with which he believes the news, as suggested in the next line.
140   *Farewell* – Iago neatly prepares for his exit here, although he remains on stage till the end of this fairly long speech. (He has probably not been recognized by Brabantio, partly because during most of this scene he would be directly underneath the balcony and therefore out of Brabantio's sight, and partly because the actors would indicate by their gestures the fact that the scene is taking place in darkness.) Iago says that as he is Othello's ensign, it would not be very prudent if he were to be identified as Othello's accuser or as a witness against him. Furthermore, as Othello is shortly going to be needed by the state, it would be expedient to pretend loyalty to him.
141   *meet:* fitting.
142   *produced:* brought forward as a witness.
144   *gall . . . check:* chafe or upset him with some rebuke. – The metaphor is taken from checking a horse with bridle or bit, and may be continued in *cast* in the next line, which could refer specifically to a horse being rejected as unfit for further service. In any case Iago is clearly still thinking in terms of his original animal imagery.
146   *loud reason:* obvious justification.
146   *wars* – often used as a singular noun in Shakespeare's day.
147   *stands in act:* has begun.
147   *for their souls:* for all they are worth. – Iago admits that Venice could not find Othello's equal anywhere.
148   *fathom:* ability – The word originally meant 'as much as could be grasped with outstretched arms' and hence a measure of length and figuratively, as here, of capability. The praise of Othello is wrung from Iago almost in spite of himself and he is quick to return to his spitefulness.
149   *business:* affairs – (i.e. the war).
152   *flag and sign:* outward show. – The image refers to Iago's rank as ensign or standard-bearer. (i.i.30).
153   *but:* only.
153   *That:* So that.
154   *Sagittary* – An inn bearing the sign of the centaur, a mythical creature, half man, half-horse, armed with bow and arrows as in the zodiacal sign of Sagittarius.
154   *raisèd search:* assembled party (gathered to discover Othello's whereabouts).
155   *S.D. nightgown:* dressing gown worn for warmth at night when getting out of bed.
156–63 The broken phrases of Brabantio's speech reflect his distraction after the discovery of his loss.
157   *my despisèd time:* the future, when I shall be held in contempt (because of Desdemona's disobedience).
165   *blood:* (i) passions; (ii) family relationships.
167   *Is:* Are.
167   *charms* – This is the first hint of a charge that is to be made publicly against Othello. The theme of magic and witchcraft is present throughout the play.
168   *property:* nature.
169   *May:* Can (also i.i.173).

BRABANTIO   Strike on the tinder,* ho!
          Give me a taper!* Call up all my people!
          This accident* is not unlike my dream.
          Belief of it oppresses me already.
          Light, I say, light!

                                        [*Exit above*

IAGO   Farewell,* for I must leave you.   140
          It seems not meet,* nor wholesome to my place,
          To be produced* – as, if I stay, I shall –
          Against the Moor. For I do know the state,
          However this may gall* him with some check,
          Cannot with safety cast him; for he's embarked   145
          With such loud reason* to the Cyprus wars,*
          Which even now stands in act,* that for their souls*
          Another of his fathom* they have none
          To lead their business;* in which regard,
          Though I do hate him as I do hell-pains,   150
          Yet, for necessity of present life,
          I must show out a flag and sign* of love,
          Which is indeed but* sign. That* you shall surely find
                                                          him,
          Lead to the Sagittary* the raisèd search,*
          And there will I be with him. So farewell.   155

                                        [*Exit*

          Enter BRABANTIO *in his nightgown,* with* SERVANTS
          and torches.

BRABANTIO It is too true an evil. Gone she is,
          And what's to come of my despisèd time*
          Is naught but bitterness. Now Roderigo,
          Where didst thou see her? – O unhappy girl! –
          With the Moor, say'st thou – Who would be a father? –   160
          How didst thou know 'twas she? – O, she deceives me
          Past thought! – What said she to you? Get more tapers!
          Raise all my kindred! – Are they married, think you?
RODERIGO Truly I think they are.
BRABANTIO O heaven! How got she out? O treason of the blood!*   165
          Fathers, from hence trust not your daughters' minds
          By what you see them act. Is* there not charms*
          By which the property* of youth and maidhood
          May* be abused? Have you not read, Roderigo,
          Of some such thing?

171   *would you had had her!*: I wish you had married her! – Brabantio had expressly forbidden Roderigo to court his daughter (I.i.93) but in his distraction he wishes that Roderigo had married her, to save her from the fate of becoming the Moor's bride.

172   *Some* – i.e, Go, some of you, my people.

177   *I may command at most* – Brabantio has the power to call for helpers from most houses, either because they are those of his kinsmen or because he is an important civic figure.

179   *deserve your pains*: recompense you for your trouble.

I.ii.   Iago tells Othello that some villain has been talking insultingly about him. He ascertains that Othello is now married to Desdemona. A party, led by Cassio, arrives with a message from the Duke summoning Othello to the council chamber as there is a threat to Cyprus from the Turkish forces. This party meets Brabantio's group and Brabantio accuses Othello of bewitching his daughter. Both groups move to the council chamber where Brabantio can make his accusation before the Duke himself.

The torch-bearers who attend on Othello in this scene would by their behaviour suggest ceremony and order in contrast to the bustle and disorder of those we have just seen surrounding Brabantio. But the greatest contrast the opening of this scene offers with what has gone before is that between the description of Othello in gross and bestial terms by Iago and Roderigo and the calm dignity of Othello's opening words. By commenting on Iago's apparently sincere outburst with a quiet but authoritative half-line, '*Tis better as it is*, Othello shows self-discipline and self-confidence; the contrast is not only with the malicious picture of him drawn earlier, but with Brabantio's near-hysterical panic.

Iago's method of gaining favour with Othello is different from that which he employed with Roderigo. Roderigo is a fool to whom Iago can afford to tell the truth about himself and his motives. With Othello he assumes the role of the honest and loyal soldier who can hardly restrain himself from violence in defending his master's honour.

2   *very stuff*: the very essence.

3   *contrived*. deliberately planned.

3–4   *I lack . . . service*: There are times when it would help if I were more unscrupulous.

5   *thought t'have*: thought of.

5   *yerked*: struck sharply, thrust.

5   *him* – i.e. Roderigo.

6   *prated*: boasted.

7   *scurvy*: low.

9   *full hard*: with great difficulty.

9   *forbear*: spare.

10   *fast*: definitely. – Othello probably answers Iago's question with a gesture. His silence when we may expect him to speak heightens our eagerness to hear him.

11   *magnifico*: Venetian nobleman, i.e. Brabantio.

12   *potential*: powerful.

13   *As double as the Duke's*: Of double power, like the Duke's. – The Duke had twice the power of the other noblemen and Iago is (falsely) asserting that Brabantio is just as influential.

14   *grievance*: hardship.

16   *cable*: scope to do. A cable is a thick rope used in ships. Although he is a soldier, Iago uses many images drawn from sailing, perhaps because a Venetian soldier would be used to fighting on land and sea.

16   *spite* – i.e. the worst that his spite can do.

17   *Signiory*: Venetian government.

18   *out-tongue . . .*: It is not yet known (that I am royally descended).

18   '*Tis yet to know*: I have yet to learn.

20   *promulgate*: proclaim.

20   *fetch*: derive.

20   *life and being*: quality and name.

RODERIGO	Yes, sir, I have indeed.	170
BRABANTIO	Call up my brother. – O, would you had had her!* –	
	Some* one way, some another. – Do you know	
	Where we may apprehend her and the Moor?	
RODERIGO	I think I can discover him, if you please	
	To get good guard and go along with me.	175
BRABANTIO	Pray you lead on. At every house I'll call;	
	I may command at most.* – Get weapons, ho!	
	And raise some special officers of night. –	
	On, good Roderigo; I will deserve your pains.*	

[*Exeunt*

scene ii

Another street outside the Sagittary.

So his first appearance
Dissipates Iago's
picture & make us
assess him afresh.

Enter OTHELLO, IAGO, ATTENDANTS *with torches.*

IAGO	Though in the trade of war I have slain men,	
	Yet do I hold it very stuff* o'th'conscience	
	To do no contrived* murder. I lack* iniquity	
	Sometime to do me service. Nine or ten times	
	I had thought t'have* yerked* him* here, under the ribs.	5
OTHELLO	'Tis better as it is.	
IAGO	Nay, but he prated,*	
	And spoke such scurvy* and provoking terms	
	Against your honour, that with the little godliness I have	
	I did full hard* forbear* him. But I pray you sir,	
	Are you fast* married? Be assured of this,	10
	That the magnifico* is much beloved,	
	And hath in his effect a voice potential*	
	As double as the Duke's.* He will divorce you,	
	Or put upon you what restraint or grievance*	
	The law, with all his might to enforce it on,	15
	Will give him cable.*	
OTHELLO	Let him do his spite.*	
	My services which I have done the Signiory*	
	Shall out-tongue* his complaints. 'Tis yet to know* –	
	Which when I know that boasting is an honour	
	I shall promulgate* – I fetch* my life and being*	20

Profession
not status

First
utterance
– theatrical

21   *siege:* rank. – Literally *siege* means a seat of power, such as a throne.
21   *demerits:* deserts, worth.
22   *unbonneted* – i.e. on equal terms. In Shakespeare's time 'to bonnet' may have meant to take one's cap *off* (as a mark of deference); hence *unbonneted* would signify the absence of such deference. The general sense is 'What I have deserved and the rewards I have obtained are a fair match for each other.'
24   *But . . . Desdemona* – If I did not (*But that*) love Desdemona I would not accept the restriction (*circumscription and confine*) of my unrestrained (*unhoused*) liberty. This is the first time Desdemona has been mentioned by name. The line shines out in its simplicity from the grand rhetoric of Othello's speech so far and gives a hint of the depth of his feeling for her.
25   *unhousèd:* unconfined.
26   *circumscription:* restriction.
27   *seas' worth:* for a vast treasure. – Perhaps there is a hint here of the fact that the fabulous wealth of Venice at this time was based on the sea.
27   *yond:* over there.
30   *parts:* attributes, capacities.
30   *perfect:* completely prepared.
32   *Janus:* Roman god with two faces.
36   *haste-posthaste:* speediest possible. – The words were sometimes written on letters requiring urgent delivery.
38   *divine:* gather, infer.
39   *heat:* urgency.
39   *galleys:* warships.
40   *sequent:* coming one after another.
42   *consuls:* councillors.
43   *hotly:* urgently. – This suggests the importance of Othello in the public affairs of Venice.
45   *several:* separate.
48   *makes:* does.
48   *he:* is he doing.
49   *boarded:* (i) taken a ship as prize; (ii) had intercourse with.
49   *land carack:* treasure ship on dry land.

From men of royal siege;* and my demerits*
May speak unbonneted* to as proud a fortune
As this that I have reached. For know, Iago,
But* that I love the gentle Desdemona,
I would not my unhousèd* free condition   25
Put into circumscription and confine
For the seas' worth.* But look, what lights come yond?*

Enter CASSIO, *with* OFFICERS *and torches.*

IAGO   Those are the raiséd father and his friends.
You were best go in.
OTHELLO   Not I. I must be found.
My parts,* my title, and my perfect* soul   30
Shall manifest me rightly. Is it they?
IAGO   By Janus,* I think no.
OTHELLO   The servants of the Duke? And my lieutenant?
The goodness of the night upon you, friends.
What is the news?
CASSIO   The Duke does greet you, general,   35
And he requires your haste-posthaste* appearance
Even on the instant.
OTHELLO   What is the matter, think you?
CASSIO   Something from Cyprus, as I may divine.*
It is a business of some heat.* The galleys*
Have sent a dozen sequent* messengers   40
This very night at one another's heels,
And many of the consuls,* raised and met,
Are at the Duke's already. You have been hotly* called
                                for.
When, being not at your lodging to be found,
The Senate hath sent about three several* quests   45
To search you out.
OTHELLO   'Tis well I am found by you.
I will but spend a word here in the house,
And go with you.
                         [*Exit*

CASSIO   Ancient, what makes* he* here?
IAGO   Faith, he tonight hath boarded* a land carack.*
If it prove lawful prize, he's made forever.   50
CASSIO   I do not understand.
IAGO   He's married.
CASSIO   To who?

52	*Marry:* By (the Virgin) Mary. – A pun on 'marry'.
52	*Have with you:* Let's go.
57	*I am for you:* I'm your man (to fight).
58	*keep up:* Put away (in their scabbards).
58	*Keep . . . them* – This line is expressive of Othello's eloquent authority. Though he probably has no sword himself (having just taken his leave of Desdemona) the others put theirs away at his bidding. There is a dignified irony in Othello's suggestion that the damp air of the night might rust the exposed swords.
59	*years* – i.e. age, seniority.
61	*stowed:* put, hidden. A contraction of 'bestowed'.
62	*enchanted:* bewitched. – Brabantio means this literally.
63	*I'll refer me . . . :* I would appeal to every aspect of common sense.
63	*sense:* common sense.
66	*opposite:* opposed.
67	*curlèd* – i.e. with curled hair.
68	*t'incur . . . mock:* to suffer public ridicule.
69	*guardage:* shelter, guardianship. In Brabantio's view, it is plain that only witchcraft could have made Desdemona, who hated marriage so much that she avoided the finest young men in Venice, run to the arms of such a frightening figure as the Moor.
71	*Judge me the world:* Let the world judge me.
71	*gross in sense:* perfectly plain.
72	*practised on her:* plotted against her.
73	*minerals* – i.e. poisonous substances.
75	*probable* – Brabantio uses the word almost in its original sense of 'capable of being proved'.
75	*palpable to thinking:* may be very easily thought.
76	*attach:* arrest.
77	*abuser:* corrupter.
78	*inhibited:* prohibited. – Brabantio is accusing Othello of practising black magic on Desdemona.
78	*out of warrant:* against the law.
80	*at his peril:* at his own risk.
80	*Hold:* Hold back.
81	*of my inclining:* on my side, of my party.
82–3	*cue . . . prompter* – Othello takes his metaphor from the stage actor who is helped by the *prompter* when he forgets his *cue*. He implies that he knows very well what 'part' he should play here.

Enter OTHELLO.

IAGO Marry,* to – Come, captain, will you go?

OTHELLO   Have with you.*

CASSIO Here comes another troop to seek for you.

Enter BRABANTIO, RODERIGO, *with* OFFICERS *and torches.*

IAGO It is Brabantio. General, be advised.
He comes to bad intent.

OTHELLO   Holla! Stand there!   55

RODERIGO Signior, it is the Moor.

BRABANTIO   Down with him, thief!
[*They draw swords*

IAGO You, Roderigo? Come, sir, I am for you.*

OTHELLO Keep* up* your bright swords, for the dew will rust them.
Good signior, you shall more command with years*
Than with your weapons.   60

BRABANTIO O thou foul thief, where hast thou stowed* my daughter?
Damned as thou art, thou hast enchanted* her!
For I'll refer me* to all things of sense,*
If she in chains of magic were not bound,
Whether a maid so tender, fair, and happy,   65
So opposite* to marriage that she shunned
The wealthy, curlèd* darlings of our nation,
Would ever have, t'incur* a general mock,
Run from her guardage* to the sooty bosom
Of such a thing as thou – to fear, not to delight?   70
Judge me the world* if 'tis not gross in sense*
That thou hast practised on her* with foul charms,
Abused her delicate youth with drugs or minerals*
That weaken motion. I'll have't disputed on;
'Tis probable,* and palpable to thinking.*   75
I therefore apprehend and do attach* thee
For an abuser* of the world, a practiser
Of arts inhibited* and out of warrant.*

[*To the* OFFICERS]

Lay hold upon him. If he do resist,
Subdue him at his peril.*

OTHELLO   Hold* your hands,   80
Both you of my inclining* and the rest.
Were it my cue* to fight, I should have known it

83   *Whither . . . go:* where do you want me to go?
85   *direct session:* immediate trial.
89   *present:* urgent.
93   *Bring:* Take.
94   *idle:* unimportant, frivolous. – Brabantio is justifying his decision to bring his personal
       ·   grievance before the state at a time of national crisis by insisting that Othello's
           action is a threat not only to him personally but to all the noblemen of Venice,
           including the Duke.
97   *passage free:* free pardon.
98   *Bondslaves and pagans* – an insulting reference to Othello's past history and faith. See the
           section on Elizabethans and Moors on page xii of the Introduction.

I.iii.   The Duke is talking with some senators in the council chamber about the conflicting
reports from Cyprus. Brabantio, Roderigo, Othello, Iago and others arrive and Brabantio
repeats his charge that Othello has bewitched his daughter. The Duke calls on Othello to
defend himself, whereupon the Moor asks that Desdemona be sent for to speak for herself.
While they wait for her Othello tells them how he wooed Desdemona. Desdemona arrives
and makes it clear that she married Othello of her own free will. Brabantio accepts the
situation with a heavy heart.

The council then discuss the Cyprus situation, and ask Othello to proceed at once to the
island and take charge of its defence. It is agreed that Othello should leave that very night
and that Desdemona will follow as soon as possible, accompanied by Iago and attended by
his wife Emilia.

When all but Iago and Roderigo have left the chamber Roderigo, in despair, threatens to
kill himself. Iago mockingly dissuades him, advising him to get enough money and come to
Cyprus and pursue his plan to win Desdemona. Roderigo agrees and leaves, whereupon
Iago tells us that he is only using Roderigo as a dupe in a plan to destroy Othello's marriage
and ruin Cassio.

This scene brings to a climax both the domestic and the political tensions which have
been set up so far. It is the first scene to take place indoors and the fact that most of the
characters are seated contrasts with the hustle and bustle of the various factions in the
previous scenes. It begins with a discussion of the numbers of ships involved, but there is
the sense of the real threat represented by the Turkish fleet to the security and prosperity
of a commercial republic such as Venice. There is also the threat of the Turk to the Christian
state, a threat which echoes Brabantio's last lines in the earlier scene and gives them a
wider reference. This part of the action comes to a pause with the entry of the Messenger
who brings the latest information regarding the invasion. Unlike the Sailor who entered
earlier and whose news served only to heighten the tension and the confusion (by creating
doubt as to whether it was Rhodes or Cyprus which was the Turks' target) this news has a
more definite tone and leads to a rapid decision on the part of the Duke. The fact that the
Messenger speaks without being asked is an indication of the urgency of the news. But the
Duke has only just time to take action on this information before Othello and Brabantio
enter and the personal issue takes the centre of the stage. This willingness to interrupt
important public business to hear Brabantio's grievance confirms the high opinion the
Venetian state has of him. (cf. I.ii. 11–13.) Now we have a chance to see Othello's action,
about which we have heard so much comment from others, as he himself sees it, and also to
see and hear Desdemona for the first time and compare our impression of her with that we
have gained from hearing Iago and Brabantio.

1   *composition:* consistency, agreement.
2   *gives them credit:* makes them (i.e. the items of news) credible. *News* is used as a plural noun
           by Shakespeare.
2   *disproportioned:* inconsistent.
5   *jump not:* do not agree.
5 ·   *a just accompt:* an exact figure.
6   *the aim reports:* the report includes an estimate.
9   *possible . . . judgment:* plausible.
10   *I . . . error:* I do not so over-confidently rely on the error (as to assume that the whole report
           is false).

Without a prompter. Whither* will you that I go
To answer this your charge?

BRABANTIO   To prison, till fit time
Of law and course of direct session*
Call thee to answer.

OTHELLO   What if I do obey?   85
How may the Duke be therewith satisfied,
Whose messengers are here about my side
Upon some present* business of the state
To bring me to him?

OFFICER   'Tis true, most worthy signior.   90
The Duke's in council, and your noble self
I am sure is sent for.

BRABANTIO   How? The Duke in council?
In this time of the night? – Bring* him away.
Mine's not an idle* cause. The Duke himself,
Or any of my brothers of the state,   95
Cannot but feel this wrong as 'twere their own;
For if such actions may have passage free,*
Bondslaves and pagans* shall our statesmen be.

                                                [*Exeunt*

scene iii

A council chamber.

The DUKE, SENATORS, *and* OFFICERS *sitting round a table,
with lights and* ATTENDANTS.

DUKE There's no composition* in these news
That gives them credit.*

FIRST SENATOR   Indeed, they are disproportioned.*
My letters say a hundred and seven galleys.

DUKE And mine a hundred forty.

SECOND SENATOR   And mine two hundred.
But though they jump not* on a just accompt* –   5
As in these cases where the aim reports*
'Tis oft with difference – yet do they all confirm
A Turkish fleet, and bearing up to Cyprus.

DUKE Nay, it is possible* enough to judgment.
I* do not so secure me in the error,   10

11–12   *The main article . . . fearful sense:* I believe the frightening news which is the chief point
         (which all these reports agree on). – The Duke says that the fact that there is a
         discrepancy in numbers between the reports does not lead him to doubt the main
         point which they have in common, i.e. the news of a Turkish attack on Cyprus.

13   *Now . . . business?* – The immediate attention to the sailor expressed by these questions
         heightens the sense of urgent expectancy.

18   *How . . . change?:* What do you think about this change? – i.e. from Cyprus to Rhodes as
         the target of the Turkish attack.

19   *assay:* test.

19   *pageant:* (false) show.

20   *keep . . . gaze:* distract us.

20–31   *Th'importancy . . . profitless:* Let us remember that not only is Cyprus more important to the
         Turks than Rhodes but also the Turks can take (*bear*) it more easily (*with more
         facile question*), since (*For that*) it has not such military readiness (*warlike brace*),
         lacking the equipment (*abilities*) that Rhodes has. Realizing this, we must not
         underestimate the Turks and expect them to put their greatest interest last
         (*latest*), deferring an easy and profitable attack (on Cyprus) in order to run a
         perhaps unrewarding risk (by attacking Rhodes first). Note the long-winded
         pomposity of the Senator's speech.

23   *more concerns:* is more important to.

24   *with more . . . bear it:* with an easier struggle capture it.

25   *warlike brace:* readiness for war. – The brace was part of a suit of armour.

27   *dressed in:* furnished with.

29   *latest:* last.

30   *attempt of ease and gain:* something that may be easily and profitably accomplished.

31   *wake:* arouse.

31   *wage:* risk.

31   *danger profitless:* crisis without chance of gain, pointless danger.

32   *in all confidence:* certainly.

34   *Ottomites:* Ottomans, Turks (cf. line 50 and note).

36   *injointed them:* joined together.

36   *after:* following.

38   *sail:* ships.

38   *restem:* steer again.

41   *servitor:* servant.

42   *With . . . recommends:* with willing service advises.

But the main article* I do approve
In fearful sense.

SAILOR [*Within*]   What, ho! What, ho! What, ho!

Enter SAILOR.

OFFICER A messenger from the galleys.
DUKE   Now?* What's the business?
SAILOR The Turkish preparation makes for Rhodes.   15
So was I bid report here to the State
By Signior Angelo.
DUKE How* say you by this change?
FIRST SENATOR   This cannot be
By no assay* of reason. 'Tis a pageant*
To keep* us in false gaze. When we consider   20
Th' importancy* of Cyprus to the Turk,
And let ourselves again but understand
That, as it more concerns* the Turk than Rhodes,
So may he with more* facile question bear it,
For that it stands not in such warlike brace,*   25
But altogether lacks th'abilities
That Rhodes is dressed in.* If we make thought of this,
We must not think the Turk is so unskilful
To leave that latest* which concerns him first,
Neglecting an attempt of ease and gain*   30
To wake* and wage* a danger profitless.*
DUKE Nay, in all confidence* he's not for Rhodes.
OFFICER Here is more news.

Enter a MESSENGER.

MESSENGER The Ottomites,* reverend and gracious,
Steering with due course toward the isle of Rhodes,   35
Have there injointed them* with an after* fleet.
FIRST SENATOR Ay, so I thought. How many, as you guess?
MESSENGER Of thirty sail;* and now they do restem*
Their backward course, bearing with frank appearance
Their purposes toward Cyprus. Signior Montano,   40
Your trusty and most valiant servitor,*
With* his free duty recommends you thus,
And prays you to believe him.
DUKE 'Tis certain then for Cyprus.
Marcus Luccicos, is not he in town?   45
FIRST SENATOR He's now in Florence.

49   *Valiant Othello* – The fact that the Duke speaks first to Othello is an indication of his importance to the state, particularly at this time of crisis.
49   *straight:* immediately.
50   *general:* public.
50   *Ottoman;* Turkish.
53   *Good your grace:* My good lord. A respectful mode of address.
54   *place:* official position.
54   *aught:* anything.
57   *so floodgate and o'erbearing nature:* such torrential nature, sweeping all before it.
58   *engluts:* engulfs.
60   *My daughter! O my daughter!* – Brabantio's grief bursts out through the more formal speech he is making.
62   *of mountebanks:* from quacks.
63   *prepost'rously:* against its normal course.
64   *lame of sense:* lacking intelligence or common sense.
65   *Sans:* without. – Brabantio keeps hammering away at the charge of witchcraft.
65   *could not* has the subject *nature* in line 63: nature could not stray from its normal course . . .
67   *beguiled:* cheated.
67   *bloody:* deadly.
70   *After . . . sense:* with your own interpretation.
70   *our proper:* our own. The Duke uses the royal plural.
71   *Stood . . . action:* faced your accusation. – *Action* is used here in its legal sense, taking 'legal action'.
73   *whom . . . brought:* who is now here (*hither*) on your specific orders (*special mandate*).
73   *mandate:* directive.
73   *state affairs:* affairs of state.
76   *Nothing . . . so* – Brabantio's interruption increases our eagerness to hear Othello speak.

NB whole setting as
City Theme — sober judgment.
Later, O cannot to bid for
himself.

DUKE Write from us to him; post-posthaste dispatch.
FIRST SENATOR Here comes Brabantio and the valiant Moor.

Enter BRABANTIO, OTHELLO, CASSIO, IAGO, RODERIGO, *and*
OFFICERS.

DUKE Valiant Othello,* we must straight* employ you
    Against the general* enemy Ottoman.*   50
    [*To* BRABANTIO] I did not see you. Welcome, gentle
                                                    signior.
    We lacked your counsel and your help tonight.
BRABANTIO So did I yours. Good your grace,* pardon me.
    Neither my place,* nor aught* I heard of business,
    Hath raised me from my bed; nor doth the general care   55
    Take hold on me; for my particular grief
    Is of so floodgate and o'erbearing nature*
    That it engluts* and swallows other sorrows,
    And it is still itself.
DUKE   Why, what's the matter?
BRABANTIO My daughter! O, my daughter!*
SENATORS   Dead?
BRABANTIO   Ay, to me.   60
    She is abused, stol'n from me, and corrupted
    By spells and medicines bought of mountebanks;*
    For nature so prepost'rously* to err,
    Being not deficient, blind, or lame of sense,*
    Sans* witchcraft could not.*   65
DUKE Whoe'er he be that in this foul proceeding
    Hath thus beguiled* your daughter of herself,
    And you of her, the bloody* book of law
    You shall yourself read in the bitter letter
    After* your own sense; yea, though our proper* son   70
    Stood* in your action.
BRABANTIO   Humbly I thank your Grace.
    Here is the man – this Moor, whom* now, it seems,
    Your special mandate* for the state affairs*
    Hath hither brought.
ALL   We are very sorry for't.
DUKE [*To* OTHELLO] What in your own part can you say to
                                                    this?   75
BRABANTIO Nothing,* but this is so.
OTHELLO Most potent, grave, and reverend signiors,

81   *head and front:* greatest extent – *head* and *front* are military terms signifying 'hostile advance' and 'foremost battle line' respectively.
82   *Rude:* rough. – There is an evident contrast between Othello's description of his language and the actual language itself. The lines have a swelling rhythm, a spaciousness of imagery and a calm dignity of tone which are characteristic of Othello before the poison of Iago has entered into him.
84   *pith:* strength.
85   *moons:* months.
85   *wasted:* past.
86   *dearest:* hardest, most important.
86   *tented field* – i.e. field of battle.
91   *round:* plain.
93   *conjuration:* magical incantation.
94   *withal:* with.
96   *motion:* impulse (cf. I.ii.74).
97   *herself:* itself. – According to Brabantio, Desdemona was so modest that she blushed at her own desires or impulses. Brabantio may here be unwittingly indicating the strength of these desires.
98   *credit:* reputation.
100–104   *It is . . . should be:* Only a warped (*maimed and most imperfect*) judgment would admit that such perfection (as Desdemona's) could fall into so unnatural an error; true judgment would be compelled to seek for an explanation of such error in devilish practices (i.e. witchcraft).
102   *and must:* and so one's judgment must.
104   *Why:* to discover why.
104   *vouch:* affirm.
105   *blood:* passions.
106   *dram:* dose.
106   *conjured:* treated with a magic spell.
107   *wrought:* worked magic.
109   *habits:* guises, pretexts.
110   *modern seeming:* trivial superficiality.
110   *prefer:* put forward (for acceptance).
112   *indirect and forced courses:* wicked and cunning means.
114   *question:* conversation.
115–22   Othello's calm self-confidence is shown by the way in which he asks that Desdemona be allowed to speak for herself and stakes his public reputation on the outcome. But his trust in Iago arouses our anxiety, as it did at the opening of the previous scene.

My very noble and approved good masters,
That I have ta'en away this old man's daughter,
It is most true; true I have married her.   80
The very head and front* of my offending
Hath this extent, no more. Rude* am I in my speech,
And little blessed with the soft phrase of peace,
For since these arms of mine had seven years' pith*
Till now some nine moons* wasted,* they have used   85
Their dearest* action in the tented field;*
And little of this great world can I speak
More than pertains to feats of broil and battle;
And therefore little shall I grace my cause
In speaking for myself. Yet, by your gracious patience,   90
I will a round* unvarnished tale deliver
Of my whole course of love – what drugs, what charms,
What conjuration,* and what mighty magic
(For such proceeding I am charged withal*)
I won his daughter.

BRABANTIO   A maiden never bold,   95
Of spirit so still and quiet that her motion*
Blushed at herself;* and she, in spite of nature,
Of years, of country, credit,* everything,
To fall in love with what she feared to look on!
It is* a judgment maimed and most imperfect   100
That will confess perfection so could err
Against all rules of nature, and must* be driven
To find out practices of cunning hell
Why* this should be. I therefore vouch* again
That with some mixtures powerful o'er the blood,*   105
Or with some dram,* conjured* to this effect,
He wrought* upon her.

DUKE   To vouch this is no proof,
Without more wider and more overt test
Than these thin habits* and poor likelihoods
Of modern seeming* do prefer* against him.   110

FIRST SENATOR But Othello, speak.
Did you, by indirect and forcèd courses*
Subdue and poison this young maid's affections?
Or came it by request, and such fair question*
As soul to soul affordeth?

OTHELLO   I do beseech you,*   115
Send for the lady to the Sagittary

118	*foul:* wicked, worthy of blame.
123–4	*as truly . . . blood* – An indication that Othello is a Christian. Regular confession of sins to a priest was a Christian practice and still prevails among Catholics.
128	*Her father loved me* – This is unexpected, in view of Brabantio's attitude, but he does not contradict Othello. It may also suggest that Othello belongs to Brabantio's generation rather than Desdemona's. – *Oft:* often.
129	*Still:* always, constantly.
132	*ran it through:* narrated it.
134	*chances:* chance happenings.
135	*moving accidents:* exciting adventures.
135	*flood and field:* water and land; the alliterative phrasing suggests a seasoned story-teller.
136	*scapes:* escapes.
136	*imminent:* instant.
136	*breach:* opening in the walls of a fortress.
138	*redemption:* being set free by payment.
139	*portance:* behaviour.
140	*antres:* caves.
140	*idle:* empty.
141	*quarries:* places where stone, slate etc. are obtained.
142	*hint:* opportunity.
142	*process:* proceeding, narrative. – The details of Othello's adventures would fascinate Shakespeare's audience among whom bizarre travellers' tales from the newly discovered lands of the New World and the East were very popular.
146	*seriously incline:* listen intently/greatly desire.
147	*still:* always.
149	*again:* back.
151	*pliant:* favourable.
153	*my pilgrimage dilate:* relate in detail all the events of my travels (*pilgrimage*).
154	*by parcels:* in bits and pieces.

And let her speak of me before her father.
If you do find me foul* in her report,
The trust, the office I do hold of you
Not only take away, but let your sentence   120
Even fall upon my life.

DUKE   Fetch Desdemona hither.
OTHELLO Ancient, conduct them; you best know the place.

[*Exit* IAGO, *with* ATTENDANTS

And till she come, as truly* as to heaven
I do confess the vices of my blood,
So justly to your grave ears I'll present   125
How I did thrive in this fair lady's love,
And she in mine.

DUKE   Say it, Othello.
OTHELLO Her father loved me,* oft invited me;

Still* questioned me the story of my life
From year to year, the battle, sieges, fortune   130
That I have passed.
I ran it through,* even from my boyish days
To th'very moment that he bade me tell it.
Wherein I spoke of most disastrous chances,*
Of moving accidents* by flood and field,*   135
Of hairbreadth scapes* i'th'imminent* deadly breach,*
Of being taken by the insolent foe
And sold to slavery, of my redemption* thence
And portance* in my travel's history,
Wherein of antres* vast and deserts idle,*   140
Rough quarries,* rocks, and hills whose heads touch
                                            heaven
It was my hint* to speak. Such was my process.*
And of the Cannibals that each other eat,
The Anthropophagi, and men whose heads
Do grow beneath their shoulders. These things to hear 145
Would Desdemona seriously incline;*
But still* the house affairs would draw her thence;
Which ever as she could with haste dispatch,
She'd come again,* and with a greedy ear
Devour up my discourse. Which I observing,   150
Took once a pliant* hour, and found good means
To draw from her a prayer of earnest heart
That I would all my pilgrimage dilate,*
Whereof by parcels* she had something heard,

155	*intentively:* with undivided attention.
156	*beguile:* rob (i.e. she shed tears unwillingly, despite herself).
160	*passing:* very.
161	*wondrous:* exceedingly (now obsolete).
163	*such a man:* a man who had endured such hardships (as Othello had).
166	*I spake* – These simple words express beautifully the moment of Othello's declaration of love, prompted by Desdemona's encouragement (*hint*). Desdemona's silent entrance just when Othello has come to the end of his case has something almost magical about it. It is almost as if his eloquent sincerity has 'conjured her up'.
172	*take . . . best:* make the best of this sad affair.
173–4	The Duke's point is that Brabantio has not completely lost his daughter, any more than a man with broken weapons is completely defenceless.
176	*bad blame:* harsh accusation.
177	*Light:* alight, fall.
179–88	*My noble father* – The position of Desdemona on the stage would reinforce the sincerity of her declaration of love and the independence of her character. She stands alone, having for the moment the shelter of neither husband nor father.
181	*education:* upbringing. – The word had a wider meaning than it does now.
182	*learn:* teach.
183	*lord of duty:* commander of obedience.
186	*preferring . . . before:* placing . . . above.
187	*challenge:* claim.
189	*Please it:* Let it please.
189	*on to:* let us proceed with.
190	*had rather:* would have preferred.
190	*get:* beget.

But not intentively.* I did consent   155
And often did beguile* her of her tears
When I did speak of some distressful stroke
That my youth suffered. My story being done,
She gave me for my pains a world of sighs.
She swore in faith 'twas strange, 'twas passing* strange;   160
'Twas pitiful, 'twas wondrous* pitiful.
She wished she had not heard it, yet she wished
That heaven had made her such a man.* She thanked me,
And bade me, if I had a friend that loved her,
I should but teach him how to tell my story,   165
And that would woo her. Upon this hint I spake.*
She loved me for the dangers I had passed,
And I loved her that she did pity them.
This only is the witchcraft I have used.
Here comes the lady. Let her witness it.   170

Enter DESDEMONA, IAGO, ATTENDANTS.

DUKE   I think this tale would win my daughter too.
Good Brabantio, take* up this mangled matter at the best.
Men do their broken weapons rather use
Than their bare hands.
BRABANTIO   I pray you hear her speak.
If she confess that she was half the wooer,   175
Destruction on my head if my bad blame*
Light* on the man. Come hither, gentle mistress.
Do you perceive in all this noble company
Where most you owe obedience?
DESDEMONA   My noble father,*
I do perceive here a divided duty.   180
To you I am bound for life and education;*
My life and education both do learn* me
How to respect you. You are the lord of duty,*
I am hitherto your daughter. But here's my husband,
And so much duty as my mother showed   185
To you, preferring* you before her father,
So much I challenge* that I may profess
Due to the Moor my lord.
BRABANTIO   God be with you. I have
                                                        done.
Please it* your Grace, on to* the state affairs.
I had rather* to adopt a child than get* it.   190

193   *but thou hast:* if you did not have.
196   *escape* – i.e. elopement.
197   *To hang clogs:* to restrict (their i.e. the children's) freedom. – This specifies the tyranny he
        has just mentioned.
198–207 *Let me speak* – It is difficult to imagine how the series of platitudes uttered by the Duke
        could *help these lovers* except perhaps by making Brabantio reconciled to his loss.
        But the heavy rhymes and the end-stopped lines emphasize the mechanical
        nature of the consolation offered, so that we are not surprised when Brabantio
        rejects it, ironically parodying the Duke's rhymes.
198   *lay a sentence:* (i) utter a comforting aphorism; (ii) pronounce a judicial verdict.
199   *grise:* pace, – i.e. pace forward.
200–201 *When remedies . . . depended:* When the possibility of improving a situation has quite
        passed, we should be reconciled to that situation by being free of the anxieties
        caused by earlier hopes.
201   *late:* until recently.
201   *depended:* was supported by.
203   *mischief:* calamity.
203   *next:* nearest. – Mourning a past calamity is the surest way to bring on fresh calamities.
204–5 *What . . . makes:* Patient acceptance can mock the injury offered by fortune in inflicting an
        unpreventable loss.
207   *spends . . . grief:* gives vent to grieving when there is no avail (*bootless*).
208   *of Cyprus us beguile:* cheat us out of, rob us of Cyprus.
211   *free comfort:* advice. Brabantio is saying that it is hard when a man has to bear his grief, not
        only with free moral consolation, but also from his own small stock of patience.
214   *to sugar* – i.e. with their tendency to sweeten.
214   *gall:* make bitter or painful.
217   *bruisèd   ear* – i.e. that mere words could ever bring consolation to one who has been
        deeply hurt. Brabantio has already made the point that the Duke's maxims can
        either sweeten or embitter, depending on how one takes them.
219–226 The change to prose produces a more detached atmosphere appropriate to public affairs.
        The Duke now speaks more formally to Othello, the general, the public figure.
220   *fortitude:* military strength.
221   *substitute:* deputy.
222   *allowed sufficiency:* acknowledged ability.
222–3 *yet opinion . . . on you:* public opinion, which effectively decides on what should be done,
        casts its judgment in your favour as the more reliable man.
224   *slubber:* tarnish.
228   *flinty:* rough.
229   *thrice-driven:* three times sifted – i.e. softest.
229   *agnize:* acknowledge, recognize.
230   *alacrity:* readiness (to welcome).

Come hither, Moor.
I here do give thee that with all my heart
Which, but thou hast* already, with all my heart
I would keep from thee. For your sake, jewel,
I am glad at soul I have no other child,   195
For thy escape* would teach me tyranny.
To hang clogs* on them. I have done, my lord.
DUKE Let me speak* like yourself and lay a sentence*
Which, as a grise* or step, may help these lovers.
When remedies* are past, the griefs are ended   200
By seeing the worst, which late* on hopes depended.*
To mourn a mischief* that is past and gone
Is the next* way to draw new mischief on.
What* cannot be preserved when fortune takes,
Patience her injury a mock'ry makes.   205
The robbed that smiles, steals something from the thief;
He robs himself that spends* a bootless grief.
BRABANTIO So let the Turk of Cyprus us beguile:*
We lose it not so long as we can smile.
He bears the sentence well that nothing bears   210
But the free comfort* which from thence he hears;
But he bears both the sentence and the sorrow
That to pay grief must of poor patience borrow.
These sentences, to sugar,* or to gall,*
Being strong on both sides, are equivocal.   215
But words are words. I never yet did hear
That the bruisèd* heart was piercèd through the ear.
I humbly beseech you, proceed to th'affairs of state.
DUKE The* Turk with a most mighty preparation makes for
Cyprus. Othello, the fortitude* of the place is best known   220
to you; and though we have there a substitute* of most
allowed sufficiency,* yet opinion,* a more sovereign
mistress of effects, throws a more safer voice on you. You
must therefore be content to slubber* the gloss of your
new fortunes with this more stubborn and boisterous   225
expedition.
OTHELLO The tyrant custom, most grave senators,
Hath made the flinty* and steel couch of war
My thrice-driven* bed of down. I do agnize*
A natural and prompt alacrity*   230
I find in hardness, and do undertake
This present wars against the Ottomites.

234 *fit disposition:* suitable arrangements.
235 *reference of place:* assignment of a fitting position.
235 *exhibition:* funds.
236 *besort:* company.
237 *levels with:* is suited to.
238 The short sharp refusals coming in quick succession offer a sudden and very effective contrast to the formality of Othello's earlier speech, reminding us of the powerful feeling that lies beneath the formal courtesies.
241 *unfolding:* recital.
241 *prosperous:* favourable.
242 *charter:* warrant, permission.
243 *simpleness:* innocence.
245 *downright violence and storm of fortunes:* the complete suddenness of my action (i.e. her elopement).
247 *quality:* nature. – But *quality* may also mean 'profession' here, so that Desdemona is saying that she is obedient both to Othello's nature and to the hardships of the military life.
249 *parts:* attributes.
252 *moth of peace* – i.e. useless and perhaps destructive.
253 *rites for why I love him:* privileges belonging to a wife.
254 *interim:* interval.
255 *dear:* costly. – i.e. because she will pay so much for it in suffering.
256 *voice:* consent.
257 *Vouch with me:* Bear witness for me.
259 *heat:* inflamed sexual passion.
259 *young affects:* youthful desires.
260 *defunct:* free from danger or penalty. – The only known use of the word in this sense.
260 *proper satisfaction* i.e. properly belonging to me as a newly married man – The consummation of the marriage. Othello says that he does not ask for Desdemona to be allowed to accompany him simply out of sexual desire, even though as a husband he is entitled to do so, but because it is Desdemona's freely expressed wish.
262 *heaven . . . think:* heaven forbid that you should think.
263 *scant:* neglect.
265 *feathered Cupid:* winged god of love.
265 *seel:* blind.
266 *speculative and officed instrument:* observant and dutiful organ – i.e. the eyes.
267 *disports:* pleasures.
268 *skillet:* saucepan.
269 *indign:* unworthy.
270 *Make head against:* attack.
270 *estimation:* reputation.

See Traversi p 104

Sensuality emerges crookedly

But this just what happens

Most humbly therefore, bending to your state,
I crave fit disposition* for my wife,
Due reference of place,* and exhibition,*   235
With such accommodation and besort"
As levels with* her breeding.
DUKE   Why, at her father's.
BRABANTIO I will not have it so.
OTHELLO   Nor I.*
DESDEMONA   Nor would I there reside,
To put my father in impatient thoughts
By being in his eye. Most gracious Duke,   240
To my unfolding* lend your prosperous* ear,
And let me find a charter* in your voice,
T'assist my simpleness.*
DUKE   What would you, Desdemona?
DESDEMONA That I did love the Moor to live with him,
My downright violence, and storm of fortunes,*   245
May trumpet to the world. My heart's subdued
Even to the very quality* of my lord;
I saw Othello's visage in his mind,
And to his honours and his valiant parts*
Did I my soul and fortunes consecrate.   250
So that, dear lords, if I be left behind,
A moth of peace,* and he go to the war,
The rites for why I love him* are bereft me,
And I a heavy interim* shall support
By his dear* absence. Let me go with him.   255
OTHELLO Let her have your voice.*
Vouch with me,* heaven, I therefore beg it not
To please the palate of my appetite,
Nor to comply with heat* the young affects*
In my defunct* and proper satisfaction;*   260
But to be free and bounteous to her mind;
And heaven* defend your good souls that you think
I will your serious and great business scant*
When she is with me. No, when light-winged toys
Of feathered Cupid* seel* with wanton dullness   265
My speculative and officed instrument,*
That my disports* corrupt and taint my business,
Let housewives make a skillet* of my helm,
And all indign* and base adversities
Make head against* my estimation!* –   270

272   *cries:* demands.
278   *things else:* other things.
278   *quality and respect:* significance and relevance.
279   *import:* concern.
281   *conveyance:* guardianship – The word often carried unfavourable connotations of trickery.
285   *delighted:* delightful.
285–89 *Adieu, brave Moor* – These two couplets, separated by a single line, emphasize two important themes of the play, Othello's spiritual grandeur and the possibility of betrayal.
290   *faith:* faithfulness, true love.
293   *best advantage:* most suitable opportunity.
295   *direction:* instructions.
297   *Iago?* – Roderigo has to attract Iago's attention as the latter is probably still gazing at Othello and Desdemona as they leave. There is a contrast in the ensuing dialogue between Roderigo's passion and Iago's cool cynicism.
301   *incontinently:* immediately.
305   *prescription:* (i) right; (ii) medical prescription.

DUKE Be it as you shall privately determine,
Either for her stay or going. Th'affair cries* haste,
And speed must answer it.

FIRST SENATOR   You must away tonight.

OTHELLO With all my heart.

DUKE At nine i'th'morning here we'll meet again.   275
Othello, leave some officer behind,
And he shall our commission bring to you,
And such things else* of quality and respect*
As doth import* you.

OTHELLO   So please your grace, my ancient;
A man he is of honesty and trust.   280
To his conveyance* I assign my wife,
With what else needful your good grace shall think
To be sent after me.

DUKE   Let it be so.
Good night to every one. [To BRABANTIO] And, noble
                                        signior,
If virtue no delighted* beauty lack,   285
Your son-in-law is far more fair than black.

FIRST SENATOR Adieu, brave Moor.* Use Desdemona well.

BRABANTIO Look to her, Moor, if thou hast eyes to see:
She has deceived her father, and may thee.
                    [Exeunt DUKE, SENATORS, OFFICERS, etc.

OTHELLO My life upon her faith.* Honest Iago,   290
My Desdemona must I leave to thee;
I prithee let thy wife attend on her,
And bring them after in the best advantage.*
Come, Desdemona, I have but an hour
Of love, of worldly matter, and direction*   295
To spend with thee. We must obey the time.
                    [Exit OTHELLO with DESDEMONA

RODERIGO Iago?*

IAGO What say'st thou, noble heart?

RODERIGO What will I do, think'st thou?

IAGO Why, go to bed and sleep.   300

RODERIGO I will incontinently* drown myself.

IAGO If thou dost, I shall never love thee after. Why, thou silly
gentleman?

RODERIGO It is silliness to live when to live is torment; and then
have we a prescription* to die when death is our   305
physician.

311   *guinea hen:* harlot.
313   *fond:* foolish, infatuated.
314   *virtue:* power.
315   *Virtue? A fig!* – Though Roderigo has just used *virtue* in the sense of power or ability, Iago in this speech also glances at its other meaning of moral action. He is suggesting that no such thing exists, and that life should be conducted entirely according to our wills, without reference to moral values. On the face of it his speech is sound Christian doctrine, emphasizing the individual's freedom to shape his life. But the tone and imagery carry the strong suggestion that it is a matter of indifference how his freedom is used. It is typical of him that he considers love to be a variety of lust. *A fig!* is an expression of contempt. A *nettle* is a weed, so that the idea of deliberately *planting* it is used by Iago as an example of the supremacy of the human will.
318   *set:* plant. – *Hyssop* and *thyme* are herbs.
319   *gender:* kind.
319   *distract:* vary.
320   *manured:* cultivated.
321   *corrigible:* able to correct.
323   *poise:* counterbalance.
326   *unbitted:* unbridled.
327   *sect or scion:* cutting or graft.
330–31   *Drown cats and blind puppies:* Malformed or unwanted animals were often drowned at birth.
333   *perdurable:* enduring.
333   *stead:* be of service to.
335   *defeat:* mar.
335   *favour:* face.
335   *usurped:* assumed.
339   *answerable sequestration:* corresponding separation.
342   *locusts:* sweet Mediterranean fruit.
343   *coloquintida:* bitter fruit used medicinally.
346   *damn thyself* – i.e. by committing suicide, which is a sin against God, who has commanded us to live out our appointed time.
347   *sanctimony:* holiness.
348   *erring:* (i) wandering; (ii) misguided.

IAGO   O villainous! I have looked upon the world for four times
seven years, and since I could distinguish betwixt a
benefit and an injury, I never found man that knew how
to love himself. Ere I would say I would drown myself for   310
the love of a guinea hen,* I would change my humanity
with a baboon.

RODERIGO   What should I do? I confess it is my shame to be so fond,*
but it is not in my virtue* to amend it.

IAGO   Virtue? A fig!* 'Tis in ourselves that we are thus, or thus.   315
Our bodies are our gardens, to the which our wills are
gardeners; so that if we will plant nettles or sow lettuce,
set* hyssop and weed up thyme, supply it with one
gender* of herbs or distract* it with many – either to have
it sterile with idleness or manured* with industry – why,   320
the power and corrigible* authority of this lies in our
wills. If the balance of our lives had not one scale of
reason to poise* another of sensuality, the blood and
baseness of our natures would conduct us to most
preposterous conclusions. But we have reason to cool our   325
raging motions, our carnal stings or unbitted* lusts,
whereof I take this that you call love to be a sect or scion.*

RODERIGO   It cannot be.

IAGO   It is merely a lust of the blood and a permission of the
will. Come, be a man! Drown thyself? Drown cats and   330
blind puppies!* I have professed me thy friend, and I
confess me knit to thy deserving with cables of
perdurable* toughness. I could never better stead* thee
than now. Put money in thy purse. Follow thou the wars;
defeat* thy favour* with an usurped* beard. I say, put   335
money in thy purse. It cannot be long that Desdemona
should continue her love to the Moor – put money in thy
purse – nor he his to her. It was a violent commencement
in her and thou shalt see an answerable sequestration* –
put but money in thy purse. These Moors are changeable   340
in their wills – fill thy purse with money. The food that to
him now is as luscious as locusts* shall be to him shortly
as bitter as coloquintida.* She must change for youth;
when she is sated with his body, she will find the errors
of her choice. Therefore, put money in thy purse. If thou   345
wilt needs damn thyself,* do it a more delicate way than
drowning. Make all the money thou canst. If sanctimony*
and a frail vow betwixt an erring* barbarian and a

349   *supersubtle:* excessively refined. The word carries the unfavourable suggestion of 'devious'.
351   *clean . . . way:* entirely the wrong thing to do.
352   *compassing:* obtaining.
357   *hearted:* rooted in (my) heart.
358   *conjunctive:* allied.
361   *Traverse:* Quick march! – Probably a military term.
365   *betimes:* early.
367   *I'll sell all my land* – Roderigo's abrupt and impulsive answer to Iago shows that the latter's reiterated advice to *Put money in thy purse* has had its effect.
368   *make my fool my purse:* use the victim of my trickery as my source of money.
369   *gained knowledge:* experience. – Iago repeatedly stresses that his knowledge of men, as of war, is practical, not theoretical.
370   *snipe:* fool. – A snipe is a small long-legged bird.
372–3 *'twixt my sheets . . . my office:* has performed my function in my bed – i.e. slept with Iago's wife.
375   *surety:* certainty. – The fact that Iago is prepared to avenge himself regardless of whether the charge against Othello could be substantiated or not suggests that he does not really need a motive for his hate, or that if he has one it must lie deeper in his nature.
375   *holds:* regards.
377   *proper:* handsome.
378   *To get his place* – Iago aims to replace Cassio as Othello's second-in-command.
378   *plume up:* set a crest on, indulge to the full.
379   *double knavery* – i.e. by doing harm to both Othello and Cassio.
380   *abuse . . . wife:* deceive Othello into thinking that Cassio is too familiar with Othello's wife.
382   *dispose:* manner.
383   *to be suspected.* to arouse suspicion. According to Iago, Cassio's outward appearance (*person*) and manners are so attractive to ladies that they would arouse suspicion, presumably among their husbands.
383   *framed:* fashioned in body.
388   *I have't!* – We see here Iago's capacity to improvise and turn whatever situation he is in to his own benefit. From *Let me see now* (l.377) we are almost watching the *monstrous birth* of his plan in his head. The imagery suggests both the depth (*Hell and night*) and the creativity (*engendered birth*) of Iago's evil, and perhaps also its connection with sexual activity.

supersubtle* Venetian be not too hard for my wits, and all
the tribe of hell, thou shalt enjoy her. Therefore, make   350
money. A pox of drowning thyself, it is clean* out of the
way. Seek thou rather to be hanged in compassing* thy
joy than to be drowned and go without her.

RODERIGO Wilt thou be fast to my hopes, if I depend on the issue?

IAGO Thou art sure of me. Go, make money. I have told thee   355
often, and I retell thee again and again, I hate the Moor.
My cause is hearted ;* thine hath no less reason. Let us be
conjunctive* in our revenge against him. If thou canst
cuckold him, thou dost thyself a pleasure, me a sport.
There are many events in the womb of time, which will   360
be delivered. Traverse,* go, provide thy money! We will
have more of this tomorrow. Adieu.

RODERIGO Where shall we meet i'th'morning?

IAGO At my lodging.

RODERIGO I'll be with thee betimes.*   365

IAGO Go to, farewell. Do you hear, Roderigo?

RODERIGO I'll sell all my land.*
                                                              [Exit

IAGO Thus do I ever make my fool my purse ;*
For I mine own gained knowledge* should profane
If I would time expend with such a snipe*   370
But for my sport and profit. I hate the Moor,
And it is thought abroad that 'twixt my sheets*
H'as done my office. I know not if't be true,
But I, for mere suspicion in that kind,
Will do, as if for surety.* He holds* me well;   375
The better shall my purpose work on him.
Cassio's a proper* man. Let me see now:
To get his place,* and to plume up* my will
In double knavery.* How? How? Let's see.
After some time, to abuse* Othello's ears   380
That he is too familiar with his wife.
He hath a person and a smooth dispose*
To be suspected* – framed* to make woman false.
The Moor is of a free and open nature
That thinks men honest that but seem to be so;   385
And will as tenderly be led by th'nose
As asses are.
I have't!* It is engendered! Hell and night
Must bring this monstrous birth to the world's light.
                                                              [Exit

II.i.   In Cyprus the governor Montano is anxiously awaiting Othello's arrival; a fierce storm is raging. The first ship to arrive brings Cassio, the next Iago, Emilia and Desdemona. Cassio greets Desdemona with deep respect and affection. At last the trumpets herald Othello's arrival ashore and the newly married pair embrace each other with many expressions of mutual love.

Once again Iago and Roderigo are left alone, and Iago tells Roderigo that Cassio has fallen in love with Desdemona. When he is quite alone on stage Iago says that he will somehow destroy Othello while still retaining his trust, although the precise details of his plan are not yet clear even to himself.

The whole of the first act takes place at night in Venice. The action now moves to Cyprus and daytime. We are reminded once more of the background of national crisis against which the personal drama of Othello's marriage is set. The opening question, and the sound effects of thunder and the stormy sea maintain the sense of urgency. The evocation of the sea is not only theatrically effective (especially in a theatre which could not boast of mechanically operated waves and moving cloud-effects) but also acts as a dramatic embodiment of the tempestuous passions which are at the heart of the play. The sea is particularly associated, in this scene and elsewhere, with Othello and his eloquence. We are given further evidence of the high public esteem in which Othello is held and we also see something of the affection and respect with which Desdemona and Cassio regard each other.

2   *high-wrought flood:* angry sea.
3   *'twixt* – shortened form of *betwixt:* between.
3   *Descry:* distinguish.
4   *Methinks:* It seems to me (now obsolete).
6   *ruffianed:* behaved violently, like a ruffian.
7   *ribs of oak* – Oak was the wood commonly used for building ships.
7   *mountains* – i.e. mountainous seas.
8   *hold the mortise:* remain joined together. A *mortise* is a socket or joint.
9   *segregation:* scattering.
11   *chidden* – literally 'rebuked'; here 'whipped up' (by the wind).
11   *pelt:* beat angrily.
12   *main:* (i) strength; (ii) ocean. – There may also be a play on the *mane* of a wild animal.
13   *burning Bear* – the brightly shining constellation known as the Little Bear.
14   *guards* – two stars of the constellation of the Little Bear known as the guardians. – They were important guides for navigation in Shakespeare's time.
15   *like molestation:* an attack like this.
16   *enchafèd:* raging.
16   *If that:* If (archaic).
17   *ensheltered and embayed:* sheltered in a bay.
20   *desperate:* fearful.
20   *banged:* beaten.
21   *designment halts:* plan (i.e. expedition) is stopped.
22   *sufferance:* suffering, damage.
25   *Veronesa:* belong to Verona – part of the Venetian state.

ACT II scene i

Cyprus.

Enter MONTANO, *Governor of Cyprus, and two*
GENTLEMEN, [*on the balcony*].

MONTANO What from the cape can you discern at sea?
FIRST GENTLEMEN Nothing at all, it is a high-wrought flood.*
  I cannot 'twixt* the heaven and the main
           Descry* a sail.
MONTANO Methinks* the wind hath spoke aloud at land;
  A fuller blast ne'er shook our battlements.
  If it hath ruffianed* so upon the sea,   5
  What ribs of oak,* when mountains* melt on them,
  Can hold the mortise?* What shall we hear of this?
SECOND GENTLEMAN A segregation* of the Turkish fleet:
  For do but stand upon the foaming shore,   10
  The chidden* billow seems to pelt* the clouds;
  The wind-shaked surge, with high and monstrous main,*
  Seems to cast water on the burning Bear*
  And quench the guards* of th'ever-fixèd pole.
  I never did like molestation* view   15
  On the enchafèd* flood.
MONTANO   If that* the Turkish fleet
  Be not ensheltered and embayed,* they are drowned;
  It is impossible to bear it out.

Enter a THIRD GENTLEMAN.

THIRD GENTLEMAN News, lads! Our wars are done.
  The desperate* tempest hath so banged* the Turks   20
  That their designment halts.* A noble ship of Venice
  Hath seen a grievous wrack and sufferance*
  On most part of their fleet.
MONTANO How? Is this true?
THIRD GENTLEMAN   The ship is here put in,
  A Veronesa;* Michael Cassio,   25
  Lieutenant to the warlike Moor Othello,
  Is come on shore; the Moor himself at sea,

A tranquil
Sea in
Cinthio

28   *in full commission:* with full authority.
31   *sadly:* gravely.
37   *throw out our eyes:* look eagerly.
38–39   *till . . . regard:* till sea and sky become indistinguishable to us.
41   *arrivance:* arrivals.
42   Cassio speaks first (having overheard them speak approvingly of Othello), which suggests
         that those on stage, who were about to leave when he enters, make a respectful
         greeting to him.
46   *well shipped:* in a strongly built ship.
47   *bark:* ship (now obsolete, but preserved in a word such as 'embark').
48   *expert and approved allowance:* experienced and with a high reputation.
49   *surfeited to death:* enlarged to the point of destruction.
50   *stand in bold cure:* have a good chance of recovery – i.e. are healthy. Cassio means that his
         hopes for Othello's safe journey, while not exaggerated, are firmly based and
         have every chance of being fulfilled.
S.D.50   *Within* – i.e. off stage.
52   *brow:* edge.
54   *My hopes . . . him:* I hope he is.
55   *shot of courtesy:* gunfire salute of welcome from shore to ship.
60   *achieved:* won.
61   *paragons description:* surpasses description, being perfection itself. – Cassio's account of
         Desdemona in ideal terms forms a centre of calm after the tension and movement
         of the storm. It suggests the depth of Cassio's regard for her and the absolute
         purity which she embodies.
61   *wild fame:* uncontrolled rumour.
62   *quirks:* clever flourishes.
62   *blazoning:* praising.

	And is in full commission* here for Cyprus.	
MONTANO	I am glad on't. 'Tis a worthy governor.	
THIRD GENTLEMAN	But this same Cassio, though he speak of comfort	30
	Touching the Turkish loss, yet he looks sadly*	
	And prays the Moor be safe, for they were parted	
	With foul and violent tempest.	
MONTANO	Pray heavens he be;	
	For I have served him, and the man commands	
	Like a full soldier. Let's to the seaside, ho!	35
	As well to see the vessel that's come in	
	As to throw out our eyes* for brave Othello,	
	Even till* we make the main and th'aerial blue	
	An indistinct regard.	
THIRD GENTLEMAN	Come, let's do so;	
	For every minute is expectancy	40
	Of more arrivance.*	

Enter CASSIO.

CASSIO	Thanks, you the valiant of the warlike isle,	
	That so approve the Moor, O, let the heavens	
	Give him defence against the elements,	
	For I have lost him on a dangerous sea.	45
MONTANO	Is he well shipped?*	
CASSIO	His bark* is stoutly timbered, and his pilot	
	Of very expert and approved allowance;*	
	Therefore my hopes, not surfeited to death,*	
	Stand in bold cure.* [*Within** A sail, a sail, a sail!]	50
CASSIO	What noise?	
FIRST GENTLEMAN	The town is empty; on the brow* o'th'sea	
	Stand ranks of people, and they cry, 'A sail!'	
CASSIO	My hopes* do shape him for the governor.	
	[*A shot*	
SECOND GENTLEMAN	They do discharge their shot of courtesy:*	55
	Our friends at least.	
CASSIO	I pray you, sir, go forth	
	And give us truth who 'tis that is arrived.	
SECOND GENTLEMAN	I shall.	
	[*Exit*	
MONTANO	But, good lieutenant, is your general wived?	
CASSIO	Most fortunately. He hath achieved* a maid	60
	That paragons description* and wild fame;*	
	One that excels the quirks* of blazoning* pens,	

O'er picturing that Venus
where at see her fancy
a work nature.

63	*essential . . . creation:* pure beauty of the human form. – The word *essential* is derived from 'essence' which in this period had the sense of the true being or nature of a person or object. Thus Desdemona's outward beauty signifies inner perfection.
64	*tire the ingener:* wears out the inventor. – Desdemona's excellence is so great that it outstrips all attempts to describe it. It is ironic that this glowing description is almost immediately followed by the entry, not of Desdemona herself but of Iago, the master *ingener.*
68	*guttered:* furrowed.
68	*congregated:* massed together. – Reefs and sandbanks are meant.
69	*ensteeped:* submerged.
69	*enclog . . . keel:* hinder the innocent ship.
70	*As having sense:* Because they are aware.
70	*omit:* disregard.
71	*mortal:* deadly.
75–6	*Whose . . . speed:* whose arrival is a week earlier than we expected.
75	*footing:* landing, arrival.
76	*se'nnight's:* week's (seven nights').
76	*Othello guard* – i.e. guard Othello.
80	*extincted:* extinguished. – Cassio's prayer looks forward to the arrival of Othello and Desdemona as a source of blessing to the entire community. And, as if in answer, Desdemona enters immediately.
82	*riches* – here used as a singular noun. There are other instances in Shakespeare.
86	*Enwheel:* encircle. – Cassio's words and actions continue the idea of the *divine Desdemona.*
88–9	*nor know I aught/But that:* to the best of my knowledge.

And in th'essential* venture of creation
Does tire the ingener.*

Enter SECOND GENTLEMAN.

                              How now? Who has put in?
SECOND GENTLEMAN 'Tis one Iago, ancient to the general.   65
        CASSIO H'as had most favourable and happy speed:
                Tempests themselves, high seas, and howling winds,
                The guttered* rocks and congregated* sands,
                Traitors ensteeped* to enclog* the guiltless keel,
                As having sense* of beauty, do omit*
                Their mortal* natures, letting go safely by
                The divine Desdemona.
       MONTANO   What is she?
        CASSIO She that I spake of, our great captain's captain,
                Left in the conduct of the bold Iago,
                Whose* footing* here anticipates our thoughts   75
                A se'nnight's* speed. Great Jove, Othello guard,*
                And swell his sail with thine own pow'rful breath,
                That he may bless this bay with his tall ship,
                Make love's quick pants in Desdemona's arms,
                Give renewed fire to our extincted* spirits,
                And bring all Cyprus comfort.   80

Enter DESDEMONA, IAGO, RODERIGO, *and* EMILIA.

                              O, behold!
                The riches* of the ship is come on shore!
                You men of Cyprus, let her have your knees.
                                              [*Kneeling*
                Hail to thee, lady! and the grace of heaven,
                Before, behind thee, and on every hand,   85
                Enwheel* thee round.
     DESDEMONA   I thank you, valiant Cassio.
                What tidings can you tell me of my lord?
        CASSIO He is not yet arrived, nor know I aught
                But that* he's well and will be shortly here.
     DESDEMONA O but I fear. How lost you company?   90
        CASSIO The great contention of sea and skies
                Parted our fellowship. [*Within* A sail, a sail!]
                [*A shot*]   But hark. A sail!
SECOND GENTLEMAN They give this greeting to the citadel;
                This likewise is a friend.

97   *'Tis my breeeding* – Cassio excuses his somewhat free behaviour to another man's wife on the grounds that he has been brought up to it; perhaps he is alluding to the fact that he is a Florentine; at any rate it is an aspect of Cassio that Iago builds on in his plot against Othello.

99 100   *would she   on me:* if she gave you her lips as readily as she gives me her tongue (scolds me).

103   *still:* always.

104   *before your ladyship, I grant:* in your presence, I admit.

106   *chides with thinking:* scolds only in thought.

107   *pictures* – i.e. silent figures.

108   *Bells* – i.e. noisy. – A shrewish woman's tongue was often compared to a bell.

108   *wildcats:* savage creatures. – Presumably their behaviour to servants is meant.

109   *Saints . . . injuries:* When you intend to do harm you put on an air of holiness.

110   *Players:* play-actors, deceivers.

110   *housewives:* (i) hard workers (cf. l.113); (ii) hussies, harlots.

111   *fie upon thee:* shame on you!

112   *Turk:* heathen.

115   *What wouldst write of me* – Desdemona's question leads us to expect a description from Iago that would contrast sharply with that given a few moments earlier by Cassio. In a way our expectations are fulfilled in Iago's comments from line 126 onwards. But it is worth noting that Iago declines to give a specific description of Desdemona and talks instead about different *types* of women. This is partly due to the deference he must show to his general's wife, but it is also a characteristic of Iago that he tends to see men and women in categories rather than as unique individuals. The *gained knowledge* of the world he is so proud of consists of this tendency to reduce the variety of life to a few cynical general principles.

118   *assay:* try.

119   *I am not merry* – Desdemona's aside explains in advance what might otherwise seem rather odd behaviour for a newly married woman waiting anxiously for her husband's safe arrival.

119   *beguile:* (i) divert; (ii) disguise.

123   *pate:* head.

123   *birdlime:* sticky substance placed in trees to trap birds.

123   *frieze:* coarse woollen cloth.

125   *And thus she is delivered* – Here is another example of Iago's skill at improvisation. The metaphor of conception and birth is the same as that which he used at the end of the previous scene.

126–7, 129–30, 133–4, 138–9, 144–56 The rhyming couplets give Iago something of the quality of theatrical clowns, who often made extempore rhymes on topics suggested by the audience.

CASSIO   See for the news.

                                    [*Exit* GENTLEMAN

Good ancient, you are welcome. [*To* EMILIA] Welcome,
                                    mistress.   95

Let it not gall your patience, good Iago,
That I extend my manners. 'Tis my breeding*
That gives me this bold show of courtesy.

                                    [*Kisses* EMILIA

IAGO Sir, would she* give you so much of her lips
As of her tongue she oft bestows on me,
You would have enough.   100

DESDEMONA   Alas, she has no speech.

IAGO In faith, too much.
I find it still* when I have leave to sleep.
Marry, before your ladyship, I grant,*
She puts her tongue a little in her heart   105
And chides with thinking.*

EMILIA   You have little cause to say so.

IAGO Come on, come on! You are pictures* out of door,
Bells* in your parlours, wildcats* in your kitchens,
Saints in your injuries,* devils being offended,
Players* in your housewifery, and housewives* in your
                                    beds.   110

DESDEMONA O, fie upon thee,* slanderer!

IAGO Nay, it is true, or else I am a Turk:*
You rise to play, and go to bed to work.

EMILIA You shall not write my praise.

IAGO   No, let me not.

DESDEMONA What wouldst write of me,* if thou shouldst praise me?   115

IAGO O gentle lady, do not put me to't,
For I am nothing if not critical.

DESDEMONA Come on, assay.* There's one gone to the harbour?

IAGO Ay, madam.

DESDEMONA [*Aside*]   I am not merry;* but I do beguile*
The thing I am by seeming otherwise. – [*To* IAGO]
Come, how wouldst thou praise me?

IAGO I am about it; but indeed my invention
Comes from my pate* as birdlime* does from frieze;*
It plucks out brains and all. But my muse labours,
And thus she is delivered:*   125
If she be fair and wise: fairness and wit,
The one's for use, the other useth it.

128   *black:* dark – i.e. a brunette.
130   *white* – with a pun on *wight:* person. (cf. l.154).
134   *folly:* wantonness.
135   *fond:* foolish.
138   *thereunto:* in addition to that.
141   *what praise . . . deserving woman indeed* – From trivial banter Desdemona moves on to a
         serious question, and one that is at the heart of the play.
142   *authority . . . merit:* deservingness of her virtue.
143   *put on the vouch:* force the approval. – Desdemona asks Iago how he would praise a woman
         whose virtue was so complete and manifest that even the most malicious persons
         would be compelled to admit it.
145   *Had tongue at will:* could speak freely.
147   *Fled . . . may:* refrained from satisfying her wishes even when she had the power to do so.
151   *To change . . . tail* – i.e. to exchange the best part of something not very valuable (a stupid
         husband) for the worst of something fine (a handsome lover). There is a play on
         tail: male sexual organ.
154   *wight:* person.
156   *chronicle small beer:* keep household accounts. – i.e. be concerned with trivialities.
157   *impotent:* feeble.
159   *liberal:* licentious.
160   *home:* directly to the point.
160   *relish . . . in:* appreciate him more as (a soldier than as a scholar).
162   *well said:* well done. – A common usage at this time. Though we have only Iago's word for
         it, it is clear that signs of affection are being exchanged between Cassio and
         Desdemona. But these are sufficiently accounted for by Desdemona's genuine
         warm regard for Cassio and his elegant manners and unselfish idolization of her.
164   *gyve:* fetter.
165   *courtship:* (i) courtly behaviour; (ii) courting
167   *kissed your three fingers* – the gesture of a courtier, originally an Italian habit.
168   *sir:* gentleman.

DESDEMONA Well praised. How if she be black* and witty?

IAGO If she be black, and thereto have a wit,
She'll find a white* that shall her blackness fit.   130

DESDEMONA Worse and worse!

EMILIA How if fair and foolish?

IAGO She never yet was foolish that was fair,
For even her folly* helped her to an heir.

DESDEMONA These are old fond* paradoxes to make fools laugh   135
i'th'alehouse. What miserable praise hast thou for her
that's foul and foolish?

IAGO There's none so foul, and foolish thereunto,*
But does foul pranks which fair and wise ones do.

DESDEMONA O heavy ignorance. Thou praisest the worst best. But   140
what praise* couldst thou bestow on a deserving woman
indeed – one that in the authority* of her merit did justly
put on the vouch* of very malice itself?

IAGO She that was ever fair, and never proud;
Had tongue at will,* and yet was never loud;   145
Never lacked gold, and yet went never gay;
Fled* from her wish, and yet said 'Now I may';
She that being angered, her revenge being nigh,
Bade her wrong stay, and her displeasure fly;
She that in wisdom never was so frail   150
To change* the cod's head for the salmon's tail;
She that could think, and nev'r disclose her mind;
See suitors following, and not look behind:
She was a wight* (if ever such wights were) –

DESDEMONA To do what?   155

IAGO To suckle fools and chronicle small beer.*

DESDEMONA O most lame and impotent* conclusion. Do not learn of
him, Emilia, though he be thy husband. How say you,
Cassio? Is he not a most profane and liberal* counsellor?

CASSIO He speaks home,* madam. You may relish* him more in   160
the soldier than in the scholar.   [They converse apart

IAGO [Aside] He takes her by the palm. Ay, well said,*
whisper! With as little a web as this will I ensnare as great
a fly as Cassio. Ay, smile upon her, do! I will gyve* thee in
thine own courtship.* – You say true; 'tis so, indeed! – If   165
such tricks as these strip you out of your lieutenantry, it
had been better you had not kissed your three fingers* so
oft – which now again you are most apt to play the sir* in.
Very good! Well kissed! An excellent courtesy! 'Tis so,

171   *clyster pipes:* tubes for injecting enemas. – Iago makes the filthiest comparison that comes
       to his mind.

172   *I know his trumpet* – Each commander had his own special trumpet call. The offstage
       trumpet is the first indication of Othello's arrival in Cyprus. Iago's words are
       confirmed by Cassio and followed by Desdemona's wish to hurry to meet him.
       The effect is to increase our excitement to see Othello, and the suspense is
       heightened by the pause that would follow Cassio's *Lo, where he comes* (Look!
       Here he comes).

176   *warrior* – Othello is tenderly referring to Desdemona's willingness to accompany him to the
       wars.

181   *bark:* ship.

182   *Olympus-high:* as high as Mount Olympus, the home of the gods.

183   *If it were now:* If now were the time.

187   *Succeeds . . . fate:* will follow in the unknown future. – Othello's words strike us as
       ominously prophetic because we are aware of Iago's machinations.

188   *loves and comforts* – The plural of abstract nouns was usually used when more than one
       person was referred to. Desdemona prays that Othello's fears will not be realized,
       and that their love and joy will increase with the passage of time.

189   *Amen:* so let it be. (A word spoken by the congregation at the end of a prayer or hymn.)

189   *powers:* gods.

192   *And this, and this* – i.e. the kisses he is giving her.

194   *set down the pegs:* loosen the screws (of a musical instrument, thereby slackening the
       strings). *set down* also means to humble. – Music as a metaphor for spiritual
       harmony is very frequent in Shakespeare.

197   *How does my old acquaintance:* How are my old friends?

198   *well desired:* very welcome.

200   *out of fashion:* incoherently.

200   *dote:* babble. – Othello's excitement at being reunited with Desdemona, together with the
       joyful news he brings of the Turkish loss, makes him talk somewhat irrationally
       to his wife and the islanders in turn, without pausing for a reply from either.

202   *coffers:* wooden chests.

indeed. Yet again your fingers to your lips? Would they   170
were clyster pipes* for your sake! [*Trumpets within*]
– The Moor! I know his trumpet.*
CASSIO 'Tis truly so.
DESDEMONA Let's meet him and receive him.
CASSIO Lo, where he comes.   175

Enter OTHELLO *and* ATTENDANTS.

OTHELLO O my fair warrior!*
DESDEMONA   My dear Othello.
OTHELLO It gives me wonder great as my content
To see you here before me. O my soul's joy,
If after every tempest come such calms,
May the winds blow till they have wakened death,   180
And let the labouring bark* climb hills of seas
Olympus-high,* and duck again as low
As hell's from heaven. If it were now* to die,
'Twere now to be most happy; for I fear
My soul hath her content so absolute   185
That not another comfort like to this
Succeeds* in unknown fate.
DESDEMONA   The heavens forbid
But that our loves and comforts* should increase
Even as our days do grow.
OTHELLO   Amen* to that, sweet powers!*
I cannot speak enough of this content;   190
It stops me here [*touches his breast*]; it is too much of joy.
And this, and this,* the greatest discords be
That e'er our hearts shall make!
                                    [*They kiss*
IAGO   [*Aside*] O, you are well tuned now;
But I'll set down the pegs* that make this music,
As honest as I am.
OTHELLO   Come, let us to the castle.   195
News, friends! Our wars are done; the Turks are
                                    drowned.
How does my old acquaintance* of this isle?
Honey, you shall be well desired* in Cyprus;
I have found great love amongst them. O my sweet,
I prattle out of fashion,* and I dote*   200
In mine own comforts. I prithee, good Iago,
Go to the bay and disembark my coffers.*

203	*master:* ship's captain.
205	*challenge:* demand.
207	*presently:* at once.
210	*list:* listen to.
211	*court of guard:* the place where the guard assembles.
212	*directly:* definitely.
215	*Lay . . . thus* – i.e. keep your mouth shut and listen to one who knows better.
216	*soul:* self.
216	*Mark me:* Remember.
218	*prating:* boasting.
220	*the devil* – another insulting reference to Othello's colour.
221	*the act of sport:* sexual intercourse. – Iago stirs Roderigo's physical desires by referring to the relations between Othello and Desdemona in very intimate terms.
222	*give . . . appetite:* renew physical urges that have already been completely satisfied.
223	*favour:* appearance.
223	*sympathy:* agreement.
225	*conveniences:* compatibilities.
226–7	*heave the gorge:* vomit.
227	*disrelish:* lose the taste for.
227	*very nature:* nature itself.
229–30	*pregnant and unforced:* full of proof and natural.
230–31	*so eminent . . . fortune:* so highly favoured in this respect. – The metaphor is drawn from the rungs of a ladder (*degrees*) in which Cassio is seen as highly placed (*eminent*).
232	*voluble:* smooth-tongued, plausible.
232	*conscionable:* ruled by his conscience.
233	*mere form . . . seeming:* outward appearance of courteous and considerate behaviour. – Here and in most of the rest of this speech Iago seems to be describing himself rather than Cassio, and secretly relishing the fact that Roderigo is unaware of this.
234	*compass:* encompass, achieve.
234	*salt:* lecherous.
234	*loose:* immoral.
235	*slipper:* slippery.
236	*occasions:* opportunities.
236	*can stamp:* (that) can coin.
237–8	*counterfeit . . . itself:* create favourable opportunities though none actually occur. – The metaphor is drawn from the minting of money.
240	*green:* unripe, inexperienced.
240	*look after:* look for.
241	*found him:* realized his true nature and intentions.

Bring thou the master* to the citadel;
He is a good one, and his worthiness
Does challenge* much respect. Come, Desdemona,   205
Once more well met at Cyprus.

Exeunt OTHELLO *and* DESDEMONA.

IAGO [*To an* ATTENDANT] Do thou meet me presently* at the
harbour. [*To* RODERIGO] Come hither. If thou be'st valiant
– as they say base men being in love have then a nobility
in their natures more than is native to them – list* me. The   210
lieutenant tonight watches on the court of guard.* First, I
must tell thee this: Desdemona is directly* in love with
him.

RODERIGO With him? Why, 'tis not possible.

IAGO Lay* thy finger thus [*puts his finger to his lips*], and let thy   215
soul* be instructed. Mark me* with what violence she
first loved the Moor but for bragging and telling her
fantastical lies. To love him still for prating?* Let not thy
discreet heart think it. Her eye must be fed. And what
delight shall she have to look on the devil?* When the   220
blood is made dull with the act of sport,* there should be
a game to inflame it and to give* satiety a fresh appetite,
loveliness in favour,* sympathy* in years, manners, and
beauties; all which the Moor is defective in. Now for
want of these required conveniences,* her delicate   225
tenderness will find itself abused, begin to heave the
gorge,* disrelish* and abhor the Moor; very nature* will
instruct her in it and compel her to some second choice.
Now sir, this granted – as it is a most pregnant and
unforced* position – who stands so eminent* in the   230
degree of this fortune as Cassio does? A knave very
voluble;* no further conscionable* than in putting on the
mere form* of civil and humane seeming for the better
compass* of his salt* and most hidden loose* affection.
Why, none, why, none! A slipper* and subtle knave, a   235
finder of occasions,* that has an eye can stamp* and
counterfeit* advantages, though true advantage never
present itself. A devilish knave. Besides, the knave is
handsome, young, and hath all those requisites in him
that folly and green* minds look after.* A pestilent   240
complete knave, and the woman hath found him*
already.

244 *condition*: disposition. -- Roderigo is moved to defend Desdemona from the charge of being sexually subtle and sophisticated, though he listens without protest to Iago's accusations against Othello and Cassio.

245 *fig's end* – a contemptuous dismissive phrase typical of Iago.

245–6 *The wine . . . grapes*: She is a human being, not a saint, and inhabits the same material world as the rest of us.

248 *paddle with*: fondle.

250 *by this hand*: I assure you.

250 *index and obscure prologue*: pointer (or table of contents) and indirect introduction. – The metaphor is that of a book and is continued in *history*. In old books noteworthy passages were sometimes identified by a pointing finger in the margin.

253 *mutualities*: intimacies. – Iago is continuing his deliberate plan of exciting Roderigo by drawing a vivid picture of Desdemona indulging in sexual intimacies.

254 *hard at hand*: close by.

254–5 *master and main exercise* – i.e. the sexual act itself.

255 *incorporate*: involving bodily union.

257–9 *for the command . . . you*: I shall give you your instructions.

258–9 *Do you find*: See that you find.

260 *tainting his discipline*: speaking slightingly of his military ability.

262 *minister*: provide.

264 *choler*: anger.

264 *haply*: perhaps.

266–8 *whose qualification . . . Cassio*: whose dissatisfaction will not be allayed except by removing Cassio from his office. – The metaphor is of tasting. *Qualification* is diluting.

270 *prefer*: promote.

278 *apt and of great credit*: likely and credible.

In this soliloquy we begin to be more deeply aware of the tangled web of motives and pseudo-motives which make up the complex character of Iago. It is impossible to be certain whether or not he believes the story he has just told Roderigo. Although he says *I do well believe't*, the tone is casual and offhand, as if it didn't matter much either way. When he talks of Othello, however, there is a genuine intensity of feeling in his recognition of the Moor's virtues – indeed it may be just this recognition which accounts for the intensity of feeling. There seems also to be an effort to define for himself the true nature of his feeling for Desdemona, though here again it is difficult to feel that his whole personality is engaged in the effort. On the other hand, the suspicion that he has been made a cuckold by Othello (to which he now adds a suspicion of Cassio on the same grounds, l.298) seems to disturb him more deeply now than it did earlier. (See his soliloquy at the end of the first act. Here the metaphor of a suspicion eating away at his soul like a poison is a powerful one, as is the ominous tread of a line like *Till I be even'd with him wife for wife*. Perhaps the real springs of Iago's behaviour lie beneath all his motives; he may be a man who uses motives only to give a keener edge to his appetite for evil.

279 *howbeit*: although.

282 *dear*: (i) loved and loving; (ii) costly.

283 *not out of absolute lust*: not only out of lust.

283 *peradventure*: perhaps.

RODERIGO   I cannot believe that in her; she's full of most blessed
            condition.*

IAGO   Blessed fig's-end!* The wine* she drinks is made of   245
        grapes. If she had been blessed, she would never have
        loved the Moor. Blessed pudding! Didst thou not see her
        paddle with* the palm of his hand? Didst not mark that?

RODERIGO   Yes, that I did; but that was but courtesy.

IAGO   Lechery, by this hand!* An index and obscure prologue*   250
        to the history of lust and foul thoughts. They met so near
        with their lips that their breaths embraced together.
        Villainous thoughts, Roderigo. When these mutualities*
        so marshal the way, hard at hand* comes the master and
        main exercise,* th'incorporate* conclusion: Pish! But, sir,   255
        be you ruled by me. I have brought you from Venice.
        Watch you tonight; for the command,* I'll lay't upon
        you. Cassio knows you not. I'll not be far from you. Do
        you find* some occasion to anger Cassio, either by
        speaking too loud, or tainting his discipline,* or from   260
        what other course you please which the time shall more
        favourably minister.*

RODERIGO   Well.

IAGO   Sir, he's rash and very sudden in choler,* and haply* may
        strike at you. Provoke him that he may; for even out of   265
        that will I cause these of Cyprus to mutiny, whose
        qualification* shall come into no true taste again but by
        the displanting of Cassio. So shall you have a shorter
        journey to your desires by the means I shall then have to
        prefer* them; and the impediment most profitably   270
        removed without the which there were no expectation of
        our prosperity.

RODERIGO   I will do this if you can bring it to any opportunity.

IAGO   I warrant thee. Meet me by and by at the citadel. I must
        fetch his necessaries ashore. Farewell.   275

RODERIGO   Adieu.

[*Exit*

IAGO   That Cassio loves her, I do well believe't;
        That she loves him, 'tis apt and of great credit.*
        The Moor, howbeit* that I endure him not,
        Is of a constant, loving, noble nature,   280
        And I dare think he'll prove to Desdemona
        A most dear* husband. Now I do love her too;
        Not out of absolute lust,* though peradventure*

284	*accountant:* accountable.
285	*diet:* feed.
286	*lusty:* lustful.
287	*leaped into my seat:* taken my place (in bed).
288	*inwards:* entrails.
290	*evened:* made equal.
294	*trace:* follow after. – A term used in hunting.
295	*putting on:* incitement.
296	*on the hip:* at my mercy. – The metaphor may come from wrestling or, more appropriately in the context, from hunting, the hip or haunch of the deer being usually the part seized by the hounds.
297	*Abuse:* slander.
297	*rank garb:* gross and direct manner.
301	*practising upon:* plotting against.

ii.ii.	To celebrate the destruction of the Turkish fleet and Othello's marriage, a period of revelry is announced in Cyprus, to last from five in the evening till eleven at night.
	This short scene has an almost cinematic effect, giving a rapid movement to the action and widening its scope by reminding us of the situation in the country as a whole. The herald's proclamation of the removal of tension in the military situation and his call to public revelry only increase our sense of the private tensions and ironically suggest that in the domestic story there will soon be little cause for revelry.
2	*certain:* sure.
2	*importing:* signifying.
3	*mere perdition:* total loss.
4	*triumph:* festive celebration.
6	*addiction:* inclination.
8	*offices* – i.e. for supplying food and drink.

I stand accountant* for as great a sin,
But partly led to diet* my revenge,   285
For that I do suspect the lusty* Moor
Hath leaped into my seat;* the thought whereof
Doth, like a poisonous mineral, gnaw my inwards;*
And nothing can or shall content my soul
Till I am evened* with him, wife for wife.   290
Or failing so, yet that I put the Moor
At least into a jealousy so strong
That judgment cannot cure. Which thing to do,
If this poor trash of Venice, whom I trace*
For his quick hunting, stand the putting on,*   295
I'll have our Michael Cassio on the hip,*
Abuse* him to the Moor in the rank garb*
(For I fear Cassio with my nightcap too),
Make the Moor thank me, love me, and reward me
For making him egregiously an ass   300
And practising upon* his peace and quiet,
Even to madness. 'Tis here, [taps his head] but yet
                                                 confused:
Knavery's plain face is never seen till used.

                                                          [Exit

scene ii

A street.

Enter OTHELLO'S HERALD, *with a proclamation.*

HERALD It is Othello's pleasure, our noble and valiant general,
that upon certain* tidings now arrived importing* the
mere perdition* of the Turkish fleet, every man put
himself into triumph.* Some to dance, some to make
bonfires, each man to what sport and revels his   5
addiction* leads him. For, besides these beneficial news,
it is the celebration of his nuptial. So much was his
pleasure should be proclaimed. All offices* are open, and

II.iii.   Having given Cassio orders about the watch, Othello retires with Desdemona. Iago persuades Cassio, who is unable to hold his drink very well, to have one drink too many, in order to incite a quarrel between Cassio and Roderigo. He tells Roderigo to provoke the drunken Cassio. When Montano tries to intervene, Cassio stabs him. The alarm bell rings, bringing Othello to the scene from his marriage bed. Iago, with apparent reluctance, implies that Cassio is chiefly to blame and Othello dismisses Cassio from his office.

Left alone with Cassio Iago tells him not to worry too much but to seek Desdemona's help in winning back Othello's favour. When Cassio leaves Iago once more mentions his intention of destroying Othello, Cassio and Desdemona. Roderigo returns and is consoled for his injuries and his diminishing funds on hearing of Cassio's dismissal. Iago, alone, expresses his intention of getting his wife to ask Desdemona to plead for Cassio.

This long and boisterous scene begins deceptively quietly. Othello, at last temporarily free of public duties, and his silently contented bride are just about to enjoy their long-awaited privacy. With the entry of Iago, who stands silent till he is spoken to, we are aware of the threat to this precarious happiness. The middle part of the scene, in which Iago succeeds in making Cassio take the second drink which is the latter's undoing, is not without a good deal of coarse and grim humour, of which the drinking songs are an example. But this humour is soured by our knowledge of Iago's sinister purpose and by the brawl which follows the drinking. The whole scene is a little play expertly stage-managed by Iago, who in his soliloquy at the end of it acts commentates on his own actions and directs our attention to the next stage of his devilish scheme.

1   *Good Michael* – Othello uses Cassio's Christian name to suggest his personal friendship for his lieutenant. It also gives a feeling that the crisis is past. Othello uses Cassio's Christian name for the last time in a very different context. (See line 174.)

1   *look you to:* take charge of.

2   *stop:* restraint.

3   *outsport:* go beyond. Othello says that merrymaking should not exceed the bounds of good sense.

6   *honest* – this fateful word seems to be always attached in Othello's mind (and in the minds of others) to Iago. Here it means 'reliable'.

7   *with your earliest:* as soon as you can.

9   *the fruits are to ensue* – i.e. the marriage has yet to be consummated.

13   *Not this hour:* Not for an hour yet.

14   *cast:* dismissed.

16   *sport for Jove* – Jove, the chief of the Olympian gods, was well known in mythology for his innumerable sexual encounters. Iago is again suggesting that Desdemona has a highly developed sexual appetite.

18   *full of game:* sexually responsive.

20   *sounds a parley to:* invites and permits. – To *sound a parley* is to give a trumpet signal proclaiming a truce.

22   *right:* very, entirely (now almost completely obsolete).

there is full liberty of feasting from this present hour of
five till the bell have told eleven. Bless the isle of Cyprus   10
and our noble general Othello!

                                                            [*Exit*

scene iii

The citadel of Cyprus.

Enter OTHELLO, DESDEMONA, CASSIO, *and* ATTENDANTS.

OTHELLO   Good Michael,* look you to* the guard tonight.
          Let's teach ourselves that honourable stop,*
          Not to outsport* discretion.
CASSIO   Iago hath direction what to do;
          But notwithstanding, with my personal eye   5
          Will I look to't.
OTHELLO   Iago is most honest.*
          Michael, good night. Tomorrow with your earliest*
          Let me have speech with you. [*To* DESDEMONA] Come, my
                                                  dear love,
          The purchase made, the fruits are to ensue,*
          That profit's yet to come 'tween me and you.   10
          [*To* CASSIO] Good night.
                    [*Exit* OTHELLO *with* DESDEMONA *and* ATTENDANTS

          Enter IAGO

CASSIO   Welcome, Iago. We must to the watch.
IAGO   Not this hour,* lieutenant; 'tis not yet ten o'th'clock. Our
          general cast* us thus early for the love of his Desdemona;
          who let us not therefore blame. He hath not yet made   15
          wanton the night with her, and she is sport for Jove.*
CASSIO   She's a most exquisite lady.
IAGO   And, I'll warrant her, full of game.*
CASSIO   Indeed, she's a most fresh and delicate creature.
IAGO   What an eye she has! Methinks it sounds a parley to*   20
          provocation.
CASSIO   An inviting eye; and yet methinks right* modest.

23	*alarum:* call to arms.
26	*stoup:* drinking vessel.
26	*here without:* waiting just outside.
27	*fain:* willingly.
29–30	*poor and unhappy brains:* a bad head (for drink). Cassio means that he gets drunk very quickly.
32	*for you:* in your place. – Iago probably means that Cassio need not drink a health more than once; he would take Cassio's place the rest of the time.
33–4	*craftily qualified:* cunningly diluted.
34	*innovation –* i.e. strange changes.
40	*it dislikes me:* I dislike it.
43	*offence –* i.e. readiness to give and take offence.
44	*my young mistress' –* i.e. any young lady's. *My* does not have a specific reference to Iago here.
47	*pottle-deep:* to the bottom of the vessel. – A *pottle* was a measure of two quarts (about 2 litres).
47	*he's to watch:* he is to be one of the guard.
48	*Three else:* three others.
48	*noble swelling:* high-spirited.
49	*That hold . . . distance:* who are sensitive about their rank and dignity.
50	*very elements:* typical spirits.
51	*flustered:* roused.
55	*consequence:* following events.
55	*approve:* bear out.
55	*dream:* plan.
57	*rouse:* full cup of liquor.
60	*canakin:* small can. – Iago shrewdly takes Cassio's mind off the second drink by plunging straight into a merry song which involves the act of drinking.

IAGO   And when she speaks, is it not an alarum* to love?
CASSIO She is indeed perfection.
IAGO   Well, happiness to their sheets! Come, lieutenant, I have   25
       a stoup* of wine, and here without* are a brace of Cyprus
       gallants that would fain* have a measure to the health of
       black Othello.
CASSIO Not tonight, good Iago. I have very poor and unhappy
       brains* for drinking; I could well wish courtesy would   30
       invent some other custom of entertainment.
IAGO   O, they are our friends. But one cup! I'll drink for you.*
CASSIO I have drunk but one cup tonight, and that was craftily
       qualified* too; and behold what innovation* it makes
       here. [*Taps his head*] I am unfortunate in the infirmity   35
       and dare not task my weakness with any more.
IAGO   What, man! 'Tis a night of revels, the gallants desire it.
CASSIO Where are they?
IAGO   Here, at the door. I pray you call them in.
CASSIO I'll do't, but it dislikes me.*   40
                                                          [*Exit*

IAGO   If I can fasten but one cup upon him
       With that which he hath drunk tonight already,
       He'll be as full of quarrel and offence*
       As my young mistress'* dog. Now, my sick fool Roderigo,
       Whom love hath turned almost the wrong side out,   45
       To Desdemona hath tonight caroused
       Potations pottle-deep;* and he's to watch.*
       Three else* of Cyprus, noble swelling* spirits,
       That hold* their honours in a wary distance,
       The very elements* of this warlike isle,   50
       Have I tonight flustered* with flowing cups,
       And they watch too. Now, 'mongst this flock of drun-
                                                          kards
       Am I to put our Cassio in some action
       That may offend the isle. But here they come.

       Enter CASSIO, MONTANO, *and* GENTLEMEN.

       If consequence* do but approve* my dream,*   55
       My boat sails freely, both with wind and stream.
CASSIO 'Fore God, they have given me a rouse* already.
MONTANO Good faith, a little one; not past a pint, as I am a soldier.
IAGO   Some wine, ho!
       [*Sings*] And let me the canakin* clink, clink;   60

63	*span:* short time – literally a handsbreadth.
68	*potting:* drinking.
68	*Your Dane* – i.e. any Dane; *your* has no specific reference.
69	*swag-bellied:* with a hanging belly.
71	*exquisite:* excellent. – A difficult word for Cassio to get his tongue round at this stage.
73	*sweats not:* does not exert himself.
73	*Almain:* German.
76	*I'll do you justice:* I'll match you (in drinking that toast).
78	*was and:* was – The *and* is added for the rhythm.
81	*lown:* rogue.
85	*take . . . about:* wrap round. The last line being common to each verse of the song, is not *directly* linked to any one verse.
85	*auld:* old.
93	*the general* – i.e. Othello. Perhaps Cassio, already drunk, is apologizing for putting himself before his superior officer.

And let me the canakin clink.
A soldier's a man;
A man's life but a span,*
Why then, let a soldier drink.
Some wine, boys!   65

CASSIO 'Fore God, an excellent song!

IAGO I learned it in England, where indeed they are most
potent in potting.* Your Dane,* your German, and your
swag-bellied* Hollander – Drink, ho! – are nothing to
your English.   70

CASSIO Is your Englishman so exquisite* in his drinking?

IAGO Why, he drinks you with facility your Dane dead drunk;
he sweats not* to overthrow your Almain;* he gives your
Hollander a vomit ere the next pottle can be filled.

CASSIO To the health of our general!   75

MONTANO I am for it, lieutenant, and I'll do you justice.*

IAGO O sweet England!

[Sings] King Stephen was and* a worthy peer;
His breeches cost him but a crown;
He held them sixpence all too dear,   80
With that he called the tailor lown.*
He was a wight of high renown,
And thou art but of low degree:
'Tis pride that pulls the country down;
And take* thine auld* cloak about thee.   85

Some wine, ho!

CASSIO 'Fore God, this is a more exquisite song than the other.

IAGO Will you hear't again?

CASSIO No, for I hold him to be unworthy of his place that does
those things. Well, God's above all; and there be souls   90
must be saved, and there be souls must not be saved.

IAGO It's true, good lieutenant.

CASSIO For mine own part – no offence to the general,* nor any
man of quality – I hope to be saved.

IAGO And so do I too, lieutenant.   95

CASSIO Ay, but by your leave, not before me. The lieutenant is to
be saved before the ancient. Let's have no more of this;
let's to our affairs. – God forgive us our sins! –
Gentlemen, let's look to our business. Do not think,
gentlemen, I am drunk. This is my ancient; this is my   100
right hand, and this is my left. I am not drunk now. I can
stand well enough, and I speak well enough.

106   *platform:* A level place for mounting heavy artillery.
106   *set the watch:* mount the guard. – Montano has to give the order because Cassio, now drunk, has forgotten to do so.
110   *just equinox:* exact balance. – During an *equinox* the day is divided into equal halves of darkness and light. (This is the only time Shakespeare uses this word.)
113   *odd time:* chance occasion.
116   *watch . . . double set:* stay awake while the clock goes round twice – i.e. for twenty-four hours.
126   *ingraft informity:* deep-rooted weakness.
134   *twiggen:* covered with wicker-work. – Cassio probably means that he would beat the knave till his body was covered with marks like woven wicker-work.

GENTLEMEN Excellent well!
CASSIO Why, very well then. You must not think then that I am
      drunk.   105
                                                        [*Exit*

MONTANO To th' platform,* masters. Come, let's set the watch.*
IAGO You see this fellow that is gone before.
      He's a soldier fit to stand by Caesar
      And give direction; and do but see his vice.
      'Tis to his virtue a just equinox,*   110
      The one as long as th'other. 'Tis pity of him.
      I fear the trust Othello puts him in,
      On some odd time* of his infirmity,
      Will shake this island.
MONTANO   But is he often thus?
IAGO 'Tis evermore his prologue to his sleep: 115
      He'll watch* the horologe a double set
      If drink rock not his cradle.
MONTANO   It were well
      The general were put in mind of it.
      Perhaps he sees it not, or his good nature
      Prizes the virtue that appears in Cassio   120
      And looks not on his evils. Is not this true?

      Enter RODERIGO.

IAGO [*Aside*] How now, Roderigo?
      I pray you after the lieutenant, go!
                                        [*Exit* RODERIGO
MONTANO And 'tis great pity that the noble Moor
      Should hazard such a place as his own second   125
      With one of an ingraft infirmity.*
      It were an honest action to say so
      To the Moor.
IAGO   Not I, for this fair island!
      I do love Cassio well and would do much
      To cure him of this evil. [*Within* Help! Help!]
                        But hark? What noise?   130

      Enter CASSIO, *pursuing* RODERIGO.

CASSIO Zounds, you rogue! You rascal!
MONTANO What's the matter, lieutenant?
CASSIO A knave teach me my duty? I'll beat the knave into a
      twiggen* bottle.

138   *mazzard:* head. – A mazzard was a drinking bowl.
141   *Away, I say* – Notice that Iago is doing everything he can to spread confusion and 'blow up' the incident. In lines 143–7 he is shouting for this purpose.
143   *God's will:* Let God's will be done. A call to stop fighting.
146   *Diablo:* Devil (Spanish).
148   *ashamed:* humiliated.
150   *He dies* – i.e. I'll kill him.
151   *Hold for your lives:* Stop, or you die.
157   *heaven . . . Ottomites* – i.e. by sending a storm heaven has prevented the Turks (Ottomites) from fighting the men of Cyprus.
159   *carve . . . rage:* gratify his own anger. – The metaphor is taken from carving food at table.
160   *Holds:* values.
160   *light:* lightly.
161   *dreadful:* frightening.
162   *propriety:* normal orderly state.
163   *that looks dead with grieving:* You look as if grief were killing you – An important clue to Iago's demeanour at this point and one that increases our interest in his response to Othello's question.
164   *On thy love I charge thee:* In the name of the loyalty you owe me I demand (to know).
165   *but now, even now:* only a moment ago.
166   *In quarter and in terms:* in their relations to each other and their manner.
167   *Devesting:* undressing.

RODERIGO Beat me?   135
CASSIO Dost thou prate, rogue?

                                        [*Beats* RODERIGO
MONTANO Nay, good lieutenant! I pray you, sir, hold your hand.
                                        [*Restrains him*
CASSIO Let me go, sir, or I'll knock you o'er the mazzard.*
MONTANO Come, come, you're drunk!
CASSIO Drunk?   140
                                        [*They fight*
IAGO [*Aside to* RODERIGO] Away, I say!* Go out and cry a
     mutiny!
                                        [*Exit* RODERIGO
     Nay, good lieutenant. God's will,* gentlemen!
     Help, ho! Lieutenant. Sir. Montano.
     Help, masters! Here's a goodly watch indeed!   145
                                        [*A bell rung*
     Who's that which rings the bell? Diablo,* ho!
     The town will rise. God's will, lieutenant,
     You'll be ashamed* for ever.

     Enter OTHELLO *and* ATTENDANTS.

OTHELLO   What is the matter here?
MONTANO Zounds, I bleed still. I am hurt to the death.
     He dies.*   150
                                        [*Attacks* CASSIO *again*
OTHELLO Hold for your lives!*
IAGO Hold, ho! Lieutenant. Sir. Montano. Gentlemen!
     Have you forgot all sense of place and duty?
     Hold! The general speaks to you. Hold, for shame!
OTHELLO Why, how now, ho? From whence ariseth this?   155
     Are we turned Turks, and to ourselves do that
     Which heaven* hath forbid the Ottomites?
     For Christian shame put by this barbarous brawl!
     He that stirs next to carve* for his own rage
     Holds* his soul light;* he dies upon his motion.   160
     Silence that dreadful* bell. It frights the isle
     From her propriety.* What is the matter, masters?
     Honest Iago, that looks dead with grieving,*
     Speak. Who began this? On thy love, I charge thee.*
IAGO I do not know. Friends all, but now, even now,*   165
     In quarter and in terms* like bride and groom
     Devesting* them for bed; and then, but now –

168	*unwitted:* driven mad. – Planets (and especially the moon) were believed to cause madness if they came too close to the earth.
171	*peevish odds:* senseless quarrel. – Iago claims to be unable to say how the fight began.
172	*would . . . I had:* I wish that I had.
172	*action glorious:* – i.e. war.
174	*you are thus forgot ?:* you have forgotten yourself like this – As the use of Cassio's first name shows, Othello speaks more in sorrow than in anger.
176	*civil:* well-mannered.
177	*stillness:* stability, steadiness.
179	*censure:* judgment.
180	*unlace:* loosen, undo.
181	*spend your rich opinion:* exchange the valuable reputation you have gained.
185	*something now offends me:* now causes me some distress.
191	*blood:* passion. – Othello says that he is beginning to lose his temper, but the measured tones in which he says it show that he has reserves of discipline still left. Later we shall see that when his *blood* really begins to rule his *safer guides,* he is incapable of dignified and rational speech.
192	*collied:* darkened: – literally blackened with coal.
193	*Assays:* attempts.
195	*sink in my rebuke:* feel the weight of my displeasure.
196	*foul rout:* shameful disturbance.
197	*approved:* proved guilty.
201	*manage:* conduct.
202	*court and guard of safety:* in the very place and office responsible for the general security.
204	*partially affined:* bound by partiality.
204	*leagued in office:* brought close together by having the same occupation.
206	*Touch . . . near:* Do not appeal in terms of something so dear to me – i e his reputation as a soldier.

hsight 1

As if some planet had unwitted* men –
Swords out, and tilting one at other's breasts
In opposition bloody. I cannot speak   170
Any beginning to this peevish odds,
And would* in action glorious* I had lost
Those legs that brought me to a part of it!

OTHELLO How comes it, Michael, you are thus forgot?*

CASSIO I pray you pardon me, I cannot speak.   175

OTHELLO Worthy Montano, you were wont to be civil;*
The gravity and stillness* of your youth
The world hath noted, and your name is great
In mouths of wisest censure.* What's the matter
That you unlace* your reputation thus   180
And spend your rich opinion* for the name
Of a night-brawler? Give me answer to it.

MONTANO Worthy Othello, I am hurt to danger.
Your officer, Iago, can inform you,
While I spare speech, which something now offends me,*   185
Of all that I do know; nor know I aught
By me that's said or done amiss this night,
Unless self-charity be sometimes a vice,
And to defend ourselves it be a sin
When violence assails us.

OTHELLO   Now, by heaven,   190
My blood* begins my safer guides to rule,
And passion, having my best judgment collied,*
Assays* to lead the way. If I once stir
Or do but lift this arm, the best of you
Shall sink in my rebuke.* Give me to know   195
How this foul rout* began, who set it on;
And he that is approved* in this offence,
Though he had twinned with me, both at a birth,
Shall lose me. What? In a town of war
Yet wild, the people's hearts brimful of fear,   200
To manage* private and domestic quarrel?
In night, and on the court and guard of safety?*
'Tis monstrous. Iago, who began't?

MONTANO If partially affined,* or leagued in office,*
Thou dost deliver more or less than truth,   205
Thou art no soldier.

IAGO   Touch* me not so near.
I had rather have this tongue cut from my mouth

209–10	*to speak . . . nothing:* that to tell the truth will in no way.
214	*this gentleman* – i.e. Montano.
215	*entreats his pause:* appeals to him to cease.
216	*Myself . . . pursue:* I myself pursued the fellow (meaning Roderigo) who was crying out. – The audience of course knows that Iago is lying.
219	*the rather:* earlier, more eagerly.
220	*For that:* Because.
221	*high in oath:* swearing fiercely.
231	*strange:* unknown – i.e. to Iago.
232	*pass:* ignore.
235	S.D. *Enter Desdemona, with Attendants* – Desdemona's entrance alters the atmosphere of the scene by reminding us that this is Othello's nuptial night and also making unnecessary an immediate response to Cassio's downfall from those on stage.

Than it should do offence to Michael Cassio.
Yet I persuade myself to speak* the truth
Shall nothing wrong him. This it is, general.   210
Montano and myself being in speech,
There comes a fellow crying out for help,
And Cassio following him with determined sword
To execute upon him. Sir, this gentleman*
Steps in to Cassio and entreats his pause.*   215
Myself* the crying fellow did pursue,
Lest by his clamour – as it so fell out –
The town might fall in fright. He, swift of foot,
Outran my purpose; and I returned the rather*
For that* I heard the clink and fall of swords,   220
And Cassio high in oath;* which till tonight
I ne'er might say before. When I came back –
For this was brief – I found them close together
At blow and thrust, even as again they were
When you yourself did part them.   225
More of this matter cannot I report;
But men are men; the best sometimes forget.
Though Cassio did some little wrong to him,
As men in rage strike those that wish them best,
Yet surely Cassio I believe received   230
From him that fled some strange* indignity,
Which patience could not pass.*

OTHELLO   I know, Iago,
Thy honesty and love doth mince this matter,
Making it light to Cassio. Cassio, I love thee,
But never more be officer of mine.   235

Enter DESDEMONA, *with* ATTENDANTS.*

Look if my gentle love be not raised up.
[*To* CASSIO] I'll make thee an example.
DESDEMONA   What is the matter, dear?
OTHELLO All's well, sweeting; come away to bed.
[*To* MONTANO] Sir, for your hurts, myself will be your
                                                        surgeon.
Lead him off.   240
                              [MONTANO *is led off*
Iago, look with care about the town
And silence those whom this vile brawl distracted.
Come, Desdemona: 'tis the soldiers' life

246   Cassio's long silence is a theatrically effective indication of the depth of his humiliation. The ensuing discussion is very close to the heart of the play. Not merely Cassio, but Iago, Othello and Desdemona herself are intimately involved in the question of *Reputation*.

253   *sense:* (i) physical sensation; (ii) reason

258   *cast in his mood:* rejected because of his frame of mind.

259   *policy:* expediency.

258–61 Iago's point is that Othello has punished Cassio not because he believes Cassio's offence to be particularly serious but merely as a temporary measure to frighten the rest and thereby prevent general disorder.

265   *fustian:* bombastic nonsense.

275   *revel, and applause:* merrymaking and the desire to have other men's approval.

279   *the devil drunkenness* – Cassio's metaphor has a relevance beyond his own situation. The idea of possession by devils runs right through the play. In a sense it applies to the central relationship between Iago and Othello and, at least in Brabantio's view, to that between Othello and Desdemona.

282   *moraller:* moralizer.

To have their balmy slumbers waked with strife.

[*Exit with* DESDEMONA *and* ATTENDANTS

IAGO What, are you hurt, lieutenant?   245

CASSIO Ay, past all surgery.*

IAGO Marry, God forbid!

CASSIO Reputation, reputation, reputation! O, I have lost my
reputation! I have lost the immortal part of myself, and
what remains is bestial. My reputation, Iago, my re-   250
putation!

IAGO As I am an honest man, I had thought you had received
some bodily wound. There is more sense* in that than in
reputation. Reputation is an idle most false imposition,
oft got without merit and lost without deserving. You   255
have lost no reputation at all unless you repute yourself
such a loser. What, man, there are more ways to recover
the general again. You are but now cast in his mood* – a
punishment more in policy* than in malice – even so as
one would beat his offenceless dog to affright an   260
imperious lion. Sue to him again, and he's yours.

CASSIO I will rather sue to be despised than to deceive so good a
commander with so slight, so drunken, and so indiscreet
an officer. Drunk! And speak parrot! And squabble!
Swagger! Swear! And discourse fustian* with one's own   265
shadow! O thou invisible spirit of wine, if thou hast no
name to be known by, let us call thee devil!

IAGO What was he that you followed with your sword?
What had he done to you?

CASSIO I know not.   270

IAGO Is't possible?

CASSIO I remember a mass of things, but nothing distinctly: a
quarrel, but nothing wherefore. O God, that men should
put an enemy in their mouths to steal away their brains!
that we should with joy, pleasance, revel, and applause*   275
transform ourselves into beasts!

IAGO Why, but you are now well enough. How came you thus
recovered?

CASSIO It hath pleased the devil drunkenness* to give place to the
devil wrath. One unperfectness shows me another, to   280
make me frankly despise myself.

IAGO Come, you are too severe a moraller.* As the time, the
place, and the condition of this country stands, I could
heartily wish this had not befall'n; but since it is as it is,

287   *Hydra* – a many-headed snake slain by Hercules.
290   *inordinate:* beyond due measure.
290   *ingredient:* main part of the mixture.
291   *familiar creature:* friendly spirit. – Animals used by witches were called familiars.
294   *approved it:* proved it (in my own case).
299   *devotement of her parts:* devotion to her qualities.
304   *splinter:* repair by applying a splint.
305   *my fortunes . . . lay:* I'll wager all I have against any worthwhile stake that . . .
309   *I think it freely:* I fully believe it.
309   *betimes:* early.
310   *undertake for me:* take up the matter on my behalf.
311   *desperate:* despairing.
311   *check:* repulse.
316   *free:* open.
317   *Probal to:* Provable by.
319   *inclining:* favourably disposed.
320   *framed:* formed.
320   *fruitful:* generous.
321   *free elements* – i.e. bountiful nature.
322   *were't:* even if it were.
323   *All . . . sin:* All signs of his Christian religion. – Iago suggests that Othello is so much in love with Desdemona that for her sake he would even give up the Christian faith he has embraced.
325   *list:* wishes.

mend it for your own good.   285

CASSIO I will ask him for my place again: he shall tell me I am a
drunkard. Had I as many mouths as Hydra,* such an
answer would stop them all. To be now a sensible man,
by and by a fool, and presently a beast! O strange! Every
inordinate* cup is unblest, and the ingredient* is a devil.   290

IAGO Come, come, good wine is a good familiar creature* if it be
well used; exclaim no more against it. And, good
lieutenant, I think you think I love you.

CASSIO I have well approved it,* sir. I drunk?

IAGO You or any man living may be drunk at a time, man. I tell   295
you what you shall do. Our general's wife is now the
general. I may say so in this respect, for that he hath
devoted and given up himself to the contemplation,
mark, and devotement of her parts* and graces. Confess
yourself freely to her; importune her help to put you in   300
your place again. She is of so free, so kind, so apt, so
blessed a disposition she holds it a vice in her goodness
not to do more than she is requested. This broken joint
between you and her husband entreat her to splinter;*
and my fortunes* against any lay worth naming, this   305
crack of your love shall grow stronger than it was before.

CASSIO You advise me well.

IAGO I protest, in the sincerity of love and honest kindness.

CASSIO I think it freely;* and betimes* in the morning I will
beseech the virtuous Desdemona to undertake for me.* I   310
am desperate* of my fortunes if they check* me.

IAGO You are in the right. Good night, lieutenant; I must to
the watch.

CASSIO Good night, honest Iago.

                                        [*Exit* CASSIO

IAGO And what's he then that says I play the villain,   315
When this advice is free* I give, and honest,
Probal to* thinking, and indeed the course
To win the Moor again? For 'tis most easy
Th'inclining* Desdemona to subdue
In any honest suit; she's framed* as fruitful*   320
As the free elements.* And then for her
To win the Moor – were't* to renounce his baptism,
All* seals and symbols of redeemèd sin –
His soul is so enfettered to her love
That she may make, unmake, do what she list,*   325

[handwritten marginalia: "Brilliant conspiracy 1) Get Cassio 2) Discredit Des. Not a strategy, but tactics"]

326–7   *Even as . . . function:* To the extent that (*Even as*) her desires (*appetite*) control all his actions (*function*).
328   *parallel* – Iago's argument is that since he is advising Cassio to ask for what Desdemona would freely perform (i.e. what would be in accordance with or *parallel* to her own inclinations) no one can justly accuse him of villainy.
329   *Divinity of hell!:* Moral teaching of the devil. – An allusion to the occasion when the Devil cited Scripture in tempting Christ (*Matthew* 4:6).
330   *put on:* encourage.
331   *suggest:* tempt.
331   *shows:* appearances.
333   *Plies:* works on.
336   *repeals:* appeals for reinstatement of.
337   *by how much . . . the Moor:* the more she tries to improve Cassio's situation, the more she will destroy Othello's faith in her.
343   *fills up the cry:* merely adds to the noise of the pack.
344   *cudgelled:* beaten, not necessarily with a cudgel.
347   *wit:* sense.
350   *by wit and not by witchcraft* – perhaps an ironic allusion to Brabantio's charge against Othello. (I.ii.62–65).
351   *dilatory:* slow-moving.
353   *cashiered:* brought about the dismissal of – with a pun on Cassio's name.
354–5   *Though other things . . . be ripe:* Though flowers flourish in the sun, yet those same flowers that blossom first will be the first to ripen (and rot). – This seems to be the consolation Iago is offering Roderigo, but it is worth noting that here, as elsewhere, Iago speaks with a sort of proverb-like authority whose actual meaning is either meagre or commonplace.
356   *By the mass* – an oath. Iago has been on stage almost the whole time.
358   *billeted:* lodged.
363   *awhile:* meanwhile. – Having 'justified' himself in the earlier part of his soliloquy, Iago now turns to the strictly practical part of his plans.

Even as* her appetite shall play the god
With his weak function. How am I then a villain
To counsel Cassio to this parallel* course,
Directly to his good? Divinity of hell!*
When devils will the blackest sins put on,*   330
They do suggest* at first with heavenly shows,*
As I do now. For whiles this honest fool
Plies* Desdemona to repair his fortune,
And she for him pleads strongly to the Moor,
I'll pour this pestilence into his ear: 335
That she repeals* him for her body's lust;
And by how much* she strives to do him good,
She shall undo her credit with the Moor.
So will I turn her virtue into pitch,
And out of her own goodness make the net   340
That shall enmesh them all. – How now, Roderigo?

Enter RODERIGO.

RODERIGO I do follow here in the chase, not like a hound that hunts,
but one that fills up the cry.* My money is almost spent; I
have been tonight exceedingly well cudgelled;* and I
think the issue will be, I shall have so much experience   345
for my pains; and so, with no money at all, and a little
more wit,* return again to Venice.

IAGO How poor are they that have not patience!
What wound did ever heal but by degrees?
Thou know'st we work by wit, and not by witchcraft;*   350
And wit depends on dilatory* time.
Does't not go well? Cassio hath beaten thee,
And thou by that small hurt hast cashiered* Cassio.
Though other things* grow fair against the sun,
Yet fruits that blossom first will first be ripe.   355
Content thyself awhile. By the mass,* 'tis morning!
Pleasure and action make the hours seem short.
Retire thee; go where thou art billeted.*
Away, I say! Thou shalt know more hereafter.
Nay, get thee gone!

[*Exit* RODERIGO

Two things are to be done: 360
My wife must move for Cassio to her mistress;
I'll set her on;
Myself awhile* to draw the Moor apart

364   *jump*: exactly.
366   *Dull not device . . . delay*: Do not weaken the effectiveness of the plan by delay.

And bring him jump* when he may Cassio find
Soliciting his wife. Ay, that's the way!   365
Dull not device* by coldness and delay.

                                        [*Exit*

III.i.   Cassio tries to regain Othello's favour by getting some musicians to play at the Moor's
          window in the morning. A clown interrupts them and is paid by Cassio to fetch Emilia. Iago
          enters and undertakes to get Othello out of the way while Cassio asks for Desdemona's
          help.
              Emilia tells Cassio that Othello and his wife have been discussing his situation. She
          promises to arrange matters so that Cassio can speak privately to Desdemona.
              After the troubled night, music marks the beginning of the new day. This scene is
          sometimes omitted in production, and most readers and audiences forget that there is a
          clown in *Othello*. The music and the clown's jokes lighten the atmosphere only
          momentarily, as Cassio's nervous impatience is evident in his words, and Iago enters as
          soon as the clown has left.

1   *content your pains:* reward you for your trouble.
2   *and bid 'Good morrow, general'* – Cassio is evidently trying to put Othello in a good humour
                  so that his suit may succeed. It was customary to play music in honour of the
                  bride and groom. *Good morrow* is an archaic form of the greeting 'Good morning'.
4   *i'th'nose:* through the nose. – The inhabitants of Naples were supposed to speak with a
                  nasal twang. There may also be an allusion to venereal disease (then associated
                  with Naples) which may affect the nose.
7   *marry, are they:* Yes, they are.
8   *a tale* – with a pun on *tail* = penis.
15   *to't* – i.e. play.
23   *keep up thy quillets:* put away your quibbles.
27–8   *seem to notify* – The clown seems to be making fun of Cassio's polite speech.

ACT III scene i

Outside the citadel.

Enter CASSIO *with* MUSICIANS.

CASSIO Masters, play here; I will content your pains.*
Something that's brief; and bid 'Good morrow, general.'*
[*They play*
Enter CLOWN.

CLOWN Why, masters, have your instruments been in Naples
that they speak i'th'nose* thus?

MUSICIAN How, sir, how?   5

CLOWN Are these, I pray you, wind instruments?

MUSICIAN Ay, marry, are they,* sir.

CLOWN O, thereby hangs a tale.*

MUSICIAN Whereby hangs a tale, sir?

CLOWN Marry, sir, by many a wind instrument that I know. But   10
masters, here's money for you; and the general so likes
your music that he desires you, for love's sake, to make
no more noise with it.

MUSICIAN Well sir, we will not.

CLOWN If you have any music that may not be heard, to't* again.   15
But, as they say, to hear music the general does not
greatly care.

MUSICIAN We have none such, sir.

CLOWN Then put up your pipes in your bag, for I'll away.
Go, vanish into air, away!   20
[*Exeunt* MUSICIANS

CASSIO Dost thou hear me, mine honest friend?

CLOWN No. I hear not your honest friend. I hear you.

CASSIO Prithee keep up thy quillets.* There's a poor piece of gold
for thee. If the gentlewoman that attends the general's
wife be stirring, tell her there's one Cassio entreats her a   25
little favour of speech. Wilt thou do this?

CLOWN She is stirring, sir. If she will stir hither, I shall seem to
notify* unto her.
[*Exit* CLOWN

79

29	*In happy time:* Well met! I am glad to see you.
33	*presently:* at once.
38	*A Florentine* – i.e. 'one of my own countrymen'. – Cassio is the native of Florence, not Iago.
40	*displeasure:* falling out of favour.
42	*stoutly:* wholeheartedly.
44	(of) *great affinity:* well connected.
44	*wholesome wisdom:* expedient common sense.
45	*might not but:* had no choice but to.
53	*bosom:* true feelings.

Enter IAGO.

CASSIO In happy time,* Iago.
IAGO   You have not been abed then?
CASSIO Why no; the day had broke before we parted.   30
          I have made bold, Iago, to send in to your wife;
          My suit to her is that she will to virtuous Desdemona
          Procure me some access.
IAGO   I'll send her to you presently,*
          And I'll devise a mean to draw the Moor
          Out of the way, that your converse and business   35
          May be more free.
CASSIO I humbly thank you for't.

                                              [*Exit* IAGO
                              I never knew
          A Florentine* more kind and honest.

          Enter EMILIA.

EMILIA Good morrow, good lieutenant. I am sorry
          For your displeasure;* but all will sure be well.   40
          The general and his wife are talking of it,
          And she speaks for you stoutly.* The Moor replies
          That he you hurt is of great fame in Cyprus
          And great affinity,* and that in wholesome wisdom*
          He might not but* refuse you. But he protests he loves
                                                    you,   45
          And needs no other suitor but his likings
          To take the safest occasion by the front
          To bring you in again.
CASSIO   Yet I beseech you,
          If you think fit, or that it may be done,
          Give me advantage of some brief discourse   50
          With Desdemona alone.
EMILIA   Pray you, come in.
          I will bestow you where you shall have time
          To speak your bosom* freely.
CASSIO   I am much bound to you.

                                              [*Exeunt*

III.ii.   Othello tells Iago to take certain despatches to a ship sailing for Venice and then join him on an inspection of the island's defences.
　　　　　This very short scene, which shows Othello conscientiously attending to his public duties, indicates that Desdemona is now alone and therefore able to meet Cassio privately as he wished, and prepares us for the long and decisive scene that follows, when we see Iago and Othello enter together.

2   *do my duties*: send my greetings.
3   *works*: fortifications.

III.iii.   Desdemona assures Cassio that she will do her utmost to plead on his behalf with Othello. Emilia adds that her husband Iago is deeply grieved by Cassio's downfall.
　　　　　Seeing Othello and Iago return, Cassio leaves hurriedly. Iago seeing this mutters 'I like not that' to himself, sowing the first seeds of disquiet in Othello's mind. Desdemona asks Othello to reinstate Cassio but Othello does not wish to discuss the matter at that time, though eventually he yields to her entreaties and promises to meet Cassio soon. When Desdemona and Emilia leave Iago takes the opportunity to intensify the doubts in Othello's mind with veiled suggestions and half-expressed thoughts, implying that Cassio's relationship with Desdemona goes beyond ordinary respect and affection. Iago warns Othello to beware of jealousy. Othello denies that he would ever be jealous without clear evidence. Iago then suggests that Othello should note how Desdemona and Cassio behave in each other's company. He also tells Othello not to restore Cassio to his former office for the moment, so that he could better observe Desdemona's reaction to his former office for the moment, so that he could better observe Desdemona's reaction to this.
　　　　　Othello is greatly disturbed but the sight of Desdemona once more restores his faith in her absolute fidelity.
　　　　　Just before dinner Othello complains of a headache and Desdemona offers to bind his head with her handkerchief. It falls to the ground and Othello tells her not to bother with it as it is too small. Emilia picks up the handkerchief, notes that it was the first present Othello gave to Desdemona, gives it to Iago, who has often expressed a desire to have it.
　　　　　Iago plans to arrange matters so that Othello will discover the handkerchief in Cassio's possession, thus inflaming the Moor's jealousy.
　　　　　Othello rebukes Iago for casting doubts on Desdemona's fidelity. He is now in such an anguish of uncertainty that only definite proof one way or the other will satisfy him. He demands that Iago furnishes this forthwith. Iago tells him how Cassio has talked in his sleep, whispering endearments to Desdemona and cursing her husband. Othello is now determined to destroy both Cassio and Desdemona but Iago asks him to be patient, while letting fall the information that he has seen Cassio with a handkerchief like the one Othello had given his wife. Othello is now convinced of Desdemona's unfaithfulness and determines to kill her, asking Iago to kill Cassio. Iago swears loyalty to the Moor who promotes him to Cassio's office of lieutenant.
　　　　　This is the crucial scene of the play. The sinister plan which has so far been only in Iago's head is here released to do its deadly work, and *knavery's plain face* is seen in all its monstrous fascination. The scene begins with deceptive lightness, in which Desdemona pleasantly and almost merrily reassures the anxious Cassio. But even at the very beginning, the ominous word *honest* applied to Iago (this time by Desdemona herself) is a warning signal. And it is not long before we see Iago, in his guise as Othello's true-hearted defender, begin his sinister work of poisoning the Moor's mind. The whole scene is a kind of horrifying mixture of both *wit* and *witchcraft*, for we are not only made aware of Iago's diabolical cunning but of the mesmerising spell he casts over Othello. By the time Iago leaves him for the first time, Othello is more than half prepared to think Desdemona unfaithful; when he and Iago meet again, he is entirely in Iago's fatal power, a noble character almost literally possessed by a devil.

2   *All my abilities*: my best.
12   *strangeness*: unfriendliness.

scene ii

The citadel.

Enter OTHELLO, IAGO *and* GENTLEMEN.

OTHELLO These letters give, Iago, to the pilot
And by him do my duties* to the Senate.
That done, I will be walking on the works;*
Repair there to me.
IAGO   Well, my good lord, I'll do't.
OTHELLO This fortification, gentlemen, shall we see't?   5
GENTLEMEN We'll wait upon your lordship.
                                          [*Exeunt*

scene iii

The citadel.

Enter DESDEMONA, CASSIO, *and* EMILIA.

DESDEMONA Be thou assured, good Cassio, I will do
All my abilities* in thy behalf.
EMILIA Good madam, do. I warrant it grieves my husband
As if the cause were his.
DESDEMONA O, that's an honest fellow. Do not doubt, Cassio,   5
But I will have my lord and you again
As friendly as you were.
CASSIO   Bounteous madam,
Whatever shall become of Michael Cassio,
He's never anything but your true servant.
DESDEMONA I know't; I thank you. You do love my lord,   10
You have known him long, and be you well assured
He shall in strangeness* stand no farther off

13   *politic:* expedient.
14   *policy:* prudent conduct.
15   *nice:* thin
16   *breed . . . circumstances:* maintain itself on day-to-day happenings and needs.
17   *supplied;* filled. – Cassio says that Othello may be tempted to maintain his unfriendly
        attitude for so long that he would get used to someone else performing his
        (Cassio's) duties and so make Cassio's dismissal permanent by force of habit
        rather than deliberate intention.
19   *doubt:* fear.
20   *warrant:* guarantee.
22   *article:* item, detail.
23   *I'll watch him tame:* I'll keep watch over him till he becomes *tame.* – Animals were tamed
        by being deprived of sleep.
24   *board:* table.
24   *shrift:* confessional.
34   *do your discretion:* do as you wish.
35   *Ha! I like not that* – This innocent-seeming half-line is the first poisonous drop in the
        hellish brew concocted by Iago. He may heighten it by staring at Cassio during
        the few seconds he has been on the scene, while Othello is preoccupied by public
        matters and perhaps documents. Iago excites Othello's curiosity by breaking off
        in mid-sentence in his answer to Othello's *What dost thou say?* suggesting that he
        knows a lot more than he wishes to say.
47   *present:* immediate.

Than in a politic* distance.

CASSIO   Ay, but, lady,
That policy* may either last so long,
Or feed upon such nice* and waterish diet,   15
Or breed* itself so out of circumstances,
That I being absent, and my place supplied,*
My general will forget my love and service.
DESDEMONA Do not doubt* that; before Emilia here
I give thee warrant* of thy place. Assure thee,   20
If I do vow a friendship, I'll perform it
To thy last article.* My lord shall never rest;
I'll watch him tame* and talk him out of patience;
His bed shall seem a school, his board* a shrift;*
I'll intermingle everything he does   25
With Cassio's suit. Therefore be merry, Cassio,
For thy solicitor shall rather die
Than give thy cause away.

Enter OTHELLO *and* IAGO *at a distance.*

EMILIA Madam, here comes my lord.
CASSIO Madam, I'll take my leave.   30
DESDEMONA Why stay, and hear me speak.
CASSIO Madam, not now. I am very ill at ease,
Unfit for mine own purposes.
DESDEMONA Well, do your discretion.*
                                            [*Exit* CASSIO

IAGO Ha! I like not that.*
OTHELLO   What dost thou say?   35
IAGO Nothing, my lord; or if – I know not what.
OTHELLO Was not that Cassio parted from my wife?
IAGO Cassio, my lord? No, sure, I cannot think it,
That he would steal away so guilty-like,
Seeing you coming.
OTHELLO   I do believe 'twas he.   40
DESDEMONA [*Coming to them*] How now, my lord?
I have been talking with a suitor here,
A man that languishes in your displeasure.
OTHELLO Who is't you mean?
DESDEMONA Why, your lieutenant, Cassio. Good my lord,   45
If I have any grace or power to move you,
His present* reconciliation take.
For if he be not one that truly loves you,

52   *I'sooth*: in truth.

60–74   Desdemona is as good as her word, and takes the first opportunity to speak on Cassio's behalf. Her short tripping phrases introduce a quicker and lighter rhythm to the scene, expressing both her unclouded happiness and her absolute confidence in her relationship with her husband. She literally *talks him out of patience*, carrying on talking till Othello accedes to her wish.

64   *trespass*: offence, transgression (archaic).

67   *T'incur a private check*: to receive a reprimand in private (let alone publicly, as happened to Cassio).

70   *mamm'ring*: hesitating.

71   *came awooing with you* – see Introduction p. xxxviii.

74   *bring him in*: reinstate him.

74   *By'r Lady*: By our Lady (i.e. the Virgin Mary). An oath.

79   *peculiar profit*: especial benefit.

82   *poise*: seriousness. – The metaphor is that of a pair of scales almost equally weighted in each pan.

84   *Whereon*: at which point.

That errs in ignorance, and not in cunning,
I have no judgment in an honest face.   50
I prithee call him back.

OTHELLO   Went he hence now?

DESDEMONA I'sooth* so humbled
That he hath left part of his grief with me
To suffer with him. Good love, call him back.

OTHELLO Not now, sweet Desdemon; some other time.   55

DESDEMONA But shall't be shortly?

OTHELLO   The sooner, sweet, for you.

DESDEMONA Shall't be tonight at supper?

OTHELLO   No, not tonight.

DESDEMONA Tomorrow dinner then?

OTHELLO   I shall not dine at home;
I meet the captains at the citadel.

DESDEMONA Why then, tomorrow night, on Tuesday morn,   60
On Tuesday noon, or night, on Wednesday morn.
I prithee name the time, but let it not
Exceed three days. In faith, he's penitent;
And yet his trespass,* in our common reason
(Save that they say the wars must make example   65
Out of her best), is not almost a fault
T'incur a private check.* When shall he come?
Tell me, Othello. I wonder in my soul
What you would ask me that I should deny,
Or stand so mamm'ring* on. What? Michael Cassio,   70
That came awooing with you,* and so many a time,
When I have spoke of you dispraisingly,
Hath ta'en your part – to have so much to do
To bring him in?* By'r Lady,* I could do much –

OTHELLO Prithee no more. Let him come when he will;   75
I will deny thee nothing.

DESDEMONA   Why, this is not a boon;
'Tis as I should entreat you wear your gloves,
Or feed on nourishing dishes, or keep you warm,
Or sue to you to do a peculiar profit*
To your own person. Nay, when I have a suit   80
Wherein I mean to touch your love indeed,
It shall be full of poise* and difficult weight,
And fearful to be granted.

OTHELLO   I will deny thee nothing!
Whereon* I do beseech thee, grant me this,

90   *wretch* – a term of affection.
90–92   *Perdition . . . thee:* I am utterly damned if I do not love you. These poignant words are Othello's last complete affirmation of his love for Desdemona, and with their hint of loss and destruction presage the tragedy to come.
92   *Chaos is come again:* It will be the end of the world (when it was believed, there would be a return to the chaos existing before Creation).
102   *aught:* anything.
103   *honest:* (i) honourable; (ii) sexually moral. – As already indicated, this is one of the key words in the play and resounds with a wide range of meanings.
106   *By heaven, thou echoest me* – Iago's technique of merely repeating Othello's words has exactly the desired effect of creating a *monster* in Othello's *thought*.
111   *of my counsel:* in my confidence.
113   *contract . . . brow:* frown.
115   *conceit:* conception, notion.

If confused,
lost.

To leave me but a little to myself.   85
DESDEMONA Shall I deny you? No. Farewell, my lord.
OTHELLO Farewell, my Desdemona; I'll come to thee straight.
DESDEMONA Emilia, come. [*To OTHELLO*] Do as your fancies teach you;
Whate'er you be, I am obedient.

[*Exit with* EMILIA
OTHELLO Excellent wretch!* Perdition* catch my soul   90
But I do love thee! And when I love thee not,
Chaos is come again.*
IAGO My noble lord –
OTHELLO   What dost thou say, Iago?
IAGO Did Michael Cassio, when you wooed my lady,
Know of your love?   95
OTHELLO He did, from first to last. Why dost thou ask?
IAGO But for a satisfaction of my thought –
No further harm.
OTHELLO   Why of thy thought, Iago?
IAGO I did not think he had been acquainted with her
OTHELLO Oh, yes, and went between us very oft.   100
IAGO Indeed?
OTHELLO Indeed? Ay, indeed! Discern'st thou aught* in that?
Is he not honest?*
IAGO   Honest, my lord?
OTHELLO   Honest? Ay, honest.
IAGO My lord, for aught I know.
OTHELLO What dost thou think?
IAGO   Think, my lord?
OTHELLO   Think, my lord?   105
By heaven, thou echoest me,*
As if there were some monster in thy thought
Too hideous to be shown. Thou dost mean something.
I heard thee say even now, thou lik'st not that,
When Cassio left my wife. What didst not like?   110
And when I told thee he was of my counsel*
Of my whole course of wooing, thou cried'st 'Indeed?'
And didst contract* and purse thy brow together,
As if thou then hadst shut up in thy brain
Some horrible conceit.* If thou dost love me,   115
Show me thy thought.
IAGO My lord, you know I love you.
OTHELLO   I think thou dost;
And, for I know thou'rt full of love and honesty

120   *stops:* pauses, hesitations.
122   *tricks of custom:* customary.
123   *close dilations:* expression of hidden thoughts. – The meaning is that pauses and hesitations which would be merely tricks of habit in an untrustworthy man would, in an honest person, be expressions of thoughts and feelings too powerful to be entirely suppressed.
127   *would . . . none* – I wish they would not bear the outward form of men.
131–2 *speak . . . ruminate:* speak to me in the very language of your own thoughts.
135   *to that* – i.e. to that which.
137   *As where's:* where, for example, is.
140   *leets and law days:* meetings of local courts of justice. – Who, Iago asks, is so pure-minded that unclean thoughts do not sometimes come to him. The imagery is of dishonourable men joining worthy magistrates on the bench (*in sessions*).
147   *jealousy:* suspicion, vigilance.
149   *conceits:* speculates. – Iago is subtly flattering Othello in the sphere where the man of action would be most susceptible to flattery – through an allusion to his *wisdom*. He suggests that Othello, in his wisdom, should ignore his (Iago's) speculations, which may well rest on dubious foundations.
151   *scattering:* haphazard, fragmentary.
152   *not for your quiet nor your good:* conducive neither to your peace of mind nor your welfare. – Now that Iago has stirred Othello's mind in vague and general terms, he proceeds to a more explicit statement of menace, provoking Othello's perturbed and instinctive question. (1. 154).

Because I can talk of
laver elements that he can
Destroy Othello's certainty
(Travesi p 113)

And weigh'st thy words before thou giv'st them breath,
Therefore these stops* of thine fright me the more;   120
For such things in a false disloyal knave
Are tricks of custom;* but in a man that's just
They're close dilations,* working from the heart,
That passion cannot rule.

IAGO   For Michael Cassio,
I dare be sworn, I think that he is honest.   125

OTHELLO I think so too.

IAGO   Men should be what they seem;
Or those that be not, would* they might seem none!

OTHELLO Certain, men should be what they seem.

IAGO Why then, I think Cassio's an honest man.

OTHELLO Nay, yet there's more in this.   130
I prithee speak* to me as to thy thinkings,
As thou dost ruminate, and give thy worst of thoughts
The worst of words.

IAGO   Good my lord, pardon me:
Though I am bound to every act of duty,
I am not bound to that* all slaves are free to.   135
Utter my thoughts? Why, say they are vile and false,
As where's* that palace whereinto foul things
Sometimes intrude not? Who has that breast so pure
But some uncleanly apprehensions
Keep leets and law days,* and in sessions sit   140
With meditations lawful?

OTHELLO Thou dost conspire against thy friend, Iago,
If thou but think'st him wronged, and mak'st his ear
A stranger to thy thoughts.

IAGO   I do beseech you –
Though I perchance am vicious in my guess   145
(As I confess it is my nature's plague
To spy into abuses, and of my jealousy*
Shape faults that are not) – that your wisdom
From one that so imperfectly conceits*
Would take no notice, nor build yourself a trouble   150
Out of his scattering* and unsure observance.
It were not for your quiet nor your good,*
Nor for my manhood, honesty, and wisdom,
To let you know my thoughts.

OTHELLO   What dost thou mean?

IAGO Good name in man and woman, dear my lord,   155

156   *immediate:* personally important. – The word *jewel* was often associated in the seventeenth century with chastity and coming so close to the phrase *man and woman* evidently provokes Othello's outburst: *By heaven, I'll know thy thoughts!* On the surface Iago is talking about himself and his good name, but underneath there are cunning innuendoes directed towards Cassio and Desdemona.

159   *filches:* steals.

166   *doth mock . . . feeds on* – i.e. the man who suffers from jealousy becomes more ridiculous as his jealousy grows more intense. This is a poignant prophecy of Othello's imminent fate.

169   *tells:* counts.

173   *fineless:* limitless.

176–92   Othello's capacity to make a long and dignified rejection of Iago's insinuations suggests that while his suspicions have been stirred in a general way, he has still not *consciously* confronted the possibility that Desdemona has been unfaithful to him with Cassio, though, as has been suggested, the seeds of this notion have been planted in his subconscious mind by Iago. Thus his interjections of *Ha!* and *O misery!* may be seen as his conscious reactions to the general drift of Iago's remarks rather than an indication of his awareness that they may apply to himself. But if this awareness has burst into his consciousness at *By heaven, I'll know thy thoughts!* then this long speech may be interpreted as his last desperate attempt to fight off a 'truth' too hideous to acknowledge. His opening questions *Why? Why is this?* certainly suggest a man shaking himself into reason out of a hypnotic trance into which he has almost fallen.

178   *still:* always. – The moon was associated with certain forms of madness.

180   *resolved:* convinced. – Othello, in his own view, is the kind of man who, once his suspicion was aroused, would immediately set about finding out the truth, whatever it was.

182   *exsufflicate:* swollen up, exaggerated. – The word means almost the same as *blown* and is therefore itself an example of 'swollen up' language.

183   *'Tis not to:* it is not sufficient to.

187–8   *Nor from . . . her revolt:* I will not in the least suspect her of infidelity (*revolt*) merely because I am so undeserving (of her love).

Is the immediate* jewel of their souls.
Who steals my purse steals trash; 'tis something, noth-
                                          ing;
'Twas mine, 'tis his, and has been slave to thousands,
But he that filches* from me my good name
Robs me of that which not enriches him   160
And makes me poor indeed.

OTHELLO By heaven, I'll know thy thoughts!

IAGO You cannot, if my heart were in your hand;
Nor shall not whilst 'tis in my custody.

OTHELLO Ha!

IAGO   O beware, my lord, of jealousy!   165
It is the green-eyed monster, which doth mock*
The meat it feeds on. That cuckold lives in bliss
Who, certain of his fate, loves not his wronger;
But O, what damnèd minutes tells* he o'er
Who dotes, yet doubts – suspects, yet strongly loves!   170

OTHELLO O misery!

IAGO Poor and content is rich, and rich enough;
But riches fineless* is as poor as winter
To him that ever fears he shall be poor.
Good God the souls of all my tribe defend   175
From jealousy!*

OTHELLO   Why? Why is this?
Think'st thou I'd make a life of jealousy,
To follow still* the changes of the moon
With fresh suspicions? No! To be once in doubt
Is once to be resolved.* Exchange me for a goat   180
When I shall turn the business of my soul
To such exsufflicate* and blown surmises,
Matching thy inference. 'Tis not to* make me jealous
To say my wife is fair, feeds well, loves company,
Is free of speech, sings, plays, and dances;   185
Where virtue is, these are more virtuous.
Nor from* mine own weak merits will I draw
The smallest fear or doubt of her revolt,
For she had eyes, and chose me. No, Iago.
I'll see before I doubt; when I doubt, prove;   190
And on the proof there is no more but this:
Away at once with love or jealousy!

IAGO I am glad of this; for now I shall have reason
To show the love and duty that I bear you

195   *as I am bound:* since it is my duty (to say it).
197   Iago is now confident enough to direct Othello explicitly (*Look to your wife*) because Othello himself has mentioned her in connection with infidelity and spoken aloud the things Iago had only hinted at.
198   *Wear your eyes thus* – It is poignantly ironical that Iago, who holds a subordinate position, now feels so confident that he is able to command Othello, his superior officer, in the smallest physical details of his behaviour. This is a vivid instance of the process by which Iago 'possesses' Othello.
200   *self-bounty:* innate generosity of mind (which would credit others with his own high standards).
201   *country disposition:* native temperament. – Iago is now playing on Othello's insecurity as an alien in Venice. Venice was notorious at this time for courtesans.
203   *best conscience:* highest notion of morality.
208   *And so she did* – The fact that Othello has come, in a few lines from his rapturous affirmation of faith (*For she had eyes and chose me*) to interpreting *this same behaviour on Desdemona's part* in a diametrically opposed manner is evidence of the deep level at which Iago's poison is working within him.
208   *go to:* so there! – a colloquial phrase.
210   *seel:* sew up. – The word is taken from falconry and refers to the sewing up of the falcon's eyelids during training.
210   *close as oak:* oak is a very close-grained wood.
211   Note how Iago deftly slips in the charge of witchcraft, this time not against Othello but Desdemona. He changes course with *But I am much to blame* perhaps to bring Othello out of the troubled reverie into which he has fallen, because something in Othello's reaction may make him feel he has gone too far.
213   *I am bound to thee for ever* – This is tragically true in more senses than the speaker is aware of. In the ensuing dialogue Iago's confidence reaches the point where he can openly refer to the effect of his words on Othello, still wearing the mask of loyal concern.
219   *grosser:* (i) plainer; (ii) more lewd. – *Larger* also has this second sense, in addition to meaning 'greater'.
222   *fall . . . success:* have such evil consequences.
225   *I do not think but:* I have no doubt that.
225   *honest:* chaste. – This is the first time in this long exchange that Desdemona has been mentioned by name.
226   *Long live . . . think so* – The second wish Iago expresses takes away the reassurance that the first seemed to offer. In the next line Othello echoes Brabantio's original explanation of his daughter's conduct (I.iii.97). Once he begins to think of Desdemona's conduct as 'unnatural' Iago's success is assured. He pounces on Othello's half-formed thought and elaborates on it (l. 228–33), ending on the key word *unnatural* and once again, solicitously begging Othello's pardon for going too far (l. 234–5); though he takes care to leave in Othello's mind the notion that when Desdemona regains her own 'nature' she is bound to regret her choice of Othello (l. 235–38). The fact that Othello does not apparently take offence at insinuations against his race and colour suggests that at some level he may have been expecting them.

	With franker spirit. Therefore, as I am bound,*	195
	Receive it from me. I speak not yet of proof.	

With franker spirit. Therefore, as I am bound,*   195
Receive it from me. I speak not yet of proof.
Look to your wife; observe her well with Cassio;
Wear your eyes thus:* not jealous nor secure.
I would not have your free and noble nature
Out of self-bounty* be abused. Look to't.   200
I know our country disposition* well:
In Venice they do let heaven see the pranks
They dare not show their husbands; their best
                        conscience*
Is not to leave't undone, but keep't unknown.

OTHELLO Dost thou say so?   205

IAGO She did deceive her father, marrying you;
And when she seemed to shake and fear your looks,
She loved them most.

OTHELLO   And so she did.*

IAGO   Why, go to* then!
She that so young could give out such a seeming
To seel* her father's eyes up close as oak* –   210
He thought 'twas witchcraft.* But I am much to blame.
I humbly do beseech you of your pardon
For too much loving you.

OTHELLO   I am bound to thee for ever.*

IAGO I see this hath a little dashed your spirits.

OTHELLO Not a jot, not a jot.

IAGO   Trust me, I fear it has.   215
I hope you will consider what is spoke
Comes from my love. But I do see y'are moved.
I am to pray you not to strain my speech
To grosser* issues, nor to larger reach
Than to suspicion.   220

OTHELLO I will not.

IAGO   Should you do so, my lord,
My speech should fall* into such vile success
Which my thoughts aimed not at. Cassio's my worthy
                       friend –
My lord, I see y'are moved.

OTHELLO   No, not much moved.
I do not think but* Desdemona's honest.*   225

IAGO Long live* she so. And long live you to think so.

OTHELLO And yet, how nature erring from itself –

IAGO Ay, there's the point; as (to be bold with you)

229   *affect:* desire.
230   *degree:* social rank.
232   *a will most rank:* (i) a very corrupt intention; (ii) a fierce lust.
233   *disproportion:* depravity.
234   *in position:* positively.
235   *Distinctly:* specifically.
237   *fall to match:* come to compare.
237   *country forms:* appearance of her countrymen.
238   *happily:* perhaps.
240   *Set on thy wife to observe* – The depths to which Othello has now sunk and the power which Iago has over him are made clear by this instruction. Iago leaves but returns immediately to give Othello further instructions, this time in a positive and business-like manner.
244   *I would I might entreat:* I wish I could persuade.
249   *means:* methods.
250   *strain his entertainment:* urge his (re-) employment.
253   *too busy in my fears:* over-suspicious.
255   *hold her free:* consider her innocent. – Iago can now offer this advice, secure in the knowledge that it will be ignored.
256   *government:* self-control.
258   *all qualities:* all types of character.
258   *learnèd:* experienced.
259   *Of:* with regard to.
259   *haggard:* wild. – A haggard is an untamed mature hawk.
260   *jesses:* leather thongs attached to the hawk's feet.
261   *whistle . . . wind* – Hawks were released for hunting against the wind. If they were released 'down wind', they seldom returned. So if the hunter wanted to get rid of a hawk he would release it with the wind behind it.
262   *prey at fortune* – i.e. to make her way in the world as best she may.
262, 4 *for:* because. – Othello torments himself with possible reasons for Desdemona's supposed unfaithfulness.
263   *soft parts of:* agreeable talents for.
263   *conversation:* social behaviour.
264   *chamberers:* ladies' men.
266   *She's gone* – Othello now takes Desdemona's infidelity as accomplished fact. The *Haply* (Perhaps) which seems to qualify the thought comes three lines earlier and might apply to the reasons for his wife's disloyalty, rather than cast doubt on the fact itself.
266   *abused:* deceived, disgraced.

Not to affect* many proposed matches
Of her own clime, complexion, and degree,*   230
Whereto we see in all things nature tends –
Foh! one may smell in such a will most rank,*
Foul disproportion,* thoughts unnatural.
But pardon me, I do not in position*
Distinctly* speak of her; though I may fear   235
Her will, recoiling to her better judgment,
May fall to match* you with her country forms,*
And happily* repent.

OTHELLO   Farewell, farewell.
If more thou dost perceive, let me know more.
Set on thy wife to observe.* Leave me, Iago.   240

IAGO My lord, I take my leave.

                                              [*Going*

OTHELLO Why did I marry? This honest creature doubtless
Sees and knows more, much more, than he unfolds.

IAGO [*Returns*] My lord, I would I might entreat*your honour
To scan this thing no farther. Leave it to time.   245
Although 'tis fit that Cassio have his place,
For sure he fills it up with great ability,
Yet, if you please to hold him off awhile,
You shall by that perceive him and his means.*
Note if your lady strain his entertainment*   250
With any strong or vehement importunity;
Much will be seen in that. In the meantime
Let me be thought too busy in my fears*
(As worthy cause I have to fear I am)
And hold her free,* I do beseech your honour.   255

OTHELLO Fear not my government.*

IAGO   I once more take my leave.

                                              [*Exit*

OTHELLO This fellow's of exceeding honesty,
And knows all qualities,* with a learnèd* spirit
Of* human dealings. If I do prove her haggard,*
Though that her jesses* were my dear heartstrings,   260
I'd whistle* her off and let her down the wind
To prey at fortune.* Haply for* I am black
And have not those soft parts of* conversation*
That chamberers* have, or for I am declined
Into the vale of years – yet that's not much –   265
She's gone.* I am abused,* and my relief

273   *Prerogatived . . . base:* They are less likely than the humbly born to escape (cuckoldry).
275   *forkèd plague* – i.e. the fate of becoming a cuckold, who was supposed to grow horns on his
      forehead visible to all but himself.
276   *do quicken:* are born.
277   Desdemona's mere presence is enough to evoke in Othello an instinctive conviction of her
      purity, but only momentarily.
279   *generous:* nobly born (from Latin *generosus*).
280   *attend:* wait.
283   *a pain upon my forehead* – Another reference to the cuckold's horns.
284   *watching:* staying awake.
286   *napkin:* handkerchief.
289–98   Emilia's soliloquy, ending with a rhyming couplet, helps to concentrate our
      interest on an apparently trivial object which is to be of such tragic significance.
290   *remembrance:* keepsake.
291   *wayward:* capricious.
293   *conjured:* solemnly instructed.
294   *reserves:* keeps.
295   *ta'en out:* copied.
298   *I nothing but:* I know only how to.
298   *fantasy:* whim. – Emilia's final words direct our attention to the use Iago may make of the
      handkerchief.

The slender basis is a deliberate + necessary part of the intention.

Must be to loathe her. O curse of marriage,
That we can call these delicate creatures ours,
And not their appetites! I had rather be a toad
And live upon the vapour of a dungeon   270
Than keep a corner in the thing I love
For others' uses. Yet 'tis the plague of great ones;
Prerogatived* are they less than the base.
'Tis destiny unshunnable, like death.
Even then this forkèd plague* is fated to us   275
When we do quicken.* Look where she comes.

Enter DESDEMONA *and* EMILIA.

If she be false, O then heaven mocks itself!
I'll not believe't.
DESDEMONA   How now, my dear Othello?
Your dinner, and the generous* islanders
By you invited, do attend* your presence.   280
OTHELLO I am to blame.
DESDEMONA   Why do you speak so faintly?
Are you not well?
OTHELLO I have a pain upon my forehead,* here.
DESDEMONA Why, that's with watching;* 'twill away again.
Let me but bind it hard, within this hour   285
It will be well.
OTHELLO   Your napkin* is too little;
            [*He brushes her handkerchief aside, and it falls*
Let it alone. Come, I'll go in with you.
DESDEMONA I am very sorry that you are not well.
                                    [*Exit with* OTHELLO
EMILIA I am glad I have found this napkin;
This was her first remembrance* from the Moor.   290
My wayward* husband hath a hundred times
Wooed me to steal it; but she so loves the token
(For he conjured* her she should ever keep it)
That she reserves* it evermore about her
To kiss and talk to. I'll have the work ta'en out*   295
And give't Iago.
What he'll do with it,
                    Heaven knows, not I;
I nothing but* to please his fantasy.*

Enter IAGO.

IAGO How now? What do you here alone?

300   *thing* – Iago pretends to take the word in its Elizabethan sense of 'female sexual organ'.
301   *common:* (i) public; (ii) ordinary.
311   *to th'advantage:* luckily.
315   *import:* importance.
317   *Be not acknown on't;* Do not admit any knowledge of it.
322   *Holy Writ:* Christian scripture.
324   *conceits:* ideas. – Iago is fond of explaining himself, even when, as here, his meaning is
           quite clear.
325   *distaste:* be distasteful.
327   *mines of sulphur:* infernal regions. – In popular belief, sulphur was associated with hell-
           fire.
327   *I did say so* – Presumably a reference to the fact that Othello's tormented appearance
           illustrates what Iago has just been saying about the ruinous effects of *dangerous
           conceits.*
328   *mandragora:* a narcotic plant. – In this and the next three lines Iago's language briefly
           assumes some of the fulness and dignity of Othello's; very soon we shall hear
           Othello's speech degenerating into the foul bestiality of Iago's.
329   *drowsy:* sleep-inducing.
331   *owedst:* possessed.

EMILIA Do not you chide, I have a thing* for you.   300
  IAGO You have a thing for me? It is a common* thing –
EMILIA Ha!
  IAGO To have a foolish wife.
EMILIA O, is that all? What will you give me now
        For that same handkerchief?
  IAGO   What handkerchief?   305
EMILIA What handkerchief?
        Why, that the Moor first gave to Desdemona,
        That which so often you did bid me steal.
  IAGO Hast stol'n it from her?
EMILIA No, but she let it drop by negligence,   310
        And to th'advantage,* I, being here, took't up.
        Look, here't is.
  IAGO   A good wench; give it me.
EMILIA What will you do with't, that you have been so earnest
        To have me filch it?
  IAGO   Why, what is that to you?
                          [*Snatches it*
EMILIA If it be not for some purpose of import,*   315
        Give't me again. Poor lady, she'll run mad
        When she shall lack it.
  IAGO   Be not acknown on't.*
        I have use for it. Go, leave me.
                      [*Exit* EMILIA
        I will in Cassio's lodging lose this napkin
        And let him find it. Trifles light as air   320
        Are to the jealous confirmations strong
        As proofs of Holy Writ.* This may do something.
        The Moor already changes with my poison:
        Dangerous conceits* are in their natures poisons,
        Which at the first are scarce found to distaste,*   325
        But with a little act upon the blood,
        Burn like the mines of sulphur.* I did say so.*

        Enter OTHELLO.

        Look where he comes! Not poppy nor mandragora,*
        Nor all the drowsy* syrups of the world,
        Shall ever medicine thee to that sweet sleep   330
        Which thou owedst* yesterday.
OTHELLO   Ha, ha! False to me?
  IAGO Why how now, general? No more of that.

333   *rack* – An instrument of torture whereby men's limbs were twisted and stretched.
340   *wanting:* missing.
343   *general:* entire.
344   *Pioners:* trench-diggers – one of the lowest forms of military labour.
345   *So:* so long as.

With the words *O now, for ever farewell the tranquil mind!* Othello expresses a terrible and magnificent vision of how his present torment will destroy both his past image of himself and his future greatness as a soldier. The heavy weight of the repeated *Farewell* falls like a drumbeat of doom. The rhythm of these lines has all the heroic dignity of Othello's public conception of himself. The extent to which that conception is rooted in his innermost nature is shown by the fact that he immediately thinks of it when he is troubled by his private grief. As he has already indicated (I.ii.24–27), Othello has had virtually no 'private life' till he met Desdemona. When that new-found bliss is threatened, *chaos* is indeed *come again*, and it shows itself first in Othello's sense that his *occupation's gone*.

348   *makes:* make – a common 17th century usage.
349   *trump:* trumpet.
351   *quality:* attributes.
352   *circumstance:* ceremony.
353   *mortal engines:* death-dealing cannons.
354   *Jove's dread clamours* – i.e. thunder.
355   *occupation:* vocation. – The word has a stronger sense than that of mere 'employment'.
357   *be sure , . . whore* – Iago's question provokes Othello to make a demand he could scarcely have framed so brutally earlier.
358   *ocular:* visible. – This is the only time Shakespeare uses this word, whose weighty air emphasizes the deadly gravity of Othello's demand.
363   *probation:* proof.
366   *If thou dost slander her and torture me* – Othello has a poignant glimpse of the possibility that Iago has deceived him and it is enough almost to stun his imagination, so that all he can do is repeat in phrase after phrase his inability even to conceive what punishment would fit such boundless villainy. Iago's response is to become the injured party and pretend to condemn himself for his excessive loyalty to Othello, knowing that the latter's *self-bounty* will compel him to banish any thought of treachery on Iago's part.

OTHELLO Avaunt, be gone! Thou hast set me on the rack.*
I swear 'tis better to be much abused
Than but to know't a little.

IAGO   How now, my lord?   335

OTHELLO What sense had I of her stol'n hours of lust?
I saw't not, thought it not, it harmed not me;
I slept the next night well, fed well, was free and merry;
I found not Cassio's kisses on her lips.
He that is robbed, not wanting* what is stol'n,   340
Let him not know't, and he's not robbed at all.

IAGO I am sorry to hear this.

OTHELLO I had been happy if the general* camp,
Pioners* and all, had tasted her sweet body,
So* I had nothing known. O now, for ever   345
Farewell the tranquil mind!* Farewell content!
Farewell the plumèd troops, and the big wars
That makes* ambition virtue! O, farewell!
Farewell the neighing steed and the shrill trump,*
The spirit-stirring drum, th'ear-piercing fife,   350
The royal banner, and all quality,*
Pride, pomp, and circumstance* of glorious war!
And O you mortal engines* whose rude throats
Th'immortal Jove's dread clamours* counterfeit,
Farewell! Othello's occupation's* gone!   355

IAGO Is't possible, my lord?

OTHELLO Villain, be sure* thou prove my love a whore!
Be sure of it; give me the ocular* proof;
Or by the worth of mine eternal soul,
Thou hadst been better have been born a dog   360
Than answer my waked wrath!

IAGO   Is't come to this?

OTHELLO Make me to see't; or at the least so prove it
That the probation* bear no hinge nor loop
To hang a doubt on – or woe upon thy life!

IAGO My noble lord –   365

OTHELLO If thou dost slander her and torture me,*
Never pray more; abandon all remorse;
On horror's head horrors accumulate;
Do deeds to make heaven weep, all earth amazed;
For nothing canst thou to damnation add   370
Greater than that.

IAGO   O grace! O heaven forgive me!

373   *God b'wi'you:* Goodbye.
373   *Take mine office:* Take away my appointment (as your ensign).
374   *to make thine honesty a vice* – i.e. to carry honesty so far that it harms himself.
377   *profit:* profitable lesson.
378   *sith:* since
378   *breeds such offence:* produces such harm (to the one who loves).
379   *Nay stay* – Another desperate attempt by Othello to remain calm and reasonable. The meaning of *shouldst* in the next sentence hovers uncertainly between 'ought to be' and 'probably are', expressing Othello's own divided mind. In his next speech (l.381–88) the division comes into the open with the series of contradictory ideas and images both of which in some sense Othello 'believes'.
381   *that:* that which.
385   *Dian's:* Diana's. – Diana was the goddess of chastity and of the moon.
386–7   *cords . . . streams* – i.e. different means of committing suicide.
392–406   There is a venomous casualness in Iago's tone which contrasts strongly with Othello's anguished cry of *Death and damnation! O!* Iago seizes on Othello's word *satisfied* and plays with it, returning to it in the last line (*satisfaction*) but not before he has conjured up a series of vividly obscene images to add to Othello's torment. The matter-of-fact tone of phrases such as *It were a tedious difficulty, I think* turns the knife in the wound.
393   *supervisor:* onlooker.
394   *topped:* with a man on top of her.
396   *prospect:* scene, situation.
397   *bolster:* lie on a pillow together.
398   *More:* Other.
       The short stabbing questions *What then? How then?* etc. are designed to force Othello to visualize the scene Iago has drawn.
401   *prime:* sexually roused. – Goats and monkeys were traditional symbols of sexual appetite.
401   *hot:* sexually eager.
402   *salt:* lecherous.
402   *pride:* sexual heat.
404   *imputation and strong circumstances:* powerful circumstantial evidence.
407   *living:* real, valid.
408   *office:* duty. – Iago's apparent reluctance before beginning his elaborate lie naturally makes Othello more inclined to believe him.
409   *cause:* subject of dispute. – The words *entered in* suggest the legal sense of *cause*, i.e. a matter for litigation. It is a word we shall hear again in a more moving context from Othello himself.
410   *Pricked:* spurred.

Are you a man? Have you a soul or sense?
God b'wi'you!* Take mine office.* O wretched fool,
That lov'st to make thine honesty a vice!*
O monstrous world! Take note, take note, O world,   375
To be direct and honest is not safe.
I thank you for this profit,* and from hence
I'll love no friend, sith* love breeds such offence.*

OTHELLO Nay stay.* Thou shouldst be honest.

IAGO I should be wise; for honesty's a fool   380
And loses that* it works for.

OTHELLO   By the world,
I think my wife be honest, and think she is not;
I think that thou art just, and think thou art not.
I'll have some proof. My name, that was as fresh
As Dian's* visage, is now begrimed and black   385
As mine own face. If there be cords,* or knives,
Poison, or fire, or suffocating streams,
I'll not endure it. Would I were satisfied!

IAGO I see you are eaten up with passion.
I do repent me that I put it to you.   390
You would be satisfied?

OTHELLO   Would? Nay, and I will.

IAGO And may; but how?* How satisfied, my lord?
Would you, the supervisor,* grossly gape on?
Behold her topped?*

OTHELLO   Death and damnation! O!

IAGO It were a tedious difficulty, I think,   395
To bring them to that prospect.* Damn them then,
If ever mortal eyes do see them bolster*
More* than their own! What then? How then?
What shall I say? Where's satisfaction?
It is impossible you should see this,   400
Were they as prime* as goats, as hot* as monkeys,
As salt* as wolves in pride,* and fools as gross
As ignorance made drunk. But yet, I say,
If imputation and strong circumstances*
Which lead directly to the door of truth   405
Will give you satisfaction, you might have't.

OTHELLO Give me a living* reason she's disloyal.

IAGO I do not like the office.*
But sith I am entered in this cause* so far,
Pricked* to't by foolish honesty and love,   410

414   *loose:* careless, indiscreet.

415   *sleeps* – The plural form is a common Shakespearian usage.

417–24   Iago changes into direct speech to make the scene more vividly present to Othello's imagination. The narration becomes more fiercely physical as he uses powerfully suggestive words like *plucked*, *roots* and *thigh* in close succession, ending by bringing Othello directly into the story on the word 'Moor' and so compelling his instinctive reaction, *O monstrous! monstrous!* Iago can then afford to 'remind' Othello that it is only in a dream that Cassio has slept with Desdemona, knowing beyond doubt that this 'dream' will haunt Othello more powerfully than any waking reality. It is ironical, though true to Othello's tormented emotional condition, that the man who insisted on nothing less than *ocular proof* should now be so convinced by a dream retold.

426   *foregone conclusion:* previously accomplished event. – This phrase is often used in modern English in the rather different sense of 'a matter of which the outcome is beyond doubt'.

427   *shrewd doubt:* (i) fearful suspicion; (ii) good guess. – The word *shrewd* often had the usual sense in Shakespeare's day of 'ominous'.

429   *I'll tear her all to pieces!* – Here we see the real operation of the nature that Othello had applied to himself earlier (II.iii.190–3). As a result of Iago's fiendish provocation, Othello's *blood* has begun to *rule* his *safer guides* and *passion, having collied* his *best judgment, assays to lead the way.* The possibility of strong passions bursting through the restraining bonds of reason, judgment and self-control was only stated in the earlier speech; throughout this scene, and particularly in these later moments, we see it in action. Having goaded Othello into a frenzy, Iago's task is now to restrain him, or rather to direct the Moor's awakened passion in the way he (Iago) wants. It is Iago who now plays the role of the man of judgment who does not wish to rush to conclusions without proper evidence.

442   *Look here, Iago* – Othello can now turn to Iago and address him calmly and with dignity, though both the calm and the dignity are precarious and short-lived. Now that Desdemona's guilt has been 'confirmed', Othello is no longer in doubt. So he can dedicate himself solemnly to the new role of avenger. To a man of Othello's character, this self-dedication takes on a formal ceremonial quality, like the rituals surrounding the assumption of certain public duties. It is a ghastly travesty of a chivalric ceremony where the knight pledges his faith to his fair lady. But the reserves of personal feeling in phrases such as *Arise, black vengeance* and *O blood, blood, blood!* beat against the ceremonial framework and almost destroy it.

443   *fond:* foolish.

446   *hearted throne* – i.e. the heart on which you were enthroned.

447   *fraught:* burden.

448   *aspics':* asps'. – An asp is a variety of poisonous snake.

448   *content:* calm.

I will go on. I lay with Cassio lately,
And being troubled with a raging tooth,
I could not sleep.
There are a kind of men so loose* of soul
That in their sleeps* will mutter their affairs.   415
One of this kind is Cassio.
In sleep I heard him say, 'Sweet Desdemona,*
Let us be wary, let us hide our loves!'
And then, sir, would he gripe and wring my hand,
Cry 'O sweet creature!' Then kiss me hard,   420
As if he plucked up kisses by the roots
That grew upon my lips; laid his leg o'er my thigh,
And sigh, and kiss, and then cry, 'Cursèd fate
That gave thee to the Moor!'

OTHELLO O monstrous! monstrous!

IAGO   Nay, this was but his dream.   425

OTHELLO But this denoted a foregone conclusion,*
'Tis a shrewd doubt,* though it be but a dream.

IAGO And this may help to thicken other proofs
That do demonstrate thinly.

OTHELLO   I'll tear her all to pieces!*

IAGO Nay, yet be wise. Yet we see nothing done;   430
She may be honest yet. Tell me but this:
Have you not sometimes seen a handkerchief
Spotted with strawberries in your wife's hand?

OTHELLO I gave her such a one; 'twas my first gift.

IAGO I know not that; but such a handkerchief –   435
I am sure it was your wife's – did I today
See Cassio wipe his beard with.

OTHELLO   If it be that –

IAGO If it be that, or any that was hers,
It speaks against her with the other proofs.

OTHELLO O, that the slave had forty thousand lives!   440
One is too poor, too weak for my revenge.
Now do I see 'tis true. Look here, Iago:*
All my fond* love thus do I blow to heaven.
'Tis gone.
Arise, black vengeance, from the hollow hell!   445
Yield up, O Love, thy crown and hearted throne*
To tyrannous hate! Swell, bosom, with thy fraught,*
For 'tis of aspics'* tongues.

IAGO   Yet be content* –

449   *blood* – Othello's thrice-repeated use of this word has strong associations. In addition to the literal meaning of the word, *blood* also signifies passion and the thirst for revenge.

451   *Pontic Sea:* Black Sea. – In Philemon Holland's translation of Pliny (Bk. II, Ch. 97) Shakespeare could have read that 'the Sea Pontus evermore floweth and runneth out into Propontis, but the Sea never retireth back again within Pontus'. Othello's words (a single sentence through eight lines) are, with their powerful rhythm an illustration of the *compulsive course* of his thoughts. His singleness of mind gives his speech a dignity and power which is his natural idiom (see, for example, his address to the Senate and to Brabantio's servants) but which has been absent while Iago tormented him with insinuations and innuendoes. Now the single, simple passion for revenge reunites his divided mind and heart.

452   *compulsive:* irresistible.
453   *retiring ebb* – See note to line 451.
454   *Propontic:* Sea of Marmora.
457   *capable:* capacious, comprehensive.
458   *marble:* glowing. – The underside of the roofed part of the Elizabethan stage was probably painted with bright streaks of colour, like marble, which formed the background for the representation of the celestial bodies (see Introduction p. xxii). The roof of the stage was known as 'the heavens'. The word also suggests hardness and firmness.

459   *In the due reverence of:* with the solemnity required by.
460   *engage:* pledge.
462   *clip:* enfold.
464   *execution:* activity.
466–7   *to obey . . . business ever:* to obey Othello will be for me an act of compassion (*remorse*) no matter what bloody deeds I may have to perform. – There is a terrible irony in these words, and the accompanying stage picture of the subordinate kneeling to pledge his loyalty to the superior; in reality the roles are exactly reversed. Iago has no trouble in matching the outward form of Othello's language.

469   *to't* – i.e. to the test.
470–71   Othello is calm and apparently in control when he gives orders for action, but as soon as Iago turns his mind towards Desdemona the mask slips and he becomes almost incoherent (l. 472).

478   *I am your own for ever* – The irony is now exact and complete, as this line ought to be uttered by Othello to correspond to the reality of the situation. Othello's 'possession' by the devil Iago is now complete.

OTHELLO O, blood,* blood, blood!
     IAGO Patience, I say. Your mind may change.
OTHELLO Never, Iago. Like to the Pontic Sea,*   450
         Whose icy current and compulsive* course
         Ne'er keeps retiring ebb,* but keeps due on
         To the Propontic* and the Hellespont,
         Even so my bloody thoughts, with violent pace,   455
         Shall ne'er look back, ne'er ebb to humble love,
         Till that a capable* and wide revenge
         Swallow them up. [He kneels] Now, by yond marble*
                                                         heaven,
         In the due reverence of* a sacred vow
         I here engage* my words.
     IAGO   Do not rise yet.   460
                                        [IAGO kneels
         Witness, you ever-burning lights above,
         You elements that clip* us round about,
         Witness that here Iago doth give up
         The execution* of his wit, hands, heart
         To wronged Othello's service. Let him command,   465
         And to obey* shall be in me remorse,
         What bloody business ever.
                                        [They rise
OTHELLO   I greet thy love,
         Not with vain thanks but with acceptance bounteous,
         And will upon the instant put thee to't.*
         Within these three days let me hear thee say   470
         That Cassio's not alive.
     IAGO My friend is dead. 'Tis done at your request.
         But let her live.
OTHELLO   Damn her, lewd minx! O, damn her!
         Damn her!
         Come, go with me apart. I will withdraw   475
         To furnish me with some swift means of death
         For the fair devil. Now art thou my lieutenant.
     IAGO I am your own for ever.*
                                        [Exeunt

III.iv.   Desdemona, attended by Emilia, meets the clown and tells him to inform Cassio that her pleas on his behalf are on the point of success. She tells Emilia that she is upset by the loss of her handkerchief, though she does not believe Othello will really mind as he is not a jealous man. Othello comes in and responds to Desdemona's renewed appeal on behalf of Cassio by asking for the handkerchief. When she says she has not got it he tells her about its magical properties and the misfortune its loss could cause. Desdemona tries to plead Cassio's case again but Othello leaves in great agitation.

Iago and Cassio enter and Desdemona tells them about Othello's strange distress. Iago leaves to look for Othello, saying that something important must be troubling him. After Emilia and Desdemona have left, Bianca, a courtesan and a former intimate of Cassio, comes in and Cassio gives her the handkerchief, which he has found in his lodging, so that she can copy the design for him.

The atmosphere of impending doom conveyed by the preceding scene is momentarily relieved at the opening of this one by the light-hearted exchange between Desdemona and the clown. Yet the tension persists, for Desdemona does not quite join in the spirit of the clowning; her mind seems to be otherwise preoccupied, and her opening inquiry about Cassio's whereabouts sets up an undercurrent of anxiety in us, as we have just heard about Cassio (in the earlier scene) in a very different and sinister connection. The discussion of jealousy between Desdemona and Emilia is loaded for us with a significance which neither speaker is aware of (a technique known as dramatic irony) and Othello's entrance makes us at once anxious and expectant. The invisible presence of the missing handkerchief is strongly felt throughout this scene, not only in Desdemona's initial anxiety about it and in Emilia's lie, but later when Othello invests it with a magical significance and Desdemona too is compelled to lie about it (*It is not lost*). When we see it in Cassio's hand, just before he gives it to the courtesan Bianca, we are almost ready to believe that *there's magic in the web of it*, for we see it change from a *trifle light as air* to a powerful and deadly weapon, like Desdemona's ill-fated pleading on Cassio's behalf.

1	*lies:* lodges – with an obvious pun in the next line.
5	*'tis stabbing:* is asking to be stabbed (by the soldier).
10–11	*lies . . . throat:* tell a deliberate lie.
12	*edified:* enlightened. – Desdemona uses a mockingly elaborate diction to match the clown's verbosity.
13	*catechize:* ask questions and get answers (in a religious context). – Desdemona's word *edified* has a religious connotation which the clown picks up in his answer.
15	*moved:* appealed to.
17	*compass:* scope.
19	*should I lose:* might I have lost.
22	*crusadoes:* gold coins. – so called because they had a cross stamped on them.
22	*but:* except that.
25	*Is he not jealous?* – Perhaps Emilia's question is prompted by her experience as Iago's wife.
27	*humours:* body fluids. – These were blood, phlegm, choler and melancholy and were supposed (depending on which was predominant) to determine a man's temperament. From this is also derived the sense of *humour* as whim or caprice.

scene iv

A street.

Enter DESDEMONA, EMILIA, *and* CLOWN.

DESDEMONA Do you know, sirrah, where Lieutenant Cassio lies?*
CLOWN I dare not say he lies anywhere.
DESDEMONA Why, man?
CLOWN He's a soldier, and for me to say a soldier lies, 'tis
stabbing.*   5
DESDEMONA Go to. Where lodges he?
CLOWN To tell you where he lodges is to tell you where I lie.
DESDEMONA Can anything be made of this?
CLOWN I know not where he lodges, and for me to devise a
lodging, and say he lies* here or he lies there, were to lie   10
in mine own throat.
DESDEMONA Can you enquire him out, and be edified* by report?
CLOWN I will catechize* the world for him; that is, make
questions, and by them answer.
DESDEMONA Seek him, bid him come hither. Tell him I have moved*   15
my lord on his behalf and hope all will be well.
CLOWN To do this is within the compass* of man's wit, and
therefore I will attempt the doing it.
                                              [*Exit* CLOWN
DESDEMONA Where should I lose* the handkerchief, Emilia?
EMILIA I know not, madam.   20
DESDEMONA Believe me, I had rather have lost my purse
Full of crusadoes.* And but* my noble Moor
Is true of mind, and made of no such baseness
As jealous creatures are, it were enough
To put him to ill thinking.
EMILIA   Is he not jealous?*   25
DESDEMONA Who, he? I think the sun where he was born
Drew all such humours* from him.
EMILIA   Look where he comes.

Enter OTHELLO.

DESDEMONA I will not leave him now till Cassio
Be called to him. How is't with you, my lord?

30   *hardness to dissemble:* (i) difficulty of deceiving; (ii) the hardened nature which can dissemble. – The first sense would be applied to himself, the second to his wife. Deception obviously does not come easily to Othello, as it does to Iago. He speaks with difficulty and prefers to express his feelings through a gesture, *Give me your hand* (l. 32).

32   *moist* – A moist hand was believed to indicate a lustful nature. It was also a sign of youth, which is the sense in which Desdemona takes it (l. 33). Age and sorrow were literally supposed to dry up the blood.

34   *argues:* is proof of.

34   *fruitfulness:* (i) fertility; (ii) liberality; (iii) amorousness.

34   *liberal:* (i) generous; (ii) licentious. – *Liberal* and *liberty,* which are important words in this and the next speech by Othello had an unfavourable sense almost entirely lost today.

36   *sequester:* restraint, separation – a word taken from legal terminology.

37   *castigation:* corrective discipline.

40   *frank:* (i) undisguised; (ii) licentious.

43   *heraldry:* heraldic emblems. – *Liberal* could imply gentle birth and this makes Othello think of the heraldic coat of arms which a gentleman was entitled to. His meaning in this and the previous line is that whereas in days gone by *hearts* and *hands* went together, nowadays the outward joining of *hands* (in marriage) does not necessarily imply a joining of *hearts* (in love). Hearts and hands are thought of as heraldic emblems.

45   *chuck* – a term of endearment.

47   *salt and sorry rheum:* miserable running cold.

48   *lend me thy handkerchief* – Perhaps it is the mention of Cassio's name by Desdemona which stirs Othello to make this direct demand.

53   *Egyptian* – often used to denote gypsies, who were believed to be descended from Egyptians and had a reputation as fortune-tellers.

54   *charmer:* one skilled in magic and prophecy.

56   *amiable:* lovable. – Stronger in meaning than the modern sense of 'friendly'.

58–9   *my father's eye . . loathèd:* she would be disgusting to my father's sight.

59   *spirits:* inclinations.

60   *fancies:* loves.

62   *I did so* – This short and simple statement is in some ways the heart of Othello's speech. In it the handkerchief comes out of the past into the troubled present, and the bare utterance, though it refers to a past action, is charged with a sense of future foreboding.

64   *perdition* – a word Othello has used once before in the previous scene (III.iii.90) so that, though the immediate reference is to the disastrous consequences to *Desdemona* of losing the handkerchief, we cannot help thinking of its effect on Othello's own fate.

OTHELLO   Well, my good lady. [*Aside*] O, hardness to dissemble!* –   30
How do you, Desdemona?
DESDEMONA   Well, my good lord.
OTHELLO   Give me your hand. This hand is moist,* my lady.
DESDEMONA   It hath felt no age nor known no sorrow.
OTHELLO   This argues* fruitfulness* and liberal* heart.
Hot, hot and moist. This hand of yours requires   35
A sequester* from liberty; fasting and prayer,
Much castigation,* exercise devout;
For here's a young and sweating devil here
That commonly rebels. 'Tis a good hand,
A frank* one.
DESDEMONA   You may, indeed, say so;   40
For 'twas that hand that gave away my heart.
OTHELLO   A liberal hand! The hearts of old gave hands,
But our new heraldry* is hands, not hearts.
DESDEMONA   I cannot speak of this. Come now, your promise.
OTHELLO   What promise, chuck?*   45
DESDEMONA   I have sent to bid Cassio come speak with you.
OTHELLO   I have a salt and sorry rheum* offends me.
Lend me thy handkerchief.*
DESDEMONA   Here, my lord.
OTHELLO   That which I gave you.
DESDEMONA   I have it not about me.
OTHELLO   Not?   50
DESDEMONA   No, indeed my lord.
                              That's a fault.
OTHELLO   That handkerchief
Did an Egyptian* to my mother give.
She was a charmer,* and could almost read
The thoughts of people. She told her, while she kept it   55
'Twould make her amiable* and subdue my father
Entirely to her love; but if she lost it
Or made a gift of it, my father's eye*
Should hold her loathèd, and his spirits* should hunt
After new fancies.* She, dying, gave it me,   60
And bid me, when my fate would have me wive
To give it her. I did so;* and take heed on't;
Make it a darling like your precious eye.
To lose't or give't away were such perdition*
As nothing else could match.
DESDEMONA   Is't possible?   65

66	*web:* weaving.
67	*sibyl:* prophetess. – The most famous of them, the Sibyl of Cumae, was supposed to have lived to a very great age, because Apollo granted her wish to live as many years as she had grains of sand in her hand.
68	*course two hundred compasses:* to cover two hundred (yearly) revolutions – i.e. two hundred years. (See preceding note.)
69	*prophetic fury:* inspired frenzy.
71	*mummy* – a preparation made from *human* flesh and used for magical purposes. In this speech in response to Desdemona's question *Is't possible?* Othello seems to cast a spell on his listeners by his resounding rhythm and evocative language.
71	*the skilful:* those trained in magical techniques.
76	*startingly and rash:* abruptly and violently.
77	*out o'th'way?:* mislaid. Othello's desperate anxiety comes out in the rush of repeated short questions which are really the same question. The quick broken exchanges that follow contrast markedly with the sustained dignity of Othello's earlier speech; throughout them the word *handkerchief* flutters ominously like a storm signal. Othello calls for it three times in succession, as if the handkerchief would, like a magical object, automatically guarantee Desdemona's innocence. We are so absorbed in Othello's reactions that we tend to forget Emilia's curious silence at this point; perhaps it may be explained partly by Emilia's natural reluctance to admit that she has told her mistress a lie (especially since it is about such a seemingly small matter as a missing handkerchief) and partly by the fact that she is probably thinking about jealous husbands. (l. 22–25).
80	*an if:* if.
89	*sufficient:* capable. – Desdemona, with her brisk *Come, come!* tries to turn Othello's mind away from thoughts of the handkerchief to Cassio's reinstatement, not realizing that in Othello's distracted mind the two subjects are inextricably linked, thanks to Iago. The more she pleads for Cassio, the more Othello is angered, till he is literally unable to stand it any longer and rushes out with the exclamation *Away!*
91	*your love:* love for you.
99	*unhappy in:* (i) distressed by; (ii) unfortunate in.
100	*'Tis not . . . a man:* we can't find out what a man is really like in a short time (like a year or two).
102	*hungerly:* hungrily. – An obsolete form. Emilia's somewhat coarse metaphor expresses her down-to-earth view of the relations between men and women. In contrast to Desdemona, there is no trace of idealism in her attitude to these relations.

OTHELLO 'Tis true. There's magic in the web* of it.
          A sibyl* that had numbered in the world
          The sun to course two hundred compasses,*
          In her prophetic fury* sewed the work;
          The worms were hallowed that did breed the silk,   70
          And it was dyed in mummy* which the skilful*
          Conserved of maidens' hearts.
DESDEMONA   Indeed? Is't true?
OTHELLO Most veritable. Therefore look to't well.
DESDEMONA Then would to God that I had never seen't!
OTHELLO Ha? Wherefore?   75
DESDEMONA Why do you speak so startingly and rash?*
OTHELLO Is't lost? Is't gone? Speak, is it out o'th'way?*
DESDEMONA Heaven bless us!
OTHELLO Say you?
DESDEMONA It is not lost. But what an if* it were?   80
OTHELLO How?
DESDEMONA I say it is not lost.
OTHELLO Fetch't, let me see't!
DESDEMONA Why, so I can; but I will not now.
          This is a trick to put me from my suit: 85
          Pray you let Cassio be received again.
OTHELLO Fetch me the handkerchief! My mind misgives.
DESDEMONA Come, come!
          You'll never meet a more sufficient* man –
OTHELLO The handkerchief! ·
DESDEMONA   A man that all his time   90
          Hath founded his good fortunes on your love,*
          Shared dangers with you –
OTHELLO The handkerchief!
DESDEMONA I'faith, you are to blame.
OTHELLO Away!   95
                                        [Exit OTHELLO

EMILIA Is not this man jealous?
DESDEMONA I ne'er saw this before.
          Sure there's some wonder in this handkerchief;
          I am most unhappy in* the loss of it.
EMILIA 'Tis not* a year or two shows us a man.   100
          They are all but stomachs, and we all but food;
          They eat us hungerly,* and when they are full,
          They belch us.

105   *happiness:* good luck. – Iago has just said to Cassio that there is *no other way* to regain his
        place except through Desdemona. Now, he says, what a stroke of good luck it is
        that they happen to meet Desdemona just then.
106   *How now:* How are you?
110   *office:* service.
112   *mortal:* deadly.
113–15 *nor . . . again:* my past service, my present grief nor the service I intend to perform in the
        future, – none of these are sufficient to regain his (Othello's) favour . . .
116   *But:* merely.
117   *forced content:* pretended satisfaction.
118–19 *And shut myself . . . fortune's alms:* And restrict myself in some other employment and to
        seek alms from fortune. – Cassio expresses his intention of leaving the military
        profession if his offence is considered so serious that he can never win back
        Othello's love and esteem.
120   *advocation:* advocacy.
122   *Were . . . altered:* If his appearance (*favour*) were as much changed as his mood (*humour*).
123   *So help me . . . As:* By all the blessed spirits I swear that . . .
125   *stood . . . displeasure:* come within range of his anger. – The *blank* was the white mark at the
        centre of the target in archery.
131–4   Iago implies that Othello was unmoved even when his own comrade was blown
        from his side by cannon fire.
135   *moment:* urgent importance.
136   *There's matter in't:* It's serious.
137   *sure:* certainly.
138   *unhatched practice:* unaccomplished plot.

Enter IAGO *and* CASSIO.

Look you, Cassio and my husband.

IAGO   There is no other way; 'tis she must do't.
And lo the happiness!* Go and importune her.   105

DESDEMONA   How now,* good Cassio? What's the news with you?

CASSIO   Madam, my former suit. I do beseech you
That by your virtuous means I may again
Exist, and be a member of his love
Whom I with all the office* of my heart   110
Entirely honour. I would not be delayed.
If my offence be of such mortal* kind
That nor* my service past, nor present sorrows,
Nor purposed merit in futurity,
Can ransom me into his love again,   115
But* to know so must be my benefit.
So shall I clothe me in a forced content,*
And shut myself* up in some other course
To fortune's alms.

DESDEMONA   Alas, thrice-gentle Cassio,
My advocation* is not now in tune.   120
My lord is not my lord; nor should I know him
Were* he in favour as in humour altered.
So help me* every spirit sanctified,
As I have spoken for you all my best,
And stood* within the blank of his displeasure   125
For my free speech. You must awhile be patient.
What I can do I will; and more I will
Than for myself I dare. Let that suffice you.

IAGO   Is my lord angry?

EMILIA   He went hence but now,
And certainly in strange unquietness.   130

IAGO   Can he be angry? I have seen the cannon
When it hath blown his ranks into the air
And, like the devil, from his very arm
Puffed his own brother. And is he angry?
Something of moment* then. I will go meet him.   135
There's matter in't* indeed if he be angry.

DESDEMONA   I prithee do so.

[*Exit* IAGO

Something sure* of state,
Either from Venice or some unhatched practice*

139   *demonstrable:* apparent.
140   *puddled:* muddied. – The metaphor is of the mind as a clear stream.
141   *wrangle:* find fault.
142   *object* – i.e. the real object of their concern.
143   *endues:* leads.
146   *observancy:* loving attention.
147   *the bridal:* the wedding day.
147   *Beshrew me much* – a mild oath.
148   *unhandsome:* unskilled. – In calling herself a *warrior* Desdemona is perhaps remembering
         Othello addressing her as *O my fair warrior!* (II.i.176).
149   *Arraigning:* indicting. – The metaphor of a trial is continued in *suborned, witness* and
         indicted.
149   *unkindness* – In addition to the modern meaning, the word has the sense of 'untrue to his
         own nature'.
152   *conception:* fantasy.
153   *toy:* trifle.
158   *Begot upon itself, born on itself* – i.e. not produced by any outward cause, but produced by
         itself.
162   *fit:* receptive.
162   *move your suit:* plead your cause.
         With the departure of Desdemona and Emilia and the arrival of Bianca, the
         atmosphere becomes lighter for a short while. But the physical presence of the
         handkerchief is sufficient to keep the imminent tragedy constantly in our minds
         even as we attend to the potentially comic scene of a lady's man making excuses
         to an importunate woman for his neglect of her.
165   *Save you* – i.e. God save you. – A form of greeting.
165   *What . . . home:* what are you doing away from home.
166   *How is't with you?* How are you?
173   *with leaden . . , pressed* – Cassio uses a metaphor taken from a form of torture in which the
         victim was pressed to death with heavy weights. This may remind us of another
         torture victim who is suffering far more than Cassio.
174   *continuate:* uninterrupted.

Made demonstrable* here in Cyprus to him,
Hath puddled* his clear spirit; and in such cases   140
Men's natures wrangle* with inferior things,
Though great ones are their object,* 'Tis even so.
For let our finger ache, and it endues*
Our other, healthful members even to a sense
Of pain. Nay, we must think men are not gods,   145
Nor of them look for such observancy*
As fits the bridal.* Beshrew me much,* Emilia,
I was, unhandsome* warrior as I am,
Arraigning* his unkindness* with my soul;
But now I find I had suborned the witness,   150
And he's indicted falsely.

EMILIA   Pray heaven it be
State matters, as you think, and no conception*
Nor no jealous toy* concerning you.

DESDEMONA   Alas the day, I never gave him cause.

EMILIA   But jealous souls will not be answered so;   155
They are not ever jealous for the cause,
But jealous for they're jealous. It is a monster
Begot upon itself, born on itself.*

DESDEMONA   Heaven keep the monster from Othello's mind!

EMILIA   Lady, amen.   160

DESDEMONA   I will go seek him. Cassio, walk here about.
If I do find him fit,* I'll move your suit*
And seek to effect it to my uttermost.

CASSIO   I humbly thank your ladyship.

                         [*Exit* DESDEMONA *with* EMILIA

Enter BIANCA.

BIANCA   Save you,* friend Cassio!

CASSIO   What* make you from home?   165
How is't with you,* my most fair Bianca?
I'faith, sweet love, I was coming to your house.

BIANCA   And I was going to your lodging, Cassio.
What, keep a week away? Seven days and nights?
Eightscore eight hours? And lovers' absent hours   170
More tedious than the dial eightscore times?
O weary reck'ning!

CASSIO   Pardon me, Bianca.
I have this while with leaden* thoughts been pressed,
But I shall in a more continuate* time

175   *Strike off this score:* pay this debt.
177   *friend:* mistress.
179   *Go to:* Get away with you!
184   *neither:* either. – The double negative for emphasis is not unusual in Shakespeare.
185   *demanded:* asked for again.
186   *like enough:* probably.
190   *addition:* sign of honour.
193   *bring me on the way:* accompany me.
194   *soon at night:* towards evening. – An Elizabethan turn of phrase with a somewhat different
          emphasis from the modern sense.
197   *circumstanced:* resign (myself) to circumstances.

Strike off this score* of absence. Sweet Bianca,   175
　　　　　　　[*Gives her Desdemona's handkerchief*
Take me this work out.

BIANÇA　　　　　　　　　O Cassio, whence came this?
This is some token from a newer friend.*
To the felt absence now I feel a cause.
Is't come to this? Well, well.

CASSIO　　　　　　　　　Go to,* woman!
Throw your vile guesses in the devil's teeth,   180
From whence you have them. You are jealous now
That this is from some mistress, some remembrance.
No, by my faith, Bianca.

BIANCA　　　　　　　　Why, whose is it?

CASSIO I know not neither;* I found it in my chamber.
I like the work well; ere it be demanded,*
As like enough* it will, I would have it copied.
Take it and do't, and leave me for this time.

BIANCA Leave you? Wherefore?

CASSIO I do attend here on the general
And think it no addition,* nor my wish,   190
To have him see me womaned.

BIANCA　　　　　　　　Why, I pray you?

CASSIO Not that I love you not.

BIANCA　　　　　　　But that you do not love me!
I pray you bring me on the way* a little,
And say if I shall see you soon at night.*

CASSIO 'Tis but a little way that I can bring you,   195
For I attend here; but I'll see you soon.

BIANCA 'Tis very good; I must be circumstanced.*
　　　　　　　　　　　　　[*Exeunt omnes*

IV.i.   Iago becomes bolder in the images of Desdemona and Cassio in bed together with which he torments Othello. The Moor, unable to bear it any longer, falls into a trance. Cassio enters but Iago tells him to come back when Othello has recovered. When Othello regains consciousness, Iago tells him to conceal himself so that he can hear Cassio talking about his intimacy with Desdemona. When Cassio returns Iago asks him about Bianca in a low voice, so that Othello cannot hear him. When Cassio, urged on by Iago, talks loosely about Bianca, Othello is convinced that Desdemona is the subject of the conversation. Bianca enters and tells Cassio that she has changed her mind about copying the design on the handkerchief. She flings it back and tells Cassio he can still come to dinner that evening if he likes. Othello recognizes the handkerchief and his fury is redoubled. Iago promises to arrange that Cassio will be dead before the night is over and suggests that it would be a fitting death for Desdemona to be strangled in her bed.

Lodovico, a kinsman of Brabantio, arrives with despatches for Othello from Venice. These instruct him to return, leaving Cassio in command. Desdemona speaks to Lodovico of the change which has come over Othello and about Cassio. Hearing her, Othello loses his temper and strikes her and a little later dismisses her. After he has gone the astounded Lodovico questions Iago about Othello's transformation but Iago professes to know nothing about its cause.

We last saw Othello rushing away from Desdemona almost convinced of her unfaithfulness. In this scene we see him totally unable to think of Desdemona except in the terms in which Iago presents her to his imagination. He can now be brutally direct and realistic in describing Desdemona's allegedly immoral behaviour. Othello, unable to bear this torment for very long, falls into a trance and Iago gloats over his achievement. Cassio's unexpected entry at this point is a challenge to Iago's presence of mind, but he proves equal to the occasion. Later in this scene we see other examples of Iago's ability to turn almost any situation to his advantage, first when he encourages Cassio to talk lightly about Bianca and contrives to make Othello believe that Cassio is referring to Desdemona, and again when he makes use of Bianca's sudden entrance to point out to Othello that the handkerchief which Bianca flings back at Cassio is the very same one that Desdemona received from Othello. By this time Othello is literally out of his mind with the torments of jealousy and the thirst for revenge, so that when Lodovico and his party arrive from Venice they see a completely different man from the noble commander who left Venice for Cyprus. Othello's self-command has weakened so much that he is capable of striking Desdemona in public and talking about her in coarse terms to Lodovico, almost as if she were a common harlot. Iago is of course ready at hand with a plausible account of the change by which Lodovico is completely convinced.

2   *unauthorized*: illicit.
6   *hypocrisy . . . devil*: hypocrisy to cheat the devil. – Ordinary hypocrites cheat men by appearing virtuous. These cheat the devil by appearing to do evil but by avoiding actual immorality (i.e. sexual intercourse).
7   *do so*: do that (i.e. lie naked in bed together).
9   *If they . . . slip*: If they commit no (other) offence, it is only a minor fault. – Iago cleverly reminds Othello of his own situation, rather than general misbehaviour, by mentioning the handkerchief in the next line.
17   *They have it*: They appear to have it.
21   *raven . . . house* – Ravens were birds of ill omen; they were believed to fly towards houses where sickness, disaster or death were present or imminent. (See *Macbeth* I.v.37–39.)
22   *Boding*: foreboding (death). – Othello compares the 'recollection' that Cassio had his handkerchief to a raven. Just as the bird signifies general disaster so the memory is an evil omen that has brought torment to Othello.
25   *as knaves be such* – i.e. as such knaves be.
26   *importunate suit*: persistent courting.
27   *voluntary dotage of*: weakness of will on the part of.
28   *Convinced or supplied*: (sexually) conquered or satisfied.
29   *blab*: chatter. – The colloquial word has an undertone of contempt. Iago talks slightingly of those men who, having taken advantage of women, either through their own persistence or the women's weakness of will, cannot help boasting about their conquests.

ACT IV scene i

A court before the citadel.

Enter OTHELLO *and* IAGO.

IAGO Will you think so?
OTHELLO   Think so, Iago?
IAGO   What,
To kiss in private?
OTHELLO   An unauthorized* kiss?
IAGO Or to be naked with her friend in bed
An hour or more, not meaning any harm?
OTHELLO Naked in bed, Iago, and not mean harm?   5
It is hypocrisy* against the devil.
They that mean virtuously, and yet do so,*
The devil their virtue tempts, and they tempt heaven.
IAGO If they* do nothing, 'tis a venial slip.
But if I give my wife a handkerchief –   10
OTHELLO What then?
IAGO Why, then 'tis hers, my lord; and being hers,
She may, I think, bestow't on any man.
OTHELLO She is protectress of her honour too.
May she give that?   15
IAGO Her honour is an essence that's not seen;
They have it* very oft that have it not.
But for the handkerchief –
OTHELLO By heaven, I would most gladly have forgot it!
Thou said'st – O, it comes o'er my memory   20
As doth the raven* o'er the infected house,
Boding* to all – he had my handkerchief.
IAGO Ay, what of that?
OTHELLO   That's not so good now.
IAGO What if I had said I had seen him do you wrong?
Or heard him say – as knaves be such* abroad   25
Who having, by their own importunate suit,*
Or voluntary dotage of* some mistress,
Convincèd or supplied* them, cannot choose
But they must blab* –

31   *unswear:* deny on oath.

32–35   The more hesitant and indefinite Iago is the more he inflames Othello's tormented imagination to fill in all the hideous details for himself (l. 36–45). But the effort is more than Othello can stand and he collapses in a fit.

37   *belie:* tell lies about. – The phrase *lie on* is no longer used in this sense.

37   *fulsome:* foul, loathsome. – Othello's language is rapidly lapsing into disconnected raving.

38   *confess:* utter a complete falsehood. – *Confess and be hanged* is a proverbial phrase whose meaning is obscure. Perhaps the sound of the word *handkerchief* and its connection in his disordered mind with confessions makes him talk of hanging. 'Hanged' may also have the sense of 'sexually satisfied'.

40   *invest:* clothe.

41   *shadowing:* darkening (the mind).

42   *instruction:* intimation (with a basis in reality). – Othello begins to feel his mind cloud over under the influence of his violent passion and says that this could not happen unless there was some basis in fact for his feelings. This is why he goes on to say *It is not words that shakes me thus.*

42   *Pish!* – an exclamation with a much stronger and more serious force in Shakespeare's day than in ours, when it is scarcely used except humorously.

43   *Noses, ears and lips?* – Othello is imagining the intimacies that have supposedly taken place between Cassio and Desdemona.

44   *O devil!* – Othello's last words are a general cry of despair, but there is unconscious irony in the fact that the creature to whom they should be addressed is right beside him.

48   *reproach:* shame. – Iago sees Cassio coming and immediately switches from gloating and moralizing to showing concern for his master.

54   *lethargy:* coma.

54   *his:* its. – The usual Shakespearian form.

58   *straight:* directly.

59   *on great occasion:* about an important matter. – Iago cleverly gets rid of Cassio but makes sure he will return later to put the next part of his plan into action. (See l. 75.)

61   *Dost thou mock me?* – Othello takes Iago's question as an allusion to the cuckold's horns

62   *Would you would:* I wish that you would.

OTHELLO   Hath he said anything?

IAGO He hath, my lord; but be you well assured,   30
No more than he'll unswear.*

OTHELLO   What hath he said?

IAGO Why, that he did – I know not what he did.

OTHELLO What? What?

IAGO Lie –

OTHELLO With her?

IAGO   With her, on her; what you will.   35

OTHELLO Lie with her? Lie on her? – We say lie on her when they
belie* her. – Lie with her! Zounds, that's fulsome.* –
Handkerchief – confessions – handkerchief! To confess,*
and be hanged for his labour – first to be hanged, and
then to confess! I tremble at it. Nature would not invest*   40
herself in such shadowing* passion without some
instruction.* It is not words that shakes me thus. – Pish!*
Noses, ears, and lips?* Is't possible? – Confess? –
Handkerchief? – O devil!*
                                        [Falls in a trance

IAGO Work on,   45
My med'cine works! Thus credulous fools are caught,
And many worthy and chaste dames even thus, .
All guiltless, meet reproach.* What ho! My lord!
My lord, I say! Othello!

Enter CASSIO.

                              How now, Cassio?

CASSIO What's the matter?   50

IAGO My lord is fall'n into an epilepsy.
This is his second fit; he had one yesterday.

CASSIO Rub him about the temples.

IAGO The lethargy* must have his* quiet course.
If not, he foams at mouth, and by and by   55
Breaks out to savage madness. Look, he stirs.
Do you withdraw yourself a little while.
He will recover straight.* When he is gone,
I would on great occasion* speak with you.
                                        [Exit CASSIO

How is it, general? Have you not hurt your head?   60

OTHELLO Dost thou mock me?*

IAGO   I mock you not, by heaven.
Would you would* bear your fortune like a man.

65	*civil*: (i) well-mannered; (ii) belonging to the city.
67	*yoked*: married. – There is also an allusion to beasts of burden who are yoked together (see next line).
68	*draw*: (i) pull a load; (ii) join. – Iago cynically asks Othello to reflect that every married man is in the same situation as himself (i.e. a cuckold). Iago is now able to treat Othello *openly* as merely an instance of a general truth.
69	*unproper*: (i) not exclusively their own; (ii) defiled.
70	*peculiar*: their own alone.
72	*lip*: kiss.
72	*secure*: free from suspicion.
74	knowing what I am – i.e. a cuckold. *shall be* has the sense of *must be, is bound to be* here.
75	Iago now puts Othello in such a position that he can observe Cassio's behaviour without hearing exactly what he says.
76	*in a patient list*: within the bounds of patience. – A list was a barrier.
79	*shifted him away*: managed to get him out of the way.
80	*laid good . . . ecstasy*: made a plausible excuse out of your trance (*ecstasy*).
82	*encave*: hide.
83	*fleers*: sneers.
83	*notable*: obvious.
87	*cope*: copulate with. – Iago is now treating Othello almost like a puppet and has no hesitation in referring directly to the details of Desdemona's alleged wantonness.
89	*all in all in spleen*: completely dominated by irrational passion. – The spleen was believed to be the seat of passion, whereas a man ought to be a creature of reason.
92	*amiss*: inappropriate.
95	*huswife*: hussy, harlot. – From this brief soliloquy we learn the details of Iago's scheme. In spite of the tragic issues which hang on it, we cannot help feeling an almost sympathetic interest in its outcome. With regard to Cassio too Iago is acting as puppet master

Degradation of the victim – which next action intensifie

OTHELLO A hornèd man's a monster and a beast.
IAGO There's many a beast then in a populous city,
    And many a civil* monster.   65
OTHELLO Did he confess it?
  IAGO   Good, sir, be a man.
    Think every bearded fellow that's but yoked*
    May draw* with you. There's millions now alive
    That nightly lie in those unproper* beds
    Which they dare swear peculiar.* Your case is better.   70
    O, 'tis the spite of hell, the fiend's arch-mock,
    To lip* a wanton in a secure* couch,
    And to suppose her chaste. No, let me know;
    And knowing what I am,* I know what she shall be.
OTHELLO O, thou art wise. 'Tis certain.
IAGO   Stand you awhile apart;   75
    Confine yourself but in a patient list.*
    Whilst you were here, o'erwhelmed with your grief –
    A passion most unsuiting such a man –
    Cassio came hither. I shifted him away*
    And laid good* 'scuse upon your ecstasy;   80
    Bade him anon return, and here speak with me;
    The which he promised. Do but encave* yourself
    And mark the fleers,* the gibes, and notable* scorns
    That dwell in every region of his face.
    For I will make him tell the tale anew: 85
    Where, how, how oft, how long ago, and when
    He hath, and is again to cope* your wife.
    I say, but mark his gesture. Marry patience,
    Or I shall say you're all in all in spleen,*
    And nothing of a man.
OTHELLO   Dost thou hear, Iago?   90
    I will be found most cunning in my patience;
    But – dost thou hear? – most bloody.
  IAGO   That's not amiss;*
    But yet keep time in all. Will you withdraw?

[OTHELLO *conceals himself where he can see but not hear.*]

[*Aside*] Now will I question Cassio of Bianca,
    A huswife* that by selling her desires   95
    Buys herself bread and cloth. It is a creature
    That dotes on Cassio (as 'tis the strumpet's plague
    To beguile many and be beguiled by one).

102	*unbookish:* ignorant.	
102	*conster:* construe, interpret.	
103	*behaviours* – The plural form, frequent in Shakespeare, is no longer used.	
105	*addition:* title. – As Cassio is no longer entitled to wear a lieutenant's uniform and Iago is, the latter's respectful address would hurt Cassio.	
107	*Ply:* Work on.	
109	*speed:* prosper.	
109	*caitiff:* wretch.	
113	*out:* off.	
115	*Go to:* That's right, get on with it.	
115	*well said:* well done.	
119	*Roman* – Othello is referring to the practice of Roman generals who entered the city in triumphal procession after a victory. Perhaps there is also an allusion to Cassio the civilized Italian. *Triumph* here has the sense of 'gloat'.	
120	*customer:* one who invites trade – i.e. a prostitute.	
120–1	*bear . . . wit:* think a little kindly of my intelligence.	
124	*cry:* rumour.	
126	*else:* otherwise.	
127	*Have you scored me?* Have you made my reckoning? – i e. have you added up my whole future?	
131	S.D.	At a signal from Iago, Othello moves close enough to hear the conversation. Our suspense is even greater now as Iago must somehow prevent Cassio from mentioning Bianca's name, in order that Othello may continue to believe that it is Desdemona who is being discussed. Iago has carefully refrained from mentioning Bianca by name after his opening reference to her.
134	*bauble:* worthless toy. – a bauble was part of the professional clown's stock-in-hand.	
134–5	*falls me thus:* falls like this (in action). – this use of *me* is now obsolete.	

He, when he hears of her, cannot restrain
From the excess of laughter. Here he comes.   100

Enter CASSIO.

As he shall smile, Othello shall go mad;
And his unbookish* jealousy must conster*
Poor Cassio's smiles, gestures, and light behaviours*
Quite in the wrong. – How do you, lieutenant? –
CASSIO The worser that you give me the addition*   105
Whose want even kills me.
IAGO Ply* Desdemona well, and you are sure on't.
Now, if this suit lay in Bianca's power,
How quickly should you speed!*
CASSIO   Alas, poor caitiff!*
OTHELLO Look how he laughs already!   110
IAGO I never knew woman love man so.
CASSIO Alas, poor rogue, I think, i'faith, she loves me.
OTHELLO Now he denies it faintly, and laughs it out.*
IAGO Do you hear, Cassio?
OTHELLO   Now he importunes him
To tell it o'er. Go to,* well said,* well said!   115
IAGO She gives it out that you shall marry her.
Do you intend it?
CASSIO Ha, ha, ha!
OTHELLO Do ye triumph, Roman?* Do you triumph?
CASSIO I marry? What, a customer?* Prithee bear* some   120
charity to my wit; do not think it so unwholesome.
Ha, ha, ha!
OTHELLO So, so, so, so. They laugh that win.
IAGO Why, the cry* goes that you marry her.
CASSIO Prithee, say true.   125
IAGO I am a very villain else.*
OTHELLO Have you scored me?* Well.
CASSIO This is the monkey's own giving out. She is persuaded I
will marry her out of her own love and flattery, not out of
my promise.
OTHELLO Iago beckons me; now he begins the story.   130
                          [OTHELLO *moves closer**
CASSIO She was here even now; she haunts me in every place. I
was the other day talking on the sea bank with certain
Venetians, and thither comes the bauble,* and falls me
thus* about my neck –   135

142   *Before me!* – i.e. Bless my soul! An exclamation of surprise.
143   *such another:* no other than.
143   *fitchew:* polecat – i.e. a stinking creature. 'Fitchew' was figuratively used to mean 'prostitute'.
143   *a perfumed one* – perfumes were often associated with prostitutes.
151   *your hobby horse:* to your whore. Bianca's language, as well as Othello's helpless ravings as he hides, brings this scene dangerously close to farce.
153   *How now:* How are you? – Cassio, by repeating the phrase, is trying to soothe Bianca.
154   *should:* must. – An anguished cry of recognition escapes from Othello as the fateful handkerchief appears again.
156   *when you are next prepared for* – i.e. never.
157   Iago is anxious to get rid of Cassio in case he says anything that might reveal that it is Bianca he had been talking about just before she entered.
158   *rail . . . else:* she will rant and rave in the streets otherwise.
161   *would very fain:* am very anxious to.
165   Othello needs no more persuading now. The only question in his mind is *How?* Iago does not answer, and this enrages Othello even more.
170   *by this hand:* I swear.

OTHELLO Crying 'O dear Cassio!' as it were. His gesture imports it.
CASSIO So hangs, and lolls and weeps upon me; so shakes and
pulls me! Ha, ha, ha!
OTHELLO Now he tells how she plucked him to my chamber. O, I
see that nose of yours, but not that dog I shall throw it to.   140
CASSIO Well, I must leave her company.
IAGO Before me!* Look where she comes.

Enter BIANCA.

CASSIO 'Tis such another* fitchew!* Marry a perfumed one?*
What do you mean by this haunting of me?
BIANCA Let the devil and his dam haunt you! What did you mean   145
by that same handkerchief you gave me even now? I was
a fine fool to take it. I must take out the work? A likely
piece of work, that you should find it in your chamber
and know not who left it there! This is some minx's
token, and I must take out the work? There! [*She throws*   150
down the handkerchief.] Give it your hobby horse.*
Wheresoever you had it, I'll take out no work on't.
CASSIO How now, my sweet Bianca? How now?* how now?
OTHELLO By heaven, that should* be my handkerchief!
BIANCA If you'll come to supper tonight, you may; if you will not,   155
come when you are next prepared for.*

[*Exit*

IAGO After her, after her!
CASSIO Faith, I must; she'll rail* in the streets else.
IAGO Will you sup there?
CASSIO Yes, I intend so.   160
IAGO Well, I may chance to see you, for I would very fain*
speak with you.
CASSIO Prithee come. Will you?
IAGO Go to, say no more.

[*Exit* CASSIO

OTHELLO [*Coming forward*] How shall I murder him, Iago?   165
IAGO Did you perceive how he laughed at his vice?
OTHELLO O Iago!
IAGO And did you see the handkerchief?
OTHELLO Was that mine?
IAGO Yours, by this hand.* And to see how he prizes the foolish   170
woman your wife! She gave it him, and he hath given it
his whore.

173   *have him nine years a-killing:* spend nine years in the act of killing him. – The verbal form *a-killing* is very rarely used in modern English.

181   *that's not your way* – i.e. that's not what you should be thinking of now.

185   *invention:* imagination. – A memory of Desdemona as he knew her before Iago poisoned his thoughts rises unbidden in Othello's mind, which gives added poignancy to the line *I do but say what she is.*

187–8   *so gentle a condition!* (i) well born; (ii) of such a gentle nature.

189   *gentle:* yielding.

192   *fond over:* foolish about.

192   *patent:* license.

194   *messes:* bits of food.

199   *unprovide my mind:* weaken my resolve.

203   *The justice of it pleases* – It is typical of Othello's nature that even as he speaks of murder in the most brutal manner he should think of himself as an agent of justice.

204   *his undertaker:* the person to deal with him. – In modern English *undertaker* is one whose occupation is the making of funeral arrangements.

206   S.D. *A trumpet* – The noise of the trumpet reminds us of the larger world outside the suffocating atmosphere of Iago's intrigues. But Iago proves more than able to deal with any threat to his plan. Lodovico's stately formal entry belongs to the public world of state affairs with its ceremony and dignity, so that Othello's act of striking Desdemona appears even more starkly cruel and uncontrolled.

OTHELLO I would have him nine years a-killing!* – A fine woman, a
fair woman, a sweet woman!

IAGO Nay, you must forget that.   175

OTHELLO Ay, let her rot, and perish and be damned tonight; for
she shall not live. No, my heart is turned to stone; I strike
it, and it hurts my hand. O, the world hath not a sweeter
creature! She might lie by an emperor's side and
command him tasks.   180

IAGO Nay, that's not your way.*

OTHELLO Hang her! I do but say what she is. So delicate with her
needle. An admirable musician. O, she will sing the
savageness out of a bear! Of so high and plenteous wit
and invention* –   185

IAGO She's the worse for all this.

OTHELLO O, a thousand, a thousand times. And then, of so gentle a
condition!*

IAGO Ay, too gentle.*

OTHELLO Nay, that's certain. But yet the pity of it, Iago. O Iago, the   190
pity of it, Iago.

IAGO If you are so fond over* her iniquity, give her patent* to
offend; for if it touch not you, it comes near nobody.

OTHELLO I will chop her into messes!* Cuckold me!

IAGO O, 'tis foul in her.   195

OTHELLO With mine officer!

IAGO That's fouler.

OTHELLO Get me some poison, Iago, this night. I'll not expostulate
with her, lest her body and beauty unprovide my mind*
again. This night, Iago!   200

IAGO Do it not with poison. Strangle her in her bed, even the
bed she hath contaminated.

OTHELLO Good, good. The justice of it pleases.* Very good.

IAGO And for Cassio, let me be his undertaker.* You shall hear
more by midnight.   205

OTHELLO Excellent good!

[A trumpet*

What trumpet is that same?

IAGO I warrant something from Venice.

Enter LODOVICO, DESDEMONA, *and* ATTENDANTS.

'Tis Lodovico.
This comes from the Duke. See, your wife's with him.

LODOVICO God save you, worthy general.

211   *the instrument of their pleasures* – i.e. the letter.
217   *unkind breach:* uncharacteristic separation.
218   Othello's question seems to burst out in spite of himself.
222   *division:* difference, separation.
224   *atone: reconcile.* – Desdemona's innocent reference to her love (i.e. affection) for Cassio inflames Othello once more.
228   *Deputing . . . government:* appointing Cassio to his (Othello's) post.
230   *mad* – i.e. openly insane and reckless (as opposed to *wise,* 225).
234   *Though:* even though.
234   *'Tis very much:* It is a terrible business. – The phrase is much stronger than in modern usage.
237   *Each drop . . . crocodile* – Crocodiles were believed to lure their intended prey by shedding false tears. Desdemona's tears of grief are for Othello signs of her treachery.

OTHELLO   With all my heart, sir.
LODOVICO The Duke and the senators of Venice greet you.   210
                                          [*Gives him a letter*
OTHELLO I kiss the instrument of their pleasures.*
                                          [*Opens the letter and reads*
DESDEMONA And what's the news, good cousin Lodovico?
     IAGO I am very glad to see you, signior.
            Welcome to Cyprus.
LODOVICO I thank you. How does Lieutenant Cassio?
     IAGO   Lives, sir.   215
DESDEMONA Cousin, there's fall'n between him and my lord
            An unkind breach;* but you shall make all well.
OTHELLO Are you sure of that?*
DESDEMONA My lord?
OTHELLO [*Reads*] 'This fail you not to do, as you will – '   220
LODOVICO He did not call; he's busy in the paper.
            Is there division* 'twixt my lord and Cassio?
DESDEMONA A most unhappy one. I would do much
            T'atone* them, for the love I bear to Cassio.
OTHELLO Fire and brimstone!
DESDEMONA   My lord?
OTHELLO   Are you wise?   225
DESDEMONA What, is he angry?
LODOVICO   May be th'letter moved him;
            For, as I think, they command him home,
            Deputing* Cassio in his government.
DESDEMONA Trust me, I am glad on't.
OTHELLO   Indeed?
DESDEMONA   My lord?
OTHELLO I am glad to see you mad.*
DESDEMONA   Why, sweet Othello –   230
OTHELLO Devil!
                                          [*Strikes her*
DESDEMONA I have not deserved this.
LODOVICO My lord, this would not be believed in Venice,
            Though* I should swear I saw't. 'Tis very much.*
            Make her amends; she weeps.
OTHELLO   O devil, devil!   235
            If that the earth could teem with woman's tears,
            Each drop* she falls would prove a crocodile.
            Out of my sight!
DESDEMONA   I will not stay to offend you.   [*Going*

243	*turn:* return.
244	*turn:* (i) change her mind; (ii) lie on her back. – Othello refers to Desdemona as if she were a prostitute, obedient to a client's whims.
248	*well-painted passion:* well-feigned grief.
251	*avaunt!* away! (archaic).
254	*Goats and monkeys!* – The sudden eruption of this phrase, with its suggestion of uncontrolled lust, shows what Othello has been really thinking about while his conscious mind has been struggling to attend to official matters.
256	*sufficient:* capable.
258	*The shot of accident . . . pierce?* – The military metaphor (cannon shot and arrows) is particularly apt to describe Othello's steadfastness in the face of unexpected danger or misfortune. Iago's reply is a shattering understatement.
260	*Are his wits safe?:* Is he not in danger of going mad?
260	*light of brain:* insane.
261	*that:* what (archaic).
261	*breathe my censure:* express my (own) opinion.
262–3	Iago's lines are puzzling and editors are not agreed as to how they should be punctuated. The general sense is, 'If he is not the man he ought to be, I wish he really were out of his mind.' There may also be a secret meaning for Iago – 'If he is not yet what he seems to be (i.e. mad enough to kill Desdemona), I wish he would be.'
264	*would:* I wish.
265	*use:* habit.
266	*blood:* passionate feelings.
267	*new-create his fault:* immediately and spontaneously give rise to this failing in him.
270	*courses:* actions.

LODOVICO Truly, an obedient lady.
    I do beseech your lordship call her back.   240
  OTHELLO Mistress!
DESDEMONA   My lord?
 OTHELLO   What would you with her, sir?
LODOVICO Who? I, my lord?
  OTHELLO Ay! You did wish that I would make her turn.*
    Sir, she can turn,* and turn, and yet go on
    And turn again; and she can weep, sir, weep;   245
    And she's obedient; as you say, obedient.
    Very obedient. Proceed you in your tears.
    Concerning this, sir – O well-painted passion!* –
    I am commanded home. – Get you away;
    I'll send for you anon. – Sir, I obey the mandate   250
    And will return to Venice. – Hence, avaunt!* –

            [*Exit* DESDEMONA

    Cassio shall have my place. And, sir, tonight
    I do entreat that we may sup together.
    You are welcome, sir, to Cyprus. – Goats and monkeys!*

            [*Exit*

LODOVICO Is this the noble Moor whom our full Senate   255
    Call all in all sufficient?* Is this the nature
    Whom passion could not shake? Whose solid virtue
    The shot of accident* nor dart of chance
    Could neither graze nor pierce?
   IAGO   He is much changed.
LODOVICO Are his wits safe?* Is he not light of brain?*   260
   IAGO He's that* he is; I may not breathe my censure.*
    What* he might be (if, what he might, he is not)
    I would to heaven he were!
LODOVICO   What, strike his wife?
   IAGO Faith, that was not so well; yet would* I knew
    That stroke would prove the worst.
LODOVICO   Is it his use?*   265
    Or did the letters work upon his blood*
    And new-create* his fault?
   IAGO   Alas, alas!
    It is not honesty in me to speak
    What I have seen and known. You shall observe him,
    And his own courses* will denote him so   270

IV.ii.   Othello questions Emilia about Desdemona's relations with Cassio. Emilia swears that she has absolute trust in Desdemona's fidelity, but Othello remains sceptical. He sends her to summon Desdemona and when Emilia returns with his wife, accuses her of being false to him. He addresses his wife as if she were a whore and Emilia as if she were a procuress. He leaves in a fury and Emilia tries in vain to comfort her mistress who asks her to lay the wedding sheets on her bed and to call Iago. Iago comes in, and, hearing from his wife how Othello has treated Desdemona, tries to assure the latter that her husband is troubled by state affairs.

When the two women have gone Roderigo comes; he angrily accuses Iago of bankrupting him by making him buy costly presents intended for Desdemona. Iago tells him that if he, Roderigo, can kill Cassio, who has just been appointed commander of Cyprus, Othello and Desdemona would be forced to remain and that Iago would then ensure Roderigo's success with Desdemona. He explains that he will help Roderigo to murder Cassio that night, on Cassio's return from dinner at Bianca's.

There is an ironic contrast and resemblance between the opening of this scene and that of the earlier one. In both, Desdemona's character and conduct are the subject, and in both Othello is one of the principal characters.

But whereas in the earlier scene he made some attempt, however feeble, to defend Desdemona against Iago's insinuations and accusations, here he has taken over Iago's role and insists on besmirching his wife while Emilia tries vainly to defend her. Even though he treats Emilia as the servant of a prostitute and Desdemona herself as a prostitute, the physical presence of the latter still moves him to a recollection of all that she has meant to him. But he flings a handful of coins in Emilia's face, for her 'fee' and storms out, leaving Emilia and Desdemona to try and understand his behaviour as best they can. When Iago enters there are moments when we almost feel that his plot will be revealed, but he manages, as usual, to keep the truth from the others. A trumpet sounds, announcing that it is time for the formal banquet in honour of Lodovico, and Desdemona leaves, followed by Emilia, leaving Iago to deal with Roderigo, whom we have almost forgotten (we last saw him at the end of Act II) and whose resentment at what he takes to be Iago's inaction is now very strong. But Iago has no trouble in calming him down once more.

5	*breath made up:* was spoken.
13	*Lay . . . stake:* wager my soul.
16	*serpent's curse:* God's curse on the serpent (for tempting Eve in Eden).
18	*happy* – i.e. in the certain knowledge that his wife is faithful.
20–1	*yet . . . as much:* it would be a very naive bawd who could not say what Emilia has said. Emilia, in Othello's view, would be unlikely to say anything damaging about her mistress. There is also a suggestion that Desdemona is so cunning a whore that even her servant doesn't know her secrets.
20	*bawd:* harlot's servant or go-between.
21	*This* – i.e. Desdemona.
22	*closet lock and key* – i.e. one who guards all her secrets closely. – A closet was a cabinet for private papers.

That I may save my speech. Do but go after
And mark how he continues.

LODOVICO I am sorry that I am deceived in him.

[*Exeunt*

scene ii

The citadel.

Enter OTHELLO *and* EMILIA

OTHELLO You have seen nothing then?

EMILIA Nor ever heard, nor ever did suspect.

OTHELLO Yes, you have seen Cassio and she together.

EMILIA But then I saw no harm, and then I heard
Each syllable that breath made up* between them.   5

OTHELLO What, did they never whisper?

EMILIA   Never, my lord.

OTHELLO Nor send you out o'th'way?

EMILIA Never.

OTHELLO To fetch her fan, her gloves, her mask, nor nothing?

EMILIA Never, my lord.   10

OTHELLO That's strange.

EMILIA I durst, my lord, to wager she is honest,
Lay* down my soul at stake. If you think other,
Remove your thought. It doth abuse your bosom.
If any wretch have put this in your head,   15
Let heaven requite it with the serpent's curse,*
For if she be not honest, chaste, and true,
There's no man happy.* The purest of their wives
Is foul as slander.

OTHELLO   Bid her come hither. Go.

[*Exit* EMILIA

She says enough; yet* she's a simple bawd*   20
That cannot say as much. This* is a subtle whore,
A closet lock and key* of villainous secrets,
And yet she'll kneel and pray; I have seen her do't.

24	*chuck* – Othello had earlier used this term of endearment (III.iv.45) but now he probably uses it in a coarser tone, as if addressing a whore.
27	*Some of your function:* Do your job (as a brothel keeper).
28	*procreants:* procreators – i.e. those about to engage in sexual intercourse.
30	*mystery:* trade.
30	*dispatch:* get on with it!
35	*being . . . heaven:* because you look like an angel.
36	*double-damned* – i.e. in being unfaithful and swearing she is not.
40	*Ah, Desdemon!* – Othello can never quite escape the sudden onrush of tenderness when Desdemona is actually before him.
42	*motive:* cause. – In her innocence Desdemona asks Othello not to blame her for his recall to Venice, if perhaps he suspects that her father was responsible for it.
45	*lost him:* lost his friendship (see I.iii.128ff).
47	*they* – i.e. heaven, which was sometimes used in the plural in Shakespeare's day.
48–54	An allusion to the torment of Job in the Bible. (*Job* 10:15 etc.) Othello says that if God had tormented him in the same way he would have shown the same patience.
49	*Steeped:* submerged.
53–4	*The fixèd figure . . . finger at:* The constant object for the scornful age to point mockingly at. – The metaphor is based on the hand of a dial which, though it moves, moves so slowly that it seems not to move at all; thus the apparently contradictory epithets *slow, unmoving* are exactly right. Othello is expressing the anguish of a man who values his reputation very highly, at the prospect of suffering general contempt.

Enter DESDEMONA *and* EMILIA.

DESDEMONA My lord, what is your will?

OTHELLO   Pray you, chuck,* come hither.

DESDEMONA What is your pleasure?

OTHELLO   Let me see your eyes.   25
Look in my face.

DESDEMONA   What horrible fancy's this?

OTHELLO [*To* EMILIA] Some of your function,* mistress:
Leave procreants* alone and shut the door;
Cough or cry 'hem' if anybody come.
Your mystery,* your mystery! Nay, dispatch!*   30
                        [*Exit* EMILIA

DESDEMONA [*kneeling*] Upon my knee, what doth your speech
                          import?
I understand a fury in your words, but not the words.

OTHELLO Why, what art thou?

DESDEMONA   Your wife, my lord; your true
And loyal wife.

OTHELLO   Come, swear it, damn thyself;
Lest, being* like one of heaven, the devils themselves   35
Should fear to seize thee. Therefore be double-damned:*
Swear thou art honest.

DESDEMONA   Heaven doth truly know it.

OTHELLO Heaven truly knows that thou art false as hell.

DESDEMONA To whom, my lord? With whom? How am I false?

OTHELLO Ah, Desdemon!* Away! Away! Away!   40

DESDEMONA Alas the heavy day! Why do you weep?
Am I the motive* of these tears, my lord?
If haply you my father do suspect
An instrument of this your calling back,
Lay not your blame on me. If you have lost him,*   45
I have lost him too.

OTHELLO   Had it pleased heaven
To try me with affliction, had they* rained
All kinds of sores and shames* on my bare head,
Steeped* me in poverty to the very lips,
Given to captivity me and my utmost hopes,   50
I should have found in some place of my soul
A drop of patience. But alas, to make me
The fixèd figure* for the time of scorn
To point his slow unmoving finger at.
Yet could I bear that too, well, very well;   55

56   *garnered up:* stored.
58   *fountain:* spring.
58   *the which:* which.
60   *cistern:* pond, pool. – In modern English the word usually means a water tank. The Geneva
            version of the Bible refers to a wife as a man's 'own cistern' and to his children as
            'rivers' flowing from it. (*Proverbs* 5:15–8.)
61   *knot and gender:* twist together and procreate. – Othello speaks of the spring of his love, to
            which he owed his very life, becoming dried up or like a foul pool in the slime of
            which toads would copulate. His consciousness is now dominated by the bestial
            imagery of Iago, though occasionally poignant visions of his earlier bliss flash
            through his mind.
61   *turn thy complexion:* turn pale. – Othello addresses patience, personified as a cherubin.
62   *cherubin:* angel. – Perhaps Othello means that Desdemona's adultery is sufficient to make
            Patience (personified as a watchful angel) change colour and look as grim as hell.
65   *shambles:* slaughterhouse.
66   *quicken . . . blowing:* come to life as soon as the eggs are laid.
71   *committed* – Othello pounces on this word, which Desdemona has innocently used in its
            sense of 'done' and plays on its other Elizabethan sense of 'committed adultery'.
72   *commoner:* prostitute.
73–5 *I should . . . thy deeds* – i.e. my cheeks would blush as fiercely as a blacksmith's forge and
            totally consume and destroy all sense of shame if I merely mentioned your
            actions. Othello's thought moves from the image of a filthy book to burning and
            thence to an unbearable stench.
76   *winks:* closes its eyes. – The moon was a symbol of chastity.
78   *the hollow mine of earth* – the cave of the winds. In Virgil's *Aeneid* (I, 50–63) there is an
            account of how Jupiter, the chief of the gods, imprisoned the winds in a dark
            cavern, laid mountains upon them to prevent them rushing off with the earth
            and sea, and put Aeolus in charge of them.
82   *vessel:* body.
87   *cry you mercy:* beg your pardon. – Othello's rage now begins to vent itself in bitter mockery
            as he pretends to mistake Desdemona for a whore and begins to treat Emilia as
            her bawd.
90   *office . . . St. Peter* – St. Peter is said to guard the pearly gates of heaven.

But there where I have garnered up* my heart,
Where either I must live or bear no life,
The fountain* from the which* my current runs
Or else dries up – to be discarded thence,
Or keep it as a cistern* for foul toads   60
To knot and gender* in – turn thy complexion* there,
Patience, thou young and rose-lipped cherubin!*
I here look grim as hell!

DESDEMONA I hope my noble lord esteems me honest.

OTHELLO O ay, as summer flies are in the shambles,*   65
That quicken* even with blowing. O thou weed,
Who art so lovely fair, and smell'st so sweet,
That the sense aches at thee, would thou hadst ne'er been
                                                      born!

DESDEMONA Alas, what ignorant sin have I committed?

OTHELLO Was this fair paper, this most goodly book,   70
Made to write 'whore' upon? What committed?*
Committed? O thou public commoner,*
I should* make very forges of my cheeks
That would to cinders burn up modesty,
Did I but speak thy deeds. What committed?   75
Heaven stops the nose at it, and the moon winks;*
The bawdy wind that kisses all it meets
Is hushed within the hollow mine of earth*
And will not hear't. What committed?

DESDEMONA By heaven, you do me wrong!   80

OTHELLO Are not you a strumpet?

DESDEMONA   No, as I am a Christian!
If to preserve this vessel* for my lord
From any other foul unlawful touch
Be not to be a strumpet, I am none.

OTHELLO What, not a whore?

DESDEMONA   No, as I shall be saved!   85

OTHELLO Is't possible?

DESDEMONA O heaven forgive us!

OTHELLO   I cry you mercy* then.
I took you for that cunning whore of Venice
That married with Othello. [*Raising his voice*] You,
                                                mistress,

Enter EMILIA.

That have the office* opposite to Saint Peter   90

92	*done our course:* finished our business – i.e. our sexual intercourse.
93	*keep our counsel:* keep our affairs secret.
96–99	Desdemona's answers to Emilia's worried questioning shows that she has been momentarily dazed by Othello's treatment.
103	*go by water:* be conveyed by tears.
105	In her desperation Desdemona decides to seek advice and help from the last person to whom she should turn.
105	*Here's a change* – i.e. in the relation of Othello and Desdemona, especially in Desdemona's present view of her husband. Desdemona is being bitterly ironical.
106	*meet:* fitting.
107	*stick . . . misuse:* base the slightest censure on my smallest fault.
113	*a child to chiding* – i.e. have no experience of being scolded. A glimpse into Desdemona, the adored and perhaps somewhat spoilt daughter.
114	*bewhored her:* accused her of whoredom.
115	*despite:* insult.
120	*laid such terms:* used such language.
120	*callet:* slut.

And keep the gate of hell! You, you, ay, you!
We have done our course;* there's money for your pains.
                                        [*Flings her some coins*
I pray you turn the key and keep our counsel,*
                                                            [*Exit*

EMILIA   Alas, what does this gentleman conceive?
          How do you, madam? How do you, my good lady?   95
DESDEMONA Faith, half asleep.*
EMILIA   Good madam, what's the matter with my lord?
DESDEMONA With who?
EMILIA   Why, with my lord, madam.
DESDEMONA Who is thy lord?
EMILIA   He that is yours, sweet lady.   100
DESDEMONA I have none. Do not talk to me, Emilia.
          I cannot weep, nor answers have I none
          But what should go by water.* Prithee tonight
          Lay on my bed my wedding sheets, remember. –
          And call thy husband hither.*
EMILIA   Here's a change* indeed!   105
                                                            [*Exit*
DESDEMONA 'Tis meet I should be used so, very meet.*
          How have I been behaved, that he might stick*
          The small'st opinion on my least misuse?

          Enter IAGO *and* EMILIA.

IAGO   What is your pleasure, madam? How is't with you?
DESDEMONA I cannot tell. Those that do teach young babes   110
          Do it with gentle means and easy tasks.
          He might have chid me so; for, in good faith,
          I am a child to chiding.*
IAGO   What is the matter, lady?
EMILIA   Alas, Iago, my lord hath so bewhored her,*
          Thrown such despite* and heavy terms upon her   115
          That true hearts cannot bear it.
DESDEMONA Am I that name, Iago?
IAGO   What name, fair lady?
DESDEMONA Such as she said my lord did say I was.
EMILIA   He called her whore. A beggar in his drink
          Could not have laid such terms* upon his callet.*   120
IAGO   Why did he so?
DESDEMONA I do not know; I am sure I am none such.
IAGO   Do not weep, do not weep. Alas the day!

127   *Beshrew:* Curse.
128   *trick:* delusion.
131   *cogging:* cheating. – *cozening* has the same sense.
133   *there is no such man* – Iago's irony directs our attention to his inhumanity as well as to the
        opposed responses of Desdemona and Emilia in the two following lines.
135   *halter.* hangman's noose.
140   *companions:* fellows, villains.
140   *thou'dst* – i.e. (I wish that) heaven would.
140   *unfold:* expose.
143   *within door:* less loudly.
144   *squire:* fellow. – The word is used contemptuously.
145   *turned . . . seamy side without:* turned your wit inside out – i.e. made a fool of you. (*Seamy:*
        with seams.)
147   *Go to:* Get away, don't talk nonsense.
152   *discourse of thought:* thinking.
154   *them:* themselves – i.e. her senses. Desdemona prays that if she ever trespassed against
        Othello's love in word or deed, or if her senses took delight in anything except
        Othello's love, or if she did not and does not still love him and will continue to do
        so even if he casts her off, she may lose peace of mind and body (*comfort*) for
        ever.
158   *forswear:* disown.
159   *defeat:* destroy.

EMILIA   Hath she forsook so many noble matches,
          Her father and her country, and her friends,   125
          To be called whore? Would it not make one weep?

DESDEMONA   It is my wretched fortune.

IAGO   Beshrcw* him for't!
          How comes this trick* upon him?

DESDEMONA   Nay, heaven doth
                                     know.

EMILIA   I will be hanged if some eternal villain,
          Some busy and insinuating rogue,   130
          Some cogging,* cozening slave, to get some office,
          Have not devised this slander. I will be hanged else.

IAGO   Fie, there is no such man!* It is impossible.

DESDEMONA   If any such there be, heaven pardon him.

EMILIA   A halter* pardon him! And hcll gnaw his bones!   135
          Why should he call her whore? Who keeps her com-
                                  pany?
          What place? What time? What form? What likelihood?
          The Moor's abused by some most villainous knave,
          Some base notorious knave, some scurvy fellow.
          O heavens, that such companions* thou'dst* unfold,*   140
          And put in every honest hand a whip
          To lash the rascals naked through the world
          Even from the east to th'west!

IAGO   Speak within door.*

EMILIA   O fie upon them! Some such squire* he was
          That turned* your wit the seamy side without   145
          And made you to suspect me with the Moor.

IAGO   You are a fool. Go to.*

DESDEMONA   Alas, Iago,
          What shall I do to win my lord again?
          Good friend, go to him, for, by this light of heaven,
          I know not how I lost him. Here I kneel: 150
          If e'er my will did trespass 'gainst his love
          Either in discourse of thought* or actual deed,
          Or that mine eyes, mine ears, or any sense
          Delighted them* in any other form;
          Or that I do not yet, and ever did,   155
          And ever will (though he do shake me off
          To beggarly divorcement) love him dearly,
          Comfort forswear* me. Unkindness may do much,
          And his unkindness may defeat* my life,

161	*It does abhor me:* It fills me with abhorrence.
162–3	*To do . . . make me:* No worldly comforts and privileges (*the world's mass of vanity*) could make me do the deed which would earn me the title (*addition*) (of a whore).
165	*does him offence:* worries him.
168	*stay the meat:* await the meal.
173	*daff'st me:* put me off – The word *daff* or 'doff' was applied to the putting off of clothes.
173	*device:* excuse.
175	*conveniency:* opportunity.
177	*put up:* endure, put up with.
181	*performances:* actions.
181	*no kin:* not related.
183–4	*wasted . . . means:* spent all I had.
185	*votarist:* person under a religious vow, nun.
187	*comforts:* encouragements.
187	*sudden respect:* immediate favour.
190	*Go to* – Roderigo interprets Iago's dismissive phrase in the sense of 'have sexual intercourse'.
192	*fopped:* duped.

But never taint my love. I cannot say 'whore'.   160
It does abhor me* now I speak the word;
To do* the act that might the addition earn
Not the world's mass of vanity could make me.
IAGO I pray you be content. 'Tis but his humour.
The business of the state does him offence.*   165
DESDEMONA If 'twere no other!
IAGO   It is but so, I warrant.
                                        [Trumpets within
Hark how these instruments summon to supper.
The messengers of Venice stay the meat.*
Go in, and weep not; all things shall be well.
                        [Exeunt DESDEMONA and EMILIA

Enter RODERIGO.

How now, Roderigo?   170
RODERIGO I do not find that thou deal'st justly with me.
IAGO What in the contrary?
RODERIGO Every day thou daff'st me* with some device,* Iago, and
         rather, as it seems to me now, keep'st from me all
         conveniency* than suppliest me with the least advantage   175
         of hope. I will indeed no longer endure it; nor am I yet
         persuaded to put up* in peace what already I have
         foolishly suffered.
IAGO Will you hear me, Roderigo?
RODERIGO I have heard too much, and your words and   180
         performances* are no kin* together.
IAGO You charge me most unjustly.
RODERIGO With naught but truth. I have wasted* myself out of my
         means. The jewels you have had from me to deliver to
         Desdemona would half have corrupted a votarist.* You   185
         have told me she hath received them, and returned me
         expectations and comforts* of sudden respect* and
         acquaintance; but I find none.
IAGO Well, go to; very well.
RODERIGO Very well? Go to?* I cannot go to, man; nor 'tis not very   190
         well. Nay, I think it is scurvy, and begin to find myself
         fopped* in it.
IAGO Very well.
RODERIGO I tell you 'tis not very well. I will make myself known to
         Desdemona. If she will return me my jewels, I will give   195

196   *solicitation:* courtship.
197   *seek satisfaction:* look for my revenge (by challenging you to a duel).
198   *You have said now?:* Have you finished?
199   *protest intendment:* declare the intention.
201   *mettle:* manliness. – Iago, sensing the danger to his own plans if Roderigo carries out his
          threat to reveal all to Desdemona, now proceeds to flatter him.
204   *exception:* disapproval, objection.
206   *It . . . appeared:* It has not been evident. – Roderigo is resentful, but willing to be
          convinced.
213   *engines for:* plots against.
214   *compass:* possibility.
219   *Mauritania* – a part of western Africa. Iago seems to have no particular evidence for his
          statement, and he quickly passes, without giving Roderigo time to reflect, on to
          his main point, the removal of Cassio.
220   *abode be lingered:* stay be delayed. – The passive use of the verb 'to linger' which in
          Shakespeare's day could be used transitively is obsolete.
222   *determinate:* decisive.
228   *harlotry:* whore.
230   *fashion to fall out:* contrive to take place.
231–2 *take him at your pleasure:* attack him in any way you like.
232   *second:* support.
233   *amazed:* bewildered – as if lost in a *maze*, rather than astonished.
236   *high:* fully.
237   *About it:* i.e. Let's get moving.

over my suit and repent my unlawful solicitation.* If not,
assure yourself I will seek satisfaction* of you.

IAGO You have said now?*

RODERIGO Ay, and said nothing but what I protest intendment* of
doing.   200

IAGO Why, now I see there's mettle* in thee, and even from this
instant do build on thee a better opinion than ever
before. Give me thy hand, Roderigo. Thou hast taken
against me a most just exception;* but yet I protest I have
dealt most directly in thy affair.   205

RODERIGO It* hath not appeared.

IAGO I grant indeed it hath not appeared, and your suspicion is
not without wit and judgment. But Roderigo, if thou hast
that in thee indeed which I have greater reason to believe
now than ever – I mean purpose, courage, and valour –   210
this night show it. If thou the next night following enjoy
not Desdemona, take me from this world with treachery
and devise engines for* my life.

RODERIGO Well, what is it? Is it within reason and compass?*

IAGO Sir, there is especial commission come from Venice to   215
depute Cassio in Othello's place.

RODERIGO Is that true? Why, then Othello and Desdemona return
again to Venice.

IAGO O, no; he goes into Mauritania* and taketh away with
him the fair Desdemona, unless his abode be lingered*   220
here by some accident; wherein none can be so
determinate* as the removing of Cassio.

RODERIGO How do you mean, removing him?

IAGO Why, by making him uncapable of Othello's place –
knocking out his brains.   225

RODERIGO And that you would have me to do?

IAGO Ay, if you dare do yourself a profit and a right. He sups
tonight with a harlotry,* and thither will I go to him. He
knows not yet of his honourable fortune. If you will
watch his going thence, which I will fashion to fall out*   230
between twelve and one, you may take him at your
pleasure.* I will be near to second* your attempt, and he
shall fall between us. Come, stand not amazed* at it, but go
along with me. I will show you such a necessity in his
death that you shall think yourself bound to put it on   235
him. It is now high* supper time, and the night grows to
waste. About it.*

IV.iii.   After the banquet is over and the guests have departed, Emilia prepares Desdemona for
bed. Desdemona seems to have a sense of her impending death and asks Emilia to see that if
she dies, her wedding sheets are used as her shroud. She speaks of her mother's maid
Barbary who died of a broken heart and sings the song Barbary sang about a false love.
They discuss unfaithful wives, Emilia playfully, Desdemona very seriously. After a while
Emilia takes her leave.

The final scene of Act IV is in many ways a still point in the dramatic action, the calm
before the storm. It begins with the leave-taking of Lodovico and his party after the formal
dinner and moves on to the intimate scene between Desdemona and Emilia while the
former undresses for bed. The physical act of disrobing would tend to emphasize
Desdemona's fragility and vulnerability. The song, as nearly always in Shakespeare, is not
a decorative addition, but heightens the pathos of the scene and embodies the theme of
betrayal in love. The scene ends with Desdemona going alone to wait expectantly for her
beloved husband, tragically ignorant of what he will bring her.

8   *Dismiss* – i.e. do not have her within call (as Desdemona usually would).
10   *He looks gentler than he did* – Emilia's remark has an ironical undertone for us, but it also
indicates that Othello's manner as he instructs Desdemona to go to bed and
dismiss Emilia is outwardly calm and composed.
11   *incontinent*: immediately.
15   *nightly wearing*: night clothes.
19   *checks*: rebukes.
22   *All's one*: It doesn't matter any more. – Desdemona is too preoccupied with her thoughts of
Othello to attend to Emilia's words immediately. She recollects herself in the
next sentence.
22   *Good faith*: upon my word – a mild oath.
24   *You talk* – i.e. talk nonsense.

RODERIGO I will hear further reason for this.

IAGO And you shall be satisfied.

[*Exeunt*

scene iii

The citadel.

Enter OTHELLO, LODOVICO, DESDEMONA, EMILIA *and*
ATTENDANTS.

LODOVICO I do beseech you, sir, trouble yourself no further.

OTHELLO O, pardon me; 'twill do me good to walk.

LODOVICO Madam, good night. I humbly thank your ladyship.

DESDEMONA Your honour is most welcome.

OTHELLO Will you walk, sir? O, Desdemona –   5

DESDEMONA My lord?

OTHELLO Get you to bed on th'instant; I will be returned
forthwith. Dismiss* your attendant there. Look't be done.

DESDEMONA I will, my lord.

[*Exit* OTHELLO, *with* LODOVICO *and* ATTENDANTS

EMILIA How goes it now? He looks gentler than he did.*   10

DESDEMONA He says he will return incontinent,*
And hath commanded me to go to bed,
And bade me to dismiss you.

EMILIA   Dismiss me?

DESDEMONA It was his bidding; therefore, good Emilia,
Give me my nightly wearing,* and adieu.   15
We must not now displease him.

EMILIA I would you had never seen him!

DESDEMONA So would not I. My love doth so approve him
That even his stubbornness, his checks,* his frowns –
Prithee unpin me – have grace and favour.   20

EMILIA I have laid those sheets you bade me on the bed.

DESDEMONA All's one.* Good faith,* how foolish are our minds!
If I do die before, prithee shroud me
In one of those same sheets.

EMILIA   Come, come! You talk.*

26   *mad* – perhaps 'wild' or 'unstable' rather than 'insane'. Desdemona's reference to her
      unfortunate maid's love affair is of course prompted by her own present
      situation.
30–31 *have much to do/But to:* can't help wanting to.
35   *proper:* (i) handsome; (ii) judicious.
37   *He speaks well* – The point of Desdemona's remark is not immediately clear. Perhaps she is
      momentarily contrasting Othello's deranged speech with Lodovico's dignified
      and lucid utterance (see IV.i.255–9). Elizabethan education was based on
      training in rhetoric, in which the connection between good speaking and sound
      judgment was much closer than we generally consider it to be today.
38–39 *walked barefoot to Palestine* – i.e. by way of penance, or punishment for sins. Such
      punishment was either imposed by the church or self-imposed by the sinners
      themselves, and often took the form of mortification of the flesh.
41   *willow* – a traditional symbol of forsaken or betrayed love.
50   *hie:* hurry.
50   *anon:* at once.
57   *moe:* more – an obsolete form.

DESDEMONA My mother had a maid called Barbary.   25
           She was in love; and he she loved proved mad*
           And did forsake her. She had a song of 'Willow';
           An old thing 'twas, but it expressed her fortune,
           And she died singing it. That song tonight ·
           Will not go from my mind; I have much to do   30
           But to* go hang my head all at one side
           And sing it like poor Barbary. Prithee dispatch.
EMILIA   Shall I go fetch your nightgown?
DESDEMONA No, unpin me here.
           This Lodovico is a proper* man.   35
EMILIA   A very handsome man.
DESDEMONA He speaks well.*
EMILIA   I know a lady in Venice would have walked barefoot to
           Palestine* for a touch of his nether lip.
DESDEMONA [Sings]
                 'The poor soul sat singing by a sycamore tree,   40
                     Sing all a green willow;*
                 Her hand on her bosom, her head on her knee,
                     Sing willow, willow, willow.
                 The fresh streams ran by her and murmured her moans;
                     Sing willow, willow, willow;   45
                 Her salt tears fell from her, and soft'ned the stones –
                     Sing willow, willow, willow – '
           Lay by these.

                                        [Gives EMILIA her clothes

                 'Willow, Willow' –
           Prithee hie* thee; he'll come anon.*   50
                 'Sing all a green willow must be my garland.
                     Let nobody blame him; his scorn I approve' –
           Nay, that's not next. Hark! Who is't that knocks?
EMILIA   It is the wind.
DESDEMONA [Sings]
                 'I called my love false love; but what said he then?   55
                     Sing willow, willow, willow:
                 If I court moe* women, you'll couch with moe men.'
           So, get thee gone; good night. Mine eyes do itch.
           Doth that bode weeping?
EMILIA   'Tis neither here nor there.
DESDEMONA I have heard it said so. O, these men, these men.   60
           Dost thou in conscience think, tell me, Emilia,

63	*such gross kind:* so greatly. The ensuing discussion shows that while Desdemona is an idealist convinced of the unique and absolute value of her love, Emilia, like her husband (though entirely lacking evil intent) tends to judge people by experience of the world, that is, by regarding them as instances of *general* truths.
65	*this heavenly light* – i.e. the moon.
73	*joint-ring:* ring with interlocking halves.
74	*lawn:* fine linen.
75	*exhibition:* allowance, payment.
77	*venture:* risk.
85	*to th'vantage:* in addition.
85	*store:* (i) fill up; (ii) populate. – The undercurrent of bawdy humour in Emilia's remarks contrasts with and complements Desdemona's innocent idealism.
88	*duties* – i.e. their sexual duties as husbands.
89	*our* – i.e. those that should rightly belong to us.
89	*foreign* – i.e. not their wives'.
91	*Throwing . . . us:* limiting our freedom.
92	*scant:* reduce.
92	*having:* allowance – with sexual reference.
92	*in despite:* out of spite.
93	*galls:* grounds for resentment. – The *gall* bladder was said to be the seat of rancour and produced bile, also called *gall*.
98	*change:* exchange.
99	*affection:* inclination.

That there be women do abuse their husbands
In such gross kind?*

EMILIA   There be some such, no question.

DESDEMONA Wouldst thou do such a deed for all the world?

EMILIA Why, would not you?

DESDEMONA   No, by this heavenly light!*   65

EMILIA Nor I neither, by this heavenly light.
I might do't as well i'th'dark.

DESDEMONA Wouldst though do such a deed for all the world?

EMILIA The world's a huge thing; it is a great price for a small
vice.   70

DESDEMONA In troth, I think thou wouldst not.

EMILIA In troth, I think I should; and undo't when I had done.
Marry, I would not do such a thing for a joint-ring,* nor
for measures of lawn,* nor for gowns, petticoats, nor
caps, nor any petty exhibition.* But for all the whole   75
world? Why, who would not make her husband a
cuckold to make him a monarch? I should venture*
purgatory for't.

DESDEMONA Beshrew me if I would do such a wrong for the whole
world.   80

EMILIA Why, the wrong is but a wrong i'th'world; and having
the world for your labour, 'tis a wrong in your own
world, and you might quickly make it right.

DESDEMONA I do not think there is any such woman.

EMILIA Yes, a dozen; and as many to th'vantage* as would store*   85
the world they played for.
But I do think it is their husbands' faults
If wives do fall. Say that they slack their duties*
And pour our* treasures into foreign* laps;
Or else break out in peevish jealousies,   90
Throwing* restraint upon us; or say they strike us,
Or scant* our former having* in despite* –
Why, we have galls;* and though we have some grace,
Yet have we some revenge. Let husbands know
Their wives have sense like them. They see, and smell,   95
And have their palates both for sweet and sour,
As husbands have. What is it that they do
When they change* us for others? Is it sport?
I think it is. And doth affection* breed it?
I think it doth. Is't frailty that thus errs?   100
It is so too. And have not we affections?

104   *ills:* misdeeds.
104   *so* – i.e. to behave like them.
105   *uses:* ways, experiences.
106   *Not . . . mend:* not to imitate bad examples but to improve (myself) by learning from them.

Desires for sport? and frailty? as men have?
Then let them use us well; else let them know,
The ills* we do, their ills instruct us so.*

DESDEMONA Good night, good night. [*Exit* EMILIA] Heaven me such   105
uses* send,
Not* to pick bad from bad, but by bad mend.

[*Exit*

v.i.   On Iago's instructions, Roderigo waits in a narrow street for Cassio to pass by in order to kill him. Iago is looking on, hiding not far away. Roderigo attacks Cassio but does not injure him, as the latter is wearing a coat of chain-mail. Instead, Cassio wounds Roderigo but is himself wounded by Iago, who then disappears into the darkness. Lodovico and Gratiano, Brabantio's brother (who has also come from Venice) find the wounded man. Iago reappears and pretending to be very anxious about Cassio, stabs his attacker Roderigo to death. Bianca appears while Iago is tending Cassio's wound and he manages to turn suspicion on her. When Emilia arrives she hears what has occurred and rushes off to tell Othello the news.

This scene, like the preceding one, takes place at night time, but the atmosphere is quite different. The conspiratorial whispering between Iago and Roderigo takes us back to the opening scene of the play. Othello's brief entrance after Cassio is injured is a grotesque parody of the earlier occasion (Act II scene iii) when he also intervened in a scene of brawling involving Cassio; on both occasions Cassio is the victim of a plot by Iago, and Othello, also duped by Iago, judges Cassio unjustly. But this time there is virtually nothing of the noble Moor in Othello's utterance; it is the speech of a man demented and sometimes verges on melodrama. The behaviour of Lodovico and Gratiano, who seem most concerned for their own safety, is less than what we would expect from men who represent the highest authority of the state. When Iago reappears with a light (having cunningly hidden himself during the actual fight between Roderigo and Cassio), it looks as if his plan is succeeding perfectly; and he helps it along by stabbing Roderigo before he has a chance to betray Iago's plot. He is even able to turn the appearance of Bianca to advantage by casting suspicion on her for Cassio's injury. The scene ends with Roderigo dead, Cassio injured, and Bianca arrested. Iago's triumph seems to be complete. But the brief aside with which he ends the scene gives us a hint, in the midst of all the confusion and disaster which he has caused, that before the night is over he may find that he is no longer the master of the situation.

1   *bulk*: projecting framework of a shop. – It would be one of the stage pillars.
1   *straight*: immediately.
2   *bare* – i.e. drawn, not in its scabbard.
2   *put it home*: thrust it in.
8   *devotion to*: enthusiasm for. – Roderigo's essential callousness is shown by the fact that though he doesn't particularly want to kill Cassio, he is quite prepared to do so; *'Tis but a man gone.* (line 10.)
11   *quat*: pimple.
11   *to the sense*: till it is raw. – Iago's contemptuous metaphor shows his opinion of Roderigo. The metaphor is continued in the next line where *angry* has the subsidiary sense of 'red, inflamed'.
14   *Live Roderigo*: If Roderigo lives.
15   *calls me to*: will demand from me.
16   *bobbed from him*: swindled him out of.
19–20   *He hath . . . me ugly* – These lines come strangely from the hard-headed Iago; hovering about them there appears to be the suggestion that the *daily beauty* is not a matter of elegance and courtesy only but of moral fineness, which Iago can recognize but feels himself cut off from. With his next reason he immediately reverts to the world of expediency.
21   *unfold*: expose.
23   *gait*: footstep.
24   *had*: would have.
25   *But that*: except for the fact that.
25   *coat* – A steel-plated garment was sometimes worn under the outer clothing for protection.
26   *make proof of*: test.

ACT V scene i

A street in front of the citadel.

Enter IAGO *and* RODERIGO.

IAGO   Here, stand behind this bulk;* straight* will he come.
      Wear thy good rapier bare,* and put it home.*
      Quick, quick! Fear nothing; I'll be at thy elbow.
      It makes us, or it mars us, think on that,
      And fix most firm thy resolution.   5
RODERIGO   Be near at hand; I may miscarry in't.
IAGO   Here, at thy hand. Be bold, and take thy stand.
                                  [Moves to one side
RODERIGO   I have no great devotion to* the deed,
      And yet he hath given me satisfying reasons.
      'Tis but a man gone. Forth my sword! He dies.   10
IAGO   *[Aside]* I have rubbed this young quat* almost to the
                                       sense,*
      And he grows angry. Now, whether he kill Cassio,
      Or Cassio him, or each do kill the other,
      Every way makes my gain. Live Roderigo,*
      He calls me to* a restitution large   15
      Of gold and jewels that I bobbed from him*
      As gifts to Desdemona.
      It must not be. If Cassio do remain,
      He hath* a daily beauty in his life
      That makes me ugly; and besides, the Moor   20
      May unfold* me to him; there stand I in much peril.
      No, he must die. But so, I hear him coming.

Enter CASSIO.

RODERIGO   I know his gait.* 'Tis he. Villain, thou diest!
                             [Thrusts at CASSIO
CASSIO   That thrust had* been mine enemy indeed
      But that* my coat* is better than thou know'st.   25
      I will make proof of* thine.
                      [Draws sword; they fight
RODERIGO   O, I am slain!

161

29   *It is even so* – Perhaps Othello's comment shows that he thinks the earlier line has been spoken by Cassio.

33   *Minion:* Hussy. – The word could also mean 'darling'.

34   *hies:* hurries on.

35   *Forth of:* Out of. – Othello means that he has wiped out of his mind the memory of Desdemona's eyes, which are like magical charms.

37   *watch:* watchman.

37   *passage:* people passing by.

38   *direful:* agonized, full of distress.

44   *come into the cry:* approach the source of the cries.

47   *Here's one . . . shirt* – Iago enters as if he has just got out of bed.

53   *What:* who.

54   *spoiled:* wounded.

54   *undone:* ruined.

CASSIO   I am maimed for ever. Help, ho! Murder! Murder!

Enter OTHELLO.

OTHELLO   The voice of Cassio. Iago keeps his word.
RODERIGO   O villain that I am!
OTHELLO   It is even so.*
CASSIO   O help, ho! Light! A surgeon!   30
OTHELLO   'Tis he. O brave Iago, honest and just,
That hast such noble sense of thy friend's wrong!
Thou teachest me. Minion,* your dear lies dead,
And your unblest fate hies.* Strumpet, I come.
Forth of* my heart those charms, thine eyes, are blotted.   35
Thy bed, lust-stained, shall with lust's blood be spotted.
                                      [*Exit* OTHELLO

Enter LODOVICO *and* GRATIANO.

CASSIO   What, ho? No watch?* No passage?* Murder! Murder!
GRATIANO   'Tis some mischance; the voice is very direful.*
CASSIO   O, help!
LODOVICO   Hark!   40
RODERIGO   O wretched villain!
LODOVICO   Two or three groan. 'Tis heavy night.
These may be counterfeits. Let's think't unsafe
To come into the cry* without more help.
RODERIGO   Nobody come? Then shall I bleed to death.   45
LODOVICO   Hark!

Enter IAGO *with a light.*

GRATIANO   Here's one* comes in his shirt, with light and weapons.
IAGO   Who's there? Whose noise is this that cries on murder?
LODOVICO   We do not know.
IAGO   Do not you hear a cry?
CASSIO   Here, here! For heaven's sake, help me!
IAGO   What's the matter?   50
GRATIANO   This is Othello's ancient, as I take it.
LODOVICO   The same indeed, a very valiant fellow.
IAGO   What* are you here that cry so grievously?
CASSIO   Iago? O, I am spoiled,* undone* by villains.
Give me some help.   55
IAGO   O me, lieutenant! What villains have done this?
CASSIO   I think that one of them is hereabout
And cannot make away.

65   *What may you be?* – From this point on, having made sure that Roderigo is dead, Iago
       directs operations, making sure that everyone plays the part assigned to them.
66   *prove:* determine by trial.
69   *cry you mercy:* I beg your pardon. (cf. line 93.)
75   *Who is't that cried* – Iago mockingly echoes Bianca to cast doubts on her sincerity.
82   *garter* – a garter to tie the bandage made from Iago's nightshirt could be provided by a man
       or a woman. The former is more likely.
82   *So:* There! That's done – uttered when the dressing of the wound is complete.
85   *trash:* worthless person.

The first thing Iago does –

IAGO   O treacherous villains!
          [*To* LODOVICO *and* GRATIANO] What are you there? Come
                              in, and give some help.
RODERIGO O, help me there!   60
CASSIO That's one of them.
IAGO   O murd'rous slave! O villain!
                              [*Stabs* RODERIGO
RODERIGO O damned Iago! O inhuman dog!
IAGO Kill men i'th'dark? – Where be these bloody thieves? –
          How silent is this town! – Ho! Murder! Murder! –
          [*To* LODOVICO *and* GRATIANO] What may you be?* Are
                              you of good or evil?   65
LODOVICO As you shall prove* us, praise us.
IAGO Signior Lodovico?
LODOVICO He, sir.
IAGO I cry you mercy.* Here's Cassio hurt by villains.
GRATIANO Cassio?   70
IAGO How is't, brother?
CASSIO My leg is cut in two.
IAGO   Marry, heaven forbid!
          Light, gentlemen. I'll bind it with my shirt.

          Enter BIANCA.

BIANCA What is the matter, ho? Who is't that cried?
IAGO Who is't that cried?*   75
BIANCA O my dear Cassio! My sweet Cassio!
          O Cassio, Cassio, Cassio!
IAGO O notable strumpet! – Cassio, may you suspect
          Who they should be that have thus mangled you?
CASSIO No.   80
GRATIANO I am sorry to find you thus. I have been to seek you.
IAGO Lend me a garter.* So.* O for a chair
          To bear him easily hence.
BIANCA Alas, he faints! O Cassio, Cassio, Cassio!
IAGO Gentlemen all, I do suspect this trash*   85
          To be a party in this injury. –
          Patience awhile, good Cassio. – Come, come.
          Lend me a light. Know we this face or no?
          Alas, my friend and my dear countryman
          Roderigo? No. – Yes, sure. – Yes, 'tis Roderigo.   90
GRATIANO What, of Venice?
IAGO Even he, sir. Did you know him?

98	*well said:* well done. – Several passers-by have probably gathered by now.
100	*For:* as for.
101	*Save . . . labour:* do nothing, stop interfering.
100–101	Bianca probably wants to help Cassio but Iago prevents her, having 'cast' her in the role of suspect.
104	*out o'th'air* – i.e. indoors.
106	*gastness of:* fear in.
109–10	*guiltiness . . . out of use* – i.e. guilt will reveal itself without speech.
117	*know of:* find out from.
119	*I therefore shake not:* I do not quake in fear because of it.
124	*dressed:* bandaged.

GRATIANO   Know him? Ay.
   IAGO Signior Gratiano? I cry your gentle pardon.
         These bloody accidents must excuse my manners
         That so neglected you.
GRATIANO   I am glad to see you.   95
   IAGO How do you, Cassio? – O, a chair, a chair!
GRATIANO Roderigo?
   IAGO He, he, 'tis he! [*A chair is brought in*] O, that's well said;*
                                                  the chair.
         Some good man bear him carefully from hence.
         I'll fetch the general's surgeon. [*To* BIANCA] For* you,
                                              mistress,   100
         Save* you your labour.* [*To* CASSIO] He that lies slain
                                              here, Cassio,
         Was my dear friend. What malice was between you?
 CASSIO None in the world; nor do I know the man.
   IAGO What, look you pale? – O bear him out o'th'air.*
                                    [CASSIO *is carried off*
         Stay you, good gentlemen. – [*To* BIANCA] Look you pale,
                                              mistress?   105
         [*To the rest*] Do you perceive the gastness of* her eye?
         Nay, if you stare, we shall hear more anon.
         Behold her well; I pray you look upon her.
         Do you see, gentlemen? Nay, guiltiness* will speak,
         Though tongues were out of use.   110

         Enter EMILIA.

 EMILIA Alas, what is the matter? What is the matter, husband?
   IAGO Cassio hath here been set on in the dark
         By Roderigo and fellows that are scaped.
         He's almost slain, and Roderigo quite dead.
 EMILIA Alas, good gentleman! Alas, good Cassio!   115
   IAGO This is the fruits of whoring. Prithee, Emilia,
         Go know of* Cassio where he supped tonight.
         [*To* BIANCA] What, do you shake at that?
 BIANCA He supped at my house; but I therefore shake not.*
   IAGO O, did he so? I charge you go with me.   120
 EMILIA Oh fie upon thee, strumpet!
 BIANCA I am no strumpet, but of life as honest
         As you that thus abuse me.
 EMILIA   As I? Foh! Fie upon thee!
   IAGO Kind gentlemen, let's go see poor Cassio dressed.*

125   *tell's:* tell us.
127   *happed:* happened.
128   *afore:* ahead.
129   *fordoes me quite:* ruins me utterly.

v.ii.   Othello enters the chamber where Desdemona lies asleep. Though he is greatly moved by her beauty, he is resolved that she must die. He kisses her and she awakes; Othello tells her to ask God's forgiveness for her sins, as she is about to die. Desdemona begs for mercy, but in vain. Othello accuses her of adultery with Cassio, and of giving his gift, the handkerchief, to her lover. In spite of his wife's anguished denials, he begins to strangle her.

He is interrupted by Emilia who rushes in with the news of Roderigo's death and Cassio's wounding. Desdemona stirs and just before she dies gasps out that she has been falsely murdered, but to the end refuses to accuse her husband. Othello tells Emilia that he has killed his wife because Iago has proved her guilt. Emilia curses her husband and calls Othello an ignorant fool.

Montano, Gratiano, Iago and others now enter. Gradually the details of Desdemona's death and the reasons for it emerge. Iago tries to keep Emilia from telling the truth, but she recounts the story of the handkerchief before Iago stabs her and runs out before Othello can attack him. Montano and others pursue him.

Emilia dies reminding Othello of his wife's absolute loyalty and love. Lodovico, Montano and others come in bringing Iago prisoner. Cassio also enters and Othello at last learns the truth about the handkerchief. Letters found on Roderigo make Iago's guilt plain, but he remains stubbornly silent. Othello reminds the assembled company to tell the truth about him and kills himself with a dagger. Lodovico confirms Cassio's appointment as governor, leaves Iago to be tortured and departs for Venice to relate the tragic events which have taken place at Cyprus.

After the noise, confusion and rapid movement of the previous scene, this one opens in an atmosphere of solemn stillness. We are in Othello's bedchamber and, figuratively, in the innermost chamber of his heart. In the Elizabethan theatre, Desdemona's bed would probably have been in the curtained area beneath the stage balcony. This method would have the disadvantage that some of the action would not be visible to part of the audience, but would solve the problem of getting the bed off the stage with Desdemona's body on it (a cumbersome business especially with a 17th century four-poster) as the curtains of the inner stage would be drawn (v.ii.362 S.D.) to conceal the bed. Though Othello is about to commit murder he approaches the task as a priest going to a ritual sacrifice, even perhaps as a lover about to consummate his passion. His still powerful love for Desdemona alternates with his terrible conviction that she must be punished. Desdemona is helpless against the combination in a single figure of plaintiff, witness, judge, jury and executioner. But to the end she remains loyal to the husband who, in the name of justice, has been so cruelly unjust to her.

With the entrance of Emilia, the need and the opportunity arise for Othello to justify his action, and the manifest impossibility of doing so is made clear by Emilia's total refusal to believe Othello's account of his wife's alleged unfaithfulness. It is not long before Emilia realizes whose villainy has been responsible for Othello's mistake and its tragic outcome, and she pays for the realization with her life.

Othello himself, now that the enormity of his error has been revealed to him, has nothing left to live for. In the manner of his death he recaptures something of the dignity which, under Iago's malignant influence, he had lost. As for Iago, though taken into custody by the representatives of the state and facing imprisonment and torture, he remains silent to the end, the living embodiment of the mystery of evil.

1   *cause:* (i) offence; (ii) legal case; (iii) reason.
4   *that whiter . . . than snow* – i.e. her skin whiter than snow.

[*To* BIANCA] Come, mistress, you must tell's* another tale.   125
Emilia, run you to the citadel
And tell my lord and lady what hath happed.*

[*Exit* EMILIA

Will you go on afore?*

[*Exeunt all but* IAGO
This is the night
That either makes me or fordoes me quite.*

[*Exit*

scene ii

Desdemona's chamber.

Enter OTHELLO *with a light; and* DESDEMONA *in her bed.*

OTHELLO   It is the cause,* it is the cause, my soul.
Let me not name it to you, you chaste stars.
It is the cause. Yet I'll not shed her blood,
Nor scar that whiter* skin of hers than snow,
And smooth as monumental alabaster.   5
Yet she must die, else she'll betray more men.
Put out the light, and then put out the light.*
If I quench thee, thou flaming minister,*
I can again thy former light restore,
Should I repent me; but once put out thy* light,   10
Thou cunning'st* pattern of excelling nature,
I know not where is that Promethean heat*
That can thy light relume.* When I have plucked the
                                                          rose,

---

7   *Put out the light, and then put out the light* – Othello wants to extinguish the taper he has
        brought in (*put out the light*) *and then* strangle Desdemona (*put out the light*). But
        the thought of the first action brings to his mind the irrevocability of the second
        (8–15).
8   *minister:* agent – i.e. the taper.
10   *thy* – i.e. Desdemona's.
11   *cunning'st . . . nature:* most exquisite work of Nature excelling herself.
12   *Promethean heat:* divine fire. – In Greek mythology, Prometheus was a Titan who stole fire
        from the gods to give it to man and was punished with everlasting torture.
13   *relume:* relight.

16   *balmy:* (i) fragrant; (ii) soothing.
17   *Justice . . . sword* – Justice was personified as a blindfold female figure with sword in one hand and scales in the other.
20   *So sweet was ne'er so fatal:* Nothing so sweet (as Desdemona's last kiss) was ever so deadly.
22   *It strikes where it doth love* – Compare a passage in the Bible: 'For the Lord disciplines those whom he loves' (*Hebrews* 12:6 – New English Bible.) Othello's *sorrow is heavenly* (21) because it comes over him when he is acting as an instrument of divine justice (or so he believes) which grieves over punishing the loved ones.
26   *bethink yourself of:* remember.
27   *Unreconciled . . . grace* – a reference to the Christian doctrine of God's forgiveness of sins repented and confessed.
28   *Solicit :* pray for pardon.
32   *forfend:* forbid. – Othello alludes to the belief that a person who dies with his or her sins unconfessed would go to Hell. (See *Hamlet* III.iii.94.)
36   In response to Desdemona's direct appeal, Othello cannot bring himself to speak. But, as Desdemona's subsequent lines (especially 38, 43 and 44) show, his body betrays the turbulence of his conflicting emotions.
37   *fatal:* ominous, portending death.
41   *Ay, and for that thou diest* – Othello's reply, which doesn't make sense literally (since there is no reason to kill Desdemona because she loves him) is evidence of his deranged state of mind at this point.
44   *frame:* body.

I cannot give it vital growth again;
It needs must wither. I'll smell thee on the tree.   15
                                          [*Kisses her*
O balmy* breath, that dost almost persuade
Justice* to break her sword. One more, one more!
Be thus when thou art dead, and I will kill thee,
And love thee after. One more, and that's the last.
So sweet was ne'er so fatal.* I must weep,   20
But they are cruel tears. This sorrow's heavenly;
It strikes where it doth love.* She wakes.

DESDEMONA Who's there? Othello?
OTHELLO   Ay, Desdemona.
DESDEMONA Will you come to bed, my lord?
OTHELLO Have you prayed tonight, Desdemon?
DESDEMONA   Ay, my lord.   25
OTHELLO If you bethink yourself of* any crime
Unreconciled* as yet to heaven and grace,
Solicit* for it straight.
DESDEMONA Alack, my lord, what may you mean by that?
OTHELLO Well, do it, and be brief; I will walk by.   30
I would not kill thy unprepared spirit.
No, heavens forfend,* I would not kill thy soul.
DESDEMONA Talk you of killing?
OTHELLO   Ay, I do.
DESDEMONA   Then heaven
Have mercy on me!
OTHELLO   Amen, with all my heart.
DESDEMONA If you say so, I hope you will not kill me.   35
OTHELLO Humh.*
DESDEMONA And yet I fear you; for you're fatal* then
When your eyes roll so. Why I should fear I know not,
Since guiltiness I know not; but yet I feel I fear.
OTHELLO Think on thy sins.
DESDEMONA   They are loves I bear to you.   40
OTHELLO Ay, and for that thou diest.*
DESDEMONA That death's unnatural that kills for loving.
Alas, why gnaw you so your nether lip?
Some bloody passion shakes your very frame.*
These are portents; but yet I hope, I hope,   45
They do not point on me.
OTHELLO   Peace, and be still.
DESDEMONA I will so. What's the matter?

53	*freely* : without reservations. – *thee* is used reflexively.
54–6	*For to deny . . . groan withal*: Even if you were to deny every particular accusation on oath, it will not remove the constriction (of your guilt) which torments me.
54	*article*: item – legal usage.
55	*conception*: (i) belief; (ii) plan. There is a play on the sense of *conception* as giving birth (cf. *groan* in the next line).
60	*general warranty*: ordinary allowance. – Desdemona asserts that her love for Cassio did not go beyond ordinary friendship and affection.
63	*stone*: turn to stone. – (This is the only time the word is used in this sense by Shakespeare.) When he thinks of Desdemona's defilement by guilt, Othello considers her unfit to be a sacrificial victim, and therefore he thinks of her impending death as murder.
72	*ta'en order for't*: arranged it.
73	*my fear interprets*: my anxiety makes it apparent to me (that he is dead).
74	*Had all his hairs been lives*: Even if he had as many lives as hairs on his head.
75	*stomach*: appetite. – Desdemona's concern for Cassio's fate inflames Othello once more so that his earlier calm is shattered. He begins to smother her almost immediately, probably on his next line.

OTHELLO   That handkerchief which I so loved and gave thee,
            Thou gav'st to Cassio.
DESDEMONA   No, by my life and soul!
            Send for the man and ask him.
OTHELLO   Sweet soul, take heed,   50
            Take heed of perjury; thou art on thy deathbed.
DESDEMONA   Ay, but not yet to die.
OTHELLO   Presently.
            Therefore confess thee freely* of thy sin,
            For to deny* each article* with oath
            Cannot remove nor choke the strong conception*   55
            That I do groan withal. Thou art to die.
DESDEMONA   Then Lord have mercy on me!
OTHELLO   I say, amen.
DESDEMONA   And have you mercy too. I never did
            Offend you in my life; never loved Cassio
            But with such general warranty* of heaven   60
            As I might love. I never gave him token.
OTHELLO   By heaven, I saw my handkerchief in's hand!
            O perjured woman! thou dost stone* my heart,
            And mak'st me call what I intend to do
            A murder, which I thought a sacrifice.   65
            I saw the handkerchief.
DESDEMONA   He found it then.
            I never gave it him. Send for him hither.
            Let him confess a truth.
OTHELLO   He hath confessed.
DESDEMONA   What, my lord?
OTHELLO   That he hath used thee.
DESDEMONA   How? Unlawfully?
OTHELLO   Ay.   70
DESDEMONA   He will not say so.
OTHELLO   No; his mouth is stopped.
            Honest Iago hath ta'en order for't.*
DESDEMONA   O, my fear interprets.* What, is he dead?
OTHELLO   Had all his hairs been lives,* my great revenge
            Had stomach* for them all.   75
DESDEMONA   Alas, he is betrayed, and I undone!
OTHELLO   Out, strumpet! Weep'st thou for him to my face?
DESDEMONA   O banish me, my lord, but kill me not!
OTHELLO   Down, strumpet!
DESDEMONA   Kill me tomorrow; let me live tonight!   80

81   *Nay, if you strive* – Desdemona's struggles make Othello even more determined.

82   *Being done . . . pause:* I have begun, and I cannot stop.

82, 84 *But:* Only.

88   *So, so* – On these words Othello smothers Desdemona again.

92   *like:* probable.

93   *high:* loud.   The commotion surrounding Cassio's 'death' is heard. The short broken phrases suggest Othello's confusion and uncertainty. But the word *wife*, four times repeated, brings him back to a sense of his inconsolable loss which he expresses with his former dignity of utterance. (98–101)

101   *yawn:* split open.

101   *alteration:* change (caused by Desdemona's death). – Important events in human affairs were believed to be heralded or accompanied by equally momentous happenings in the natural world. (See *King Lear* I.ii.107–117.)

109   *error:* wandering off course. – Othello is still continuing his earlier imaginings and hardly seems to have attended fully to Emilia's news.

Heavenly bodies are not symbols of man's spirit – isolated phenomena, sublimely decorative (wh)

OTHELLO Nay, if you strive* –
DESDEMONA But* half an hour!
OTHELLO   Being done,* there is no pause.
DESDEMONA But while I say one prayer!
OTHELLO   It is too late.
                                    [*Smothers her*

            EMILIA *at the door.*

    EMILIA [*Calls within*] My lord, my lord! What, ho, my lord, my
                                              lord!

OTHELLO What noise is this? Not dead? Not yet quite dead?   85
            I that am cruel am yet merciful;
            I would not have thee linger in thy pain.
            So, so.*
    EMILIA [*Within*] What, ho! My lord, my lord!
OTHELLO   Who's there?
    EMILIA [*Within*] O, good my lord, I would speak a word with
                                              you.   90

OTHELLO Yes, 'tis Emilia. – By and by. – She's dead. –
            'Tis like* she comes to speak of Cassio's death.
            The noise was high.* Ha! No more moving?
            Still as the grave. – Shall she come in? Were't good? –
            I think she stirs again. No. – What's best to do?   95
            If she come in, she'll sure speak to my wife.
            My wife! My wife! What wife? I have no wife.
            O, insupportable! O heavy hour!
            Methinks it should be now a huge eclipse
            Of sun and moon, and that th'affrighted globe   100
            Should yawn* at alteration.*
    EMILIA   [*Within*] I do beseech you
            That I may speak with you, O good my lord!
OTHELLO I had forget thee. O, come in Emilia.
            Soft, by and by. – Let me the curtains draw. –
                          [*Draws bed hangings, then opens door*
            Where art thou?

            Enter EMILIA.

                          What's the matter with thee now?   105
    EMILIA O my good lord, yonder's foul murders done!
OTHELLO What? Now?
    EMILIA But now, my lord.
OTHELLO It is the very error* of the moon.

115–16 *murder's . . . harsh:* The murder has had the wrong effect and revenge, from which I expected sweet satisfaction, has brought only confusion and discord.

125   *Commend me:* Give my love.

126   *how should she:* how is it possible for her to have been.

129   *like a liar·* like the liar that she is.

130   *the more angel she:* (her guiltless death) makes her even more angelic.

129–30   These lines embody Othello's self-division as regards Desdemona. The same action is evidence to him of her falseness and (at a level of which he is not consciously aware) of her utter loyalty.

135   *false –* i.e. unstable.

136   *top –* Othello reverts to Iago's language.

136   *else:* if that is not true.

139   *extremity:* last violent act.

| | She comes more nearer earth than she was wont | 110 |

She comes more nearer earth than she was wont   110
And makes men mad.

EMILIA   Cassio, my lord, hath killed a young Venetian
Called Roderigo.

OTHELLO   Roderigo killed?
And Cassio killed?

EMILIA   No, Cassio is not killed.

OTHELLO   Not Cassio killed? Then murder's* out of tune,   115
And sweet revenge grows harsh.

DESDEMONA   O, falsely, falsely murdered!

EMILIA   O Lord! What cry is that?

OTHELLO   That? What?

EMILIA   Out and alas, that was my lady's voice!
Help! Help, ho! Help! [*Draws back bed hangings.*] O lady,
speak again!   120
Sweet Desdemona! O sweet mistress, speak!

DESDEMONA   A guiltless death I die.

EMILIA   O who hath done this deed?

DESDEMONA   Nobody – I myself. Farewell.
Commend me* to my kind lord. O, farewell!   125
[*She dies*

OTHELLO   Why, how should she* be murd'red?

EMILIA   Alas, who knows?

OTHELLO   You heard her say herself, it was not I.

EMILIA   She said so. I must needs report the truth.

OTHELLO   She's like a liar* gone to burning hell!
'Twas I that killed her.*

EMILIA   O, the more angel she,*   130
And you the blacker devil!

OTHELLO   She turned to folly, and she was a whore.

EMILIA   Thou dost belie her, and thou art a devil.

OTHELLO   She was false as water.

EMILIA   Thou art rash as fire to say
That she was false.* O, she was heavenly true!   135

OTHELLO   Cassio did top* her. Ask thy husband else.*
O I were damned beneath all depth in hell,
But that I did proceed upon just grounds
To this extremity.* Thy husband knew it all.

EMILIA   My husband?

OTHELLO   Thy husband.

EMILIA   That she was false to wed-
lock?   140

Perfectian is not life, but a chill stone

143   *entire:* unmixed, pure.
143   *chrysolite:* topaz – a precious stone.
148   *iterance:* repetition.
149   *made mocks with:* made a mockery of.
155   *her most filthy bargain*   i.e. her husband, for whom she had sacrificed her wealth and
         position in society as well as her father's love.
157   *Do thy worst:* I'm not afraid of you. – Emilia is facing up to Othello's threatening (Hah?)
         (line 156).
159   *Peace, you were best:* You had better keep quiet.
160–1 *Thou hast not . . . hurt –* i.e. I can endure far more than you can inflict.
168   *lay . . . on your neck:* blame you for . . .
175   *apt:* probable.

OTHELLO Ay, with Cassio. Had she been true,
    If heaven would make me such another world
    Of one entire* and perfect chrysolite,*
    I'd not have sold her for it.

EMILIA   My husband?

OTHELLO Ay, 'twas he that told me on her first.   145
    An honest man he is, and hates the slime
    That sticks on filthy deeds.

EMILIA   My husband?

OTHELLO What needs this iterance?* Woman, I say thy husband.

EMILIA O mistress, villainy hath made mocks with* love!
    My husband say she was false?

OTHELLO   He, woman.   150
    I say, thy husband. Dost understand the word?
    My friend, thy husband; honest, honest Iago.

EMILIA If he say so, may his pernicious soul
    Rot half a grain a day! He lies to th'heart.
    She was too fond of her most filthy bargain.*   155

OTHELLO Hah?

EMILIA Do thy worst.*
    This deed of thine is no more worthy heaven
    Than thou wast worthy her.

OTHELLO   Peace, you were best.*

EMILIA Thou hast not* half that pow'r to do me harm   160
    As I have to be hurt. O gull! O dolt!
    As ignorant as dirt! Thou hast done a deed –
          [OTHELLO *touches his sword*
    I care not for thy sword; I'll make thee known,
    Though I lost twenty lives. Help! Help ho! Help!
    The Moor hath killed my mistress! Murder! murder!   165

Enter MONTANO, GRATIANO, IAGO *and others.*

MONTANO What is the matter? How now, general?

EMILIA O, are you come, Iago? You have done well,
    That men must lay* their murders on your neck.

GRATIANO What is the matter?

EMILIA Disprove this villain, if thou be'st a man.   170
    He says thou told'st him that his wife was false.
    I know thou didst not; thou'rt not such a villain.
    Speak, for my heart is full.

IAGO I told him what I thought, and told no more
    Than what he found himself was apt* and true.   175

181   *charm:* cast a spell on – i.e. control.
194   *proper I obey him* – obey Iago's order to go home.
196   The sight of Desdemona dead is too much for Othello. Perhaps Emilia's scattered
          remarks have given him a glimmer of the truth.
199   *know:* recognize = A wife's uncle was also regarded as the husband's.
203   *match:* marriage.
203   *mortal:* fatal.
204   *Shore . . . twain:* cut the thread of his life in two. *Shore* is an obsolete form of 'sheared'.
204–7 *Did he . . . to reprobation;* If he were alive now, this sight would drive him to kill himself (*do
          a desperate turn*) by driving from his side with curses his guardian angel who
          would otherwise have prevented him from falling into damnation (*reprobation*)
          (by committing the unforgivable sin of suicide).
207   *reprobation:* damnation.
211   *gratify:* reward.
212   *recognizance:* token.

EMILIA But did you ever tell him she was false?
IAGO   I did.
EMILIA You told a lie, an odious damnèd lie!
        Upon my soul, a lie! A wicked lie!
        She false with Cassio? Did you say with Cassio?   180
IAGO   With Cassio, mistress. Go to, charm* your tongue.
EMILIA I will not charm my tongue; I am bound to speak;
        My mistress here lies murdered in her bed.
ALL   O heavens forfend!
EMILIA And your reports have set the murder on.   185
OTHELLO Nay, stare not, masters. It is true indeed.
GRATIANO 'Tis a strange truth.
MONTANO O monstrous act!
EMILIA   Villainy, villainy, villainy!
        I think upon't – I think I smell't! – O villainy!
        I thought so then. – I'll kill myself for grief. –   190
        O villainy, villainy!
IAGO   What, are you mad? I charge you get you home.
EMILIA Good gentlemen, let me have leave to speak
        'Tis proper I obey him,* but not now.
        Perchance, Iago, I will ne'er go home.   195
OTHELLO O! O! O!*   [Falls on the bed
EMILIA   Nay, lay thee down and roar,
        For thou hast killed the sweetest innocent
        That e'er did lift up eye.
OTHELLO   O, she was foul!
                 [Rises. To GRATIANO.]
        I scarce did know* you, uncle. There lies your niece,
        Whose breath, indeed, these hands have newly stopped.   200
        I know this act shows horrible and grim.
GRATIANO Poor Desdemon! I am glad thy father's dead.
        Thy match* was mortal* to him, and pure grief
        Shore* his old thread in twain. Did he* live now,
        This sight would make him do a desperate turn;   205
        Yea, curse his better angel from his side,
        And fall to reprobation.*
OTHELLO 'Tis pitiful; but yet Iago knows
        That she with Cassio hath the act of shame
        A thousand times committed. Cassio confessed it;   210
        And she did gratify* his amorous works
        With that recognizance* and pledge of love,
        Which I first gave her. I saw it in his hand.

217   *hold your peace:* be silent.
217   *'Twill out:* It (the truth) must come out.
218   *as liberal as the north:* as freely and bitterly as the north wind.
224   *by fortune:* by chance.
227   *Villainous whore!* – The violence of Iago's outburst shows that now he can no longer hope
         to conceal his villainy, even though he makes one more desperate attempt with
         Filth, thou liest! before he kills her.
231   *coxcomb:* fool.
232–3 *Are there . . . thunder?:* Are the thunderbolts (*stones*) in heaven only for thunderstorms? –
         An allusion to the belief that the gods hurled thunderbolts to punish offenders.
237   *notorious:* evident, obvious.
241   *I am not . . . neither:* I too lack manliness. – Othello is implying that he too is a *damned slave.*
242   *puny whipster:* whipper-snapper, small contemptible fellow.

It was a handkerchief, an antique token
My father gave my mother.   215
EMILIA O God! O heavenly God!
IAGO Zounds, hold your peace!*
EMILIA   'Twill out,* 'twill out! I
                                        peace?
No, I will speak as liberal as the north.*
Let heaven and men and devils, let them all,
All, all, cry shame against me, yet I'll speak.   220
IAGO Be wise, and get you home.
EMILIA   I will not.
                [IAGO *threatens* EMILIA *with his sword*
GRATIANO Fie! Your sword upon a woman?
EMILIA O thou dull Moor, that handkerchief thou speak'st of
I found by fortune,* and did give my husband;
For often with a solemn earnestness –   225
More than indeed belonged to such a trifle –
He begged of me to steal't.
IAGO   Villainous whore!*
EMILIA She give it Cassio? No, alas, I found it,
And I did give't my husband.
IAGO   Filth, thou liest!
EMILIA By heaven, I do not, I do not, gentlemen.   230
[*To* OTHELLO] O murd'rous coxcomb!* What should such
                                        a fool
Do with so good a wife?
OTHELLO   Are there* no stones in heaven
But what serves for the thunder! Precious villain!
[*The Moor runs at* IAGO, *but is disarmed by* MONTANO.
IAGO *kills his wife.*]
GRATIANO The woman falls. Sure he hath killed his wife.
EMILIA Ay, ay. O, lay me by my mistress' side.   235
                                [*Exit* IAGO
GRATIANO He's gone, but his wife's killed.
MONTANO 'Tis a notorious* villain. Take you this weapon,
Which I have recovered from the Moor.
Come, guard the door without. Let him not pass,
But kill him rather. I'll after that same villain,   240
For 'tis a damnèd slave.
                [*Exit with all but* OTHELLO *and* EMILIA
OTHELLO   I am not* valiant neither;
But every puny whipster* gets my sword.

243	*But why . . . honesty?* why should honour as a soldier (which goes *with* his sword) survive longer than honour as a man (*honesty,* which I have already lost)?
245–6	*swan . . . music* – The swan was believed to sing only once, just before dying.
248	*come my soul:* may my soul come.
251	*ice-brook's temper:* tempered (hardened) by being plunged in a very cold stream.
256	*naked:* unarmed.
265	*butt:* target.
266	*seamark:* limit. – Literally, an object placed in the sea to guide sailors.
267	*lost:* baseless.
268	*Man but a rush:* Point only a reed. *Man* = provide a man with.
271	*at compt:* at the reckoning – i.e. on Judgment Day. Othello's final thoughts once more take on a Christian tinge.
278	*steep-down:* sheer, precipitous. – At the end of his speech Othello may fall down in a swoon as Lodovico does not appear to see him immediately.

	But why* should honour outlive honesty?	
	Let it go all.	
EMILIA	What did thy song bode, lady?	
	Hark, canst thou hear me? I will play the swan,*	245
	And die in music. [*Sings*] 'Willow, willow, willow.'	
	Moor, she was chaste. She loved thee, cruel Moor,	
	So come my soul* to bliss as I speak true.	
	So speaking as I think, alas, I die.	

[*She dies*

OTHELLO	I have another weapon in this chamber;	250
	It was a sword of Spain, the ice-brook's temper.*	
	O, here it is. – Uncle, I must come forth.	
GRATIANO	[*Within*] If thou attempt it, it will cost thee dear.	
	Thou hast no weapon, and perforce must suffer.	
OTHELLO	Look in upon me then and speak with me,	255
	Or, naked* as I am, I will assault thee.	

[*Enter* GRATIANO]

GRATIANO	What is the matter?	
OTHELLO	Behold, I have a weapon;	
	A better never did itself sustain	
	Upon a soldier's thigh. I have seen the day	
	That with this little arm and this good sword	260
	I have made my way through more impediments	
	Than twenty times your stop. But O vain boast!	
	Who can control his fate? 'Tis not so now.	
	Be not afraid, though you do see me weaponed.	
	Here is my journey's end, here is my butt,*	265
	And very seamark* of my utmost sail.	
	Do you go back dismayed? 'Tis a lost* fear.	
	Man but a rush* against Othello's breast,	
	And he retires. Where should Othello go	
	Now? How dost thou look now? O ill-starred wench,	270
	Pale as thy smock! When we shall meet at compt,*	
	This look of thine will hurl my soul from heaven,	
	And fiends will snatch at it. Cold, cold, my girl?	
	Even like thy chastity.	
	O cursèd, cursèd slave! Whip me, ye devils,	275
	From the possession of this heavenly sight!	
	Blow me about in winds, roast me in sulphur,	
	Wash me in steep-down* gulfs of liquid fire!	
	O Desdemon! Dead Desdemon; dead. O! O!	

283   *that's a fable* – i.e. the belief that a devil has cloven hoofs.
287   *in my sense:* as I feel now.
289   *practice:* plot.
303   *thou dost best:* you are wise to stay silent.
307   *imports:* gives details of.
311   *discontented paper* – i.e. a letter expressing discontent.

Enter LODOVICO, CASSIO, *wounded,* MONTANO, *and* IAGO,
as prisoner, with OFFICERS.

LODOVICO Where is this rash and most unfortunate man?   280
OTHELLO That's he that was Othello; here I am.
LODOVICO Where is that viper? Bring the villain forth.
OTHELLO I look down towards his feet – but that's a fable.*
   If that thou be'st a devil, I cannot kill thee.
            [*Wounds* IAGO
LODOVICO Wrench his sword from him.
       [OTHELLO's *sword is taken from him*
  IAGO   I bleed, sir, but not killed.   285
OTHELLO I am not sorry neither. I'd have thee live;
   For in my sense,* 'tis happiness to die.
LODOVICO O thou Othello that was once so good,
   Fall'n in the practice* of a cursèd slave,
   What shall be said to thee?
OTHELLO   Why, anything: 290
   An honourable murderer, if you will;
   For naught I did in hate, but all in honour.
LODOVICO This wretch hath part confessed his villainy.
   Did you and he consent in Cassio's death?
OTHELLO Ay.   295
CASSIO Dear general, I never gave you cause.
OTHELLO I do believe it, and I ask your pardon.
   Will you, I pray, demand that demi-devil
   Why he hath thus ensnared my soul and body?
  IAGO Demand me nothing. What you know, you know.   300
   From this time forth I never will speak word.
LODOVICO What, not to pray?
GRATIANO   Torments will ope your lips.
OTHELLO [*To* IAGO] Well, thou dost best.*
LODOVICO Sir, you shall understand what hath befall'n,
   Which, as I think, you know not. Here is a letter   305
   Found in the pocket of the slain Roderigo;
   And here another. The one of them imports*
   The death of Cassio to be undertook
   By Roderigo.
OTHELLO O villain!
CASSIO   Most heathenish and most gross!   310
LODOVICO Now here's another discontented paper*
   Found in his pocket too; and this, it seems,

314   *belike:* probably.
315   *pernicious caitiff:* evil wretch.
320   *wrought to his desire:* worked according to his plan.
323   *Brave:* challenge, provoke.
323   *whereon it came:* as a result of which it happened.
324   *cast:* dismissed from office.
329   *this slave* – i.e. Iago.
331   *hold him:* keep him alive.
332   *rest:* remain.
334   *bring away:* lead (them) out.
335   *Soft you* – i.e. Stay a moment.
338   *unlucky:* unfortunate, ill-starred. – The word has a much more definite sense of evil
          destiny here than it does in modern usage.
342   *wrought:* worked up, provoked.
343   *Perplexed:* bewildered. – Another word whose meaning has weakened in modern usage.
344   *Indian* – i.e. American Indian. The American Indians were well known for their ignorance
          of the value of gold and jewels. The Folio gives *Judean,* which is taken to refer to
          Judas, who betrayed Christ. But Othello does not accuse himself of treachery,
          only of not realizing the true worth of she whom he once possessed.
348   *med'cinable:* usable as medicine. – The gum referred to is *myrrh,* a substance whose incense
          was associated with atonement and sacrifice.
          In the lines that follow, Othello, by fixing his imagination on a moment of his
          past when he was the noble Moor serving the Venetian State against its enemy,
          the heathen Turk, re-enacts the event and becomes both his former self (the
          noble warrior) and his present degraded self (an 'enemy' to the State).

Roderigo meant t'have sent this damnèd villain;
But that, belike,* Iago in the interim
Came in and satisfied him.

OTHELLO   [*To* IAGO] O thou pernicious caitiff!*   315
How came you, Cassio, by that handkerchief
That was my wife's?

CASSIO   I found it in my chamber;
And he himself confessed it but even now
That there he dropped it for a special purpose
Which wrought to his desire.*

OTHELLO   O fool! Fool! Fool!   320

CASSIO There is besides in Roderigo's letter,
How he upbraids Iago that he made him
Brave* me upon the watch; whereon it came*
That I was cast;* and even but now he spake;
After long seeming dead – Iago hurt him –   325
Iago set him on.

LODOVICO You must forsake this room and go with us.
Your power and your command is taken off,
And Cassio rules in Cyprus. For this slave,*
If there be any cunning cruelty   330
That can torment him much and hold him* long,
It shall be his. You shall close prisoner rest*
Till that the nature of your fault be known
To the Venetian state. Come, bring away.*

OTHELLO Soft you,* a word or two before you go.   335
I have done the state some service, and they know't.
No more of that. I pray you, in your letters,
When you shall these unlucky* deeds relate,
Speak of me as I am. Nothing extenuate,
Nor set down aught in malice. Then must you speak   340
Of one that loved not wisely, but too well;
Of one not easily jealous, but being wrought,*
Perplexed* in the extreme; of one whose hand,
Like the base Indian,* threw a pearl away
Richer than all his tribe; of one whose subdued eyes,   345
Albeit unusèd to the melting mood,
Drops tears as fast as the Arabian trees
Their med'cinable* gum. Set you down this.*
And say besides that in Aleppo once,
Where a malignant and a turbaned Turk   350
Beat a Venetian and traduced the state,

354   *period:* stop, conclusion.
358   *Spartan dog* – A variety of bloodhound noted for its ferocity and silence.
359   *fell:* deadly, terrible.
362   *keep:* stay in, guard.
363   *seize upon:* confiscate.
364   *succeed on you:* rightfully descend to you.
364   *lord governor* – i.e. Cassio.
365   *censure:* judgment, trial.
368   The very deliberate rhythm and the sighing alliteration heighten the atmosphere
              of a solemn funeral procession with which the play ends.

          I took by th'throat the circumcisèd dog
          And smote him – thus.

                                    [He stabs himself

LODOVICO O bloody period!*
GRATIANO   All that is spoke is marred.
OTHELLO I kissed thee ere I killed thee. No way but this,   355
          Killing myself, to die upon a kiss.

                        [He dies falling on DESDEMONA

CASSIO This did I fear, but thought he had no weapon;
          For he was great of heart.
LODOVICO   *[To* IAGO] O Spartan dog,*
          More fell* than anguish, hunger, or the sea,
          Look on the tragic loading of this bed.   360
          This is thy work. The object poisons sight;
          Let it be hid.

                          [Bed curtains drawn
          Gratiano, keep* the house,
          And seize upon* the fortunes of the Moor,
          For they succeed on you.* To you, lord governor,*
          Remains the censure* of this hellish villain,   365
          The time, the place, the torture, O enforce it!
          Myself will straight aboard, and to the state
          This heavy act with heavy heart relate.*

                                  [Exeunt

Glossary

(S.D. = Stage direction)

A

abhor (v.), fill with disgust IV.ii.161
ability, equipment I.iii.26
   power III.iii.2
abode, stay IV.ii.220
about it, (let us) get on with it IV.ii.237
abroad, in the outside world I.iii.372
abuse (v.), corrupt I.i.169, I.i.73
   deceive I.iii.61, 380, III.iii.200, 266, 334,
     IV.ii.14, 138, IV.iii.62
   slander II.i.226, 297, V.i.123
abuser, corrupter, deceiver I.ii.77
accent, tone of voice I.i.72
accident, event, happening I.i.138, I.iii.135,
   IV.ii.221, V.i.94
accommodation, suitable provision I.iii.236
accompt, figure, reckoning I.iii.5
accountant (adj.), accountable II.i.284
achieve, win II.i.60
acknown, acknowledged III.iii.317
act of sport, sexual act II.i.221
action, legal proceeding I.iii.71
addiction, inclination II.ii.6
addition, rank, title IV.i.105, IV.ii.162
   sign of honour III.iv.190
advantage, opportunity I.iii.293
advocation, advocacy, pleading III.iv.120
affect (n.), desire I.iii.259
   (v.), desire III.iii.229
affection, favouritism I.i.33
   inclination IV.iii.99, 101
   desire II.i.234
affined, bound I.i.36, II.iii.204
affinity, (family) connection III.i.44
afore, ahead V.i.128
after (adj.), following I.iii.36
agnize, acknowledge I.iii.229
aim, guess I.iii.6
alacrity, readiness I.iii.230
alarum, call to arms II.iii.23
albeit, although V.ii.346
all in all, in every respect IV.i.256
allowance, consent I.i.123
   reputation II.i.48
allowed (adj.), acknowledged I.iii.222
Almain, German II.iii.73
amazed, dumbfounded III.iii.369
   bewildered IV.ii.233
amiable, lovable III.iv.56

amiss, inappropriate IV.i.92
an; an if, if III.iv.80
ancient (n.), ensign, standard-bearer I.i.30,
   I.iii.122, I.iii.279
anon, by and by IV.i.250
   at once IV.iii.50
answerable, agreeing with, corresponding
   I.iii.339
Anthropophagi, cannibals I.iii.144
antre, cave I.iii.140
apprehend, arrest I.i.173, I.ii.76
apprehension, idea III.iii.139
appetite, desire I.iii.258, II.iii.326
approve, believe I.iii.11
   bear out II.iii.55, II.iii.294, IV.iii.52
   prove II.iii.197, II.iii.294
   esteem II.i.43, IV.iii.18
apt, likely II.i.278, V.ii.175
   willing II.iii.301
argue, indicate III.iv.34
arithmetician, (i) theorist; (ii) book-keeper
   I.i.16
arraign, indict III.iv.149
arrivance, arrivals II.i.41
article, item, detail I.iii.11, III.iii.22, V.ii.54
ashamed, humiliated II.iii.148
aspic,asp III.iii.448
assay (n.), test I.iii.19
   (v.), try II.i.118, III.iii.193
atone, reconcile IV.i.224
attach, arrest I.ii.76
attend, await III.iii.280, III.iv.189, 196
aught, anything I.iii.53, II.i.88, III.iii.102
auld, old II.iii.92
avaunt!, away! III.iii.332, IV.i.260
awhile, meanwhile II.iii.386

B

balmy, (i) fragrant; (ii) soothing V.ii.16
bang (v.), beat II.i.21
Barbary, a country on the North African
   coast I.i.108
bark (n.), ship II.i.48, II.i.181
battle, army, battalion I.i.20
bauble, worthless toy IV.i.134
bawd, procuress IV.ii.20
Bear, constellation as the Little Bear II.i.13
Before me!, Bless my soul! IV.i.142

193

beguile, rob (by distracting attention) I.iii.67, 156, 208
  disguise II.i.119
belee'd, cut off from the wind I.i.27
belie, tell lies about IV.i.37, V.ii.133
belike, probably V.ii.314
beshrew, curse IV.ii.127
Beshrew me much, I am to blame (an oath) III.iv.147
besort, company I.iii.236
bethink (yourself of), remember V.ii.26
betimes, early I.iii.365, II.iii.309
bewhore, accuse of whoredom IV.ii.114
billet (v.), lodge II.iii.358
birdlime, sticky substance for trapping birds II.i.123
blab (v.), chatter IV.i.29
black, (i) dark, brunette; (ii) wicked II.i.128, 129
blame, accusation I.iii.176
blank (n.), centre of target III.iv.125
blazon (v.), paint armorial bearings, hence praise II.i.62
blood, (i) passion; (ii) family relationship I.i.165
  (i) passion; (ii) revenge III.iii.449
  natural impulses I.iii.105, 124, 323, 329, II.i.221, II.iii.191, IV.i.266
bloody, deadly II.iii.67
  violent III.iii.467
blowing, depositing of eggs IV.ii.66
board (n.), table III.iii.24
bob (v.), swindle V.i.16
bode (v.), forebode IV.i.22
bolster (v.), lie together on a pillow III.iii.397
bombast, inflated, pompous (literally padded) I.i.12
bookish, learned I.i.21
bootless, fruitless, unavailing I.iii.207
bosom, true feelings III.i.53
bounteous, full III.iii.468
brace, state of defence I.iii.25
brave (v.), provoke V.i.323
breach, opening in a fortress wall I.iii.136
  separation IV.i.217
bridal, wedding day III.iv.147
bring away, lead out V.ii.334
bring in, reinstate III.iii.74
bring on the way, accompany III.iv.193
broil, tumult, confusion I.iii.88
brow, edge II.i.52
bulk, projecting framework of a shop V.i.1
burning, shining II.i.13
  ever-burning III.iii.461
business, affairs I.i.149
but, that I.i.61
  than I.i.121
  but that, except for the fact that III.iii.139, 225, III.iv.22, V.i.25
  merely II.i.217
  only III.iv.101, 116, V.ii.52, 60
  not to IV.iii.31

butt, (i) target; (ii) boundary V.ii.265
by this hand, I swear IV.i.170

C

cable, scope I.ii.16
  strong rope I.iii.332
caitiff, wretch IV.i.109, V.ii.315
callet, slut IV.ii.120
calmed, becalmed (figuratively thwarted) I.i.27
canakin, small can II.iii.60, 61
capable, comprehensive III.iii.457
carack, treasure ship I.ii.49
carry, bring off, achieve I.i.64
carve for (i) strike according to; (ii) indulge II.iii.159
cashiered, dismissed I.i.45
cast, reject I.i.145, III.iii.258
  dismiss II.iii.14, V.ii.324
castigation, corrective discipline III.iv.37
catechize, question III.iv.13
cause, subject of dispute III.iii.409
  (i) offence; (ii) legal case; (iii) reason V.ii.1, 3
censure, judgment II.iii.179
  opinion IV.i.261
  legal sentence V.ii.365
certes, certainly I.i.14
challenge, claim I.iii.187, II.i.205
chamberer, one who frequents ladies' chambers III.iii.264
chance (n.), accident I.iii.134
change, exchange I.iii.311, 343, II.i.151, IV.iii.98
charge, order I.i.93
charm (n.), spell I.i.167, I.ii.73, I.iii.92, V.i.35
  (v.), cast a spell on V.ii.181, 182
charmer, enchantress III.iv.54
charter, warrant, official permission I.iii.242
check (n.), rebuke I.i.144, III.iii.67, IV.iii.19
  (v.) repulse II.iii.311
cherubin, angel IV.ii.62
chidden, rebuked II.i.11
chiding, being rebuked IV.ii.113
choler, anger II.i.264
chronicle (v.), record II.i.156
chrysolite, topaz V.ii.143
chuck, sweetheart (term of endearment) III.iv.45, IV.ii.24
circumscription, restriction, confinement I.ii.26
circumstance, long-winded story I.i.12
  ceremony III.iii.352
circumstanced, resigned to circumstances III.iv.197
circumstances, existing situation III.iii.16
  circumstantial evidence III.iii.404
cistern, pond, pool IV.ii.60
civil, courteous II.i.233, II.iii.176 (i) well-mannered; (ii) belonging to the city IV.i.65

civility, decency, civilized behaviour I.i.127
clasps, embraces I.i.122
clean, completely I.iii.351
climate, clime, country I.i.67, III.iii.270
clip (v.), embrace, enfold III.iii.462
clog, restraint (literally a wooden block) I.iii.197
close (adj.), secret III.iii.123
    tight III.iii.210
closet (adj.), belonging to a closet (cabinet for private papers) IV.ii.22
clyster pipe, enema tube II.i.177
cod's head, (i) literal meaning; (ii) fool II.i.151
coffer, wooden chest II.i.202
cog (v.), cheat IV.ii.131
collied, darkened II.iii.192
coloquintida, bitter medicinal fruit I.iii.343
come into, intervene v.i.44
come near, closely affect IV.i.193
comfort, satisfaction I.iii.211, II.i.30
    joy II.i.81, 188, 201, IV.ii.158
    encouragement IV.ii.187
commission, mandate I.iii.277, II.i.28, IV.ii.215
commit, (i) perform; (ii) commit adultery IV.ii.69–79
common, (i) public; (ii) ordinary III.iii.301
commoner (n.), prostitute IV.ii.72
companion, fellow, villain IV.ii.140
compass (v.), obtain I.iii.352
    (n.), encompassing, achievement II.i.234
    scope III.iv.17
    circuit, revolution III.iv.68
    possibility IV.ii.214
complement, completeness (of appearance) I.i.60
composition, consistency, agreement I.iii.1
compt (n.), (last) reckoning v.ii.271
compulsive, forcing onward III.iii.452
conceit (n.), conception, notion III.iii.115, 324
    (v.), speculate III.iii.149
conception, fantasy III.iv.152
    (i) belief; (ii) plan v.ii.55
condition, disposition II.i.244
    (i) situation; (ii) nature IV.i.188
confidence, certainty I.iii.32
confine (n.), confinement, restriction I.ii.26
congregate, mass together II.i.68
conjunctive, allied I.iii.358
conjuration, magical incantation I.iii.93
conjure, cast a spell on I.iii.106
    adjure, instruct III.iii.293
conscionable, ruled by conscience II.i.232
consequence, following events II.iii.55
conster, construe, interpret IV.i.102
content (v.), reward II.i.1
    (adj.), calm III.iii.448
continuate (adj.), uninterrupted III.iv.174
contrived, deliberately planned I.ii.3
convenience, compatibility II.i.225

conveniency, opportunity IV.ii.175
conversation, social behaviour III.iii.263
converse, conversation III.i.35
conveyance, escort, protection I.iii.281
convince, conquer IV.i.28
cope (v.), copulate with IV.i.87
corrigible, capable of correction I.iii.321
couch (v.), lie IV.iii.57
counsel, confidence III.iii.111, IV.ii.93
counter-caster, book-keeper (used contemptuously) I.i.28
course (n.), action I.ii.85, I.iii.112, IV.i.270
    business IV.ii.92
    (v.), follow its set course III.iv.68
courser, swift horse I.i.109
courtship, (i) courtly behaviour; (ii) courting II.i.165
cousin, grandchild I.i.109
    kinsman IV.i.216
cover (v.), mate (used of animals) I.i.108
coxcomb, fool v.ii.231
cozen, cheat IV.ii.131
credit, reputation I.iii.98
    credibility I.iii.2, II.i.278
crusado, Portuguese gold coin III.iv.22
cry (v.), call for I.iii.272
    (n.), pack (of hounds) II.iii.343
cry on, exclaim v.i.48
cry you mercy, beg your pardon! IV.ii.87, v.i.69
cudgel (v.), beat II.iii.344
cue, last words of an actor's speech, as a signal to the next speaker I.ii.83
cure (n.), capable of being cured II.i.50
curlèd, with curled hair I.ii.67
customer, prostitute IV.i.120

D

daff (v.), doff, put off (usually clothing) IV.ii.173
daw, jackdaw (figuratively) fool I.i.62
dear, difficult, important I.iii.86
    dire, grievous I.iii.255
    beloved II.i.176
    (i) loving; (ii) costly II.i.282
debitor-and-creditor, book-keeper I.i.28
defeat (v), disfigure, disguise I.iii.335
    destroy IV.ii.159
defend, forbid I.iii.262
defunct, free from danger or penalty I.iii.260
degree, social rank III.iii.230
delicate, agreeable I.iii.346
    delightful III.iii.268
delighted, delightful I.iii.285
deliver, tell I.iii.91, III.iii.205
    bring to birth I.iii.361
demerit, worth, merit I.ii.21
demonstrable, evident III.iv.139
depend, be supported by I.iii.201

instrument, bodily organ I.iii.266
  written authority IV.i.211
  agent, instigator IV.ii.44
intendment, intention IV.ii.199
intentively, with full attention I.iii.155
interim, interval I.iii.254
intimation, hint IV.i.42
invention, imagination II.i.122, IV.i.185
invest, clothe IV.i.40
inwards (n.), entrails II.i.288
iterance, repetition V.ii.148

J

Janus, two-faced Roman god I.ii.32
jealous, suspicious (merging into modern
  sense of envious as well as in a
  specifically sexual sense) III.iii.183 etc.
jealousy, suspicion, vigilance (merging into
  a specifically sexual sense) III.iii.147
  etc.
jess, leather or silken thong tied to a hawk's
  foot III.iii.260
joint-ring, ring with interlocking halves
  IV.iii.73
jump (v.), agree I.iii.5
  (adv.), exactly II.iii.364
just, exact I.iii.5, II.iii.110
(do) justice, drink a health II.iii.76

K

keep, preside over III.iii.140
  stay in, manage V.ii.362
keep up, sheathe I.ii.58
  hold back III.i.23
knave, servant I.i.41, 120
  (i) servant; (ii) rascal I.i.46
knavery, villainy I.i.97
knee-crooking, obsequious I.i.42
knot (v.), twist together, copulate IV.ii.61

L

law day, meeting day for a court of law
  III.iii.140
lawn, fine linen IV.iii.74
lay (n.), wager II.iii.305
lay upon (v.), give a task to II.i.257
leaden, heavy, sad III.iv.173
leagued, joined together II.iii.204
learn, teach I.iii.192
learnèd, experienced, expert III.iii.258
leet, meeting of special court III.iii.140
lethargy, coma IV.i.54
level with, be suited to I.iii.237
lewd, vile, worthless III.iii.473
liberal (adj.), licentious II.i.159
  (i) generous; (ii) licentious III.iv.34, 42
  (adv.), freely V.ii.218

lie (v.), lodge III.iv.1, 10
  tell lies III.iv.2, 4, 7, 10
lie with, be sexually intimate with IV.i.34–37
lieutenantry, office of lieutenant II.i.166
light, worthless II.iii.100
light of brain, deranged IV.i.260
like, probable V.ii.92
like enough, probably III.iv.186
line (v.), provide a lining I.i.50
linger, prolong IV.ii.220
lip (v.), kiss IV.i.72
list (v.), listen to II.i.210
  wishes II.iii.325
  (n.), limit, barrier IV.i.76
living, real, valid III.iii.407
locust, sweet Mediterranean fruit I.iii.342
look after, look for, demand II.i.240
loose, immoral II.i.234
  careless, indiscreet III.iii.414
lost, unfounded V.ii.267
loud, urgent I.i.146
lown, rogue II.iii.81
lusty, lustful II.i.286

M

mad, reckless IV.i.230
  wild, unstable IV.iii.26
magnifico, Venetian magnate I.ii.11
maidhood, maidenhood I.i.168
main (n.), (i) strength; (ii) mane (crest of
  wave or hair)
make, do I.ii.48, III.iv.165
make after, go after I.i.65
make away, get away V.i.58
make proof of, test V.i.26
make mocks with, make a mockery of
  V.ii.149
malignant, rebellious, heathen V.ii.350
mammer, hesitate III.iii.70
man (v.), provide a man for V.ii.268
manage, conduct II.iii.201
mandate, directive I.iii.73
mandragora, mandrake, a narcotic plant
  III.iii.328
mangled, confused I.iii.172
manifest (v.), declare I.ii.31
manners, moral sense I.i.125
manure (v.), cultivate I.iii.320
marble (adj.), shining III.iii.458
Marry, By (the Virgin) Mary (an oath) I.ii.52,
  III.i.7
master, ship's captain II.i.203
masterly (adv.), authoritatively I.i.23
match (n.), marriage V.ii.203
matter, significance III.iv.136
Mauritania, part of western Africa IV.ii.219
mazzard, head (literally, drinking bowl)
  II.iii.138
means, methods III.iii.249
mediator, supporter I.i.14

pelt (v.), beat fiercely II.i.11
peradventure, perhaps II.i.283
perdition, destruction II.ii.3
    damnation III.iii.90
    loss, disaster III.iv.64
perdurable, lasting I.iii.333
perfect, completely prepared I.ii.30
performance, action IV.ii.181
peril, (own) risk I.ii.80
period, stop, conclusion V.ii.354
pernicious, evil V.ii.153, 315
perplex, confuse, bewilder V.ii.343
pioner, military trench-digger III.iii.344
Pish, nonsense! II.i.255
    expression of strong disgust IV.i.42
pith, strength I.iii.84
place, position (in society and public
    life) I.i.100, I.iii.54
    lodging I.iii.235
platform, level place for mounting guns
    II.iii.106
player, (i) play-actor; (ii) deceiver II.i.110
pleasance, pleasure II.iii.275
pliant, suitable, favourable I.iii.151
pluck, pull, drag IV.i.139
plume up, set a crest on, fully indulge
    I.iii.378
ply (v.), work on II.iii.333, IV.i.107
poise (v.), counterbalance I.iii.323.
    (n.), weight, seriousness III.iii.82
Pole, pole star II.i.14
policy, expediency II.iii.259, III.iii.14
politic (adj.), expedient III.iii.13
Pontic Sea, Black Sea III.iii.451
portance, bearing, behaviour I.iii.139
position, proposition, assertion II.i.230
post; post-haste, as fast as possible I.iii.47
potent; potential, powerful I.ii.12, I.iii.76
potting, drinking II.iii.68
pottle, two-quart measure II.iii.74
pottle-deep, to the bottom of the two-quart
    tankard II.iii.47
pox, a pox of, a plague on (an oath)
    I.iii.351
practice (n.), plot I.iii.103, III.iv.138, V.ii.289
practise (v.), plot I.ii.72, II.i.301
prate, talk boastfully, I.ii.6, II.i.218, II.iii.136
prefer, put forward, promote I.iii.110, II.i.270
preferment, promotion I.i.33
pregnant, cogent, meaningful II.i.229
preparation, hostile activity (hence) fleet
    I.iii.15, 219
preposterous, unnatural I.iii.325
prepost'rously, unnaturally I.iii.63
prerogatived, privileged III.iii.273
prescription, (i) right; (ii) medical
    prescription I.iii.305
present, urgent I.ii.89
    immediate III.iii.47
presently, at once III.i.33, V.ii.52
    very soon II.i.207, II.iii.289
price, value I.i.10

prick (v.), spur on III.iii.410
pride, sexual desire III.iii.402
prime, sexually roused III.iii.401
prithee, please (= I pray thee) I.iii.292,
    III.iii.51
prize, booty, I.ii.50
probable, demonstrable I.ii.75
probal to, provable by II.iii.317
probation, proof III.iii.363
process, proceeding, stratagem I.iii.142
proclaim, denounce I.i.66
procreant, procreator IV.ii.28
profane (adj.), foul-mouthed I.i.111, II.i.159
    (v.), insult, scorn I.iii.369
profit, benefit III.iii.79, IV.ii.227
    profitable lesson III.iii.377
Promethean, deriving from Prometheus
    V.ii.12
    Promethean heat = fire of life
prompter, stage assistant who whispers the
    words to an actor who has forgotten
    them I.ii.83
promulgate, make known I.ii.21
proof, trial I.i.25
proper, own, rightfully belonging to one
    I.iii.70, 260
    handsome I.iii.377
    (i) handsome; (ii) judicious IV.iii.35
prophetic, inspired III.iv.69
Propontic, Sea of Marmora III.iii.454
propose, (i) make suggestions; (ii) discourse
    I.i.22
propriety, normal condition II.iii.162
prospect, scene, situation III.iii.396
prosperous, favourable I.iii.241
protest (v.), declare II.iii.308, IV.ii.199
prove, test V.i.66
provender, food and drink I.i.45
pudding, (literally) stuffed pig's entrail
    (hence) stuff and nonsense! II.i.247
puddle (v.), make muddy, disturb III.iv.140
puny, petty, small V.ii.242
purchase, acquisition (not necessarily
    involving payments) II.iii.9
put from, divert, distract III.iv.85
put . . . home, thrust in V.i.2
put on, incite, encourage II.i.143, II.iii.330
put to't, test to the utmost II.i.116, III.iii.469
put up, put up with, endure IV.ii.177
putting on, incitement II.i.295

Q

qualification, dilution II.i.267
qualify, dilute II.iii.34
quality, (i) nature; (ii) profession I.iii.247
    significance I.iii.278
    character III.iii.258
    attributes III.iii.351
quarter, in quarter and in terms, in relations
    with one another II.iii.166

quat, pimple v.i.11
quest, search, search party I.ii.46
question, trial by force, struggle I.iii.24
    consideration, conversation I.iii.114
quicken, give or receive life III.iii.276,
    IV.ii.66
quiet (n.), peace of mind III.iii.152
quillet (n.), quibble III.i.23
quirk, clever flourish II.i.62

R

rack (n.), instrument of torture III.iii.333
raised, aroused, I.i.154, I.ii.28, 42, II.iii.236
rank (adj.), gross, lewd, II.i.297, III.iii.232
rash (adj.), excitedly III.iv.76
rather, earlier, more eagerly II.iii.219
recognizance, token v.ii.212
recoil (v.), (i) spring back in horror; (ii)
    return III.iii.236
recommend, advise I.iii.42
recover, reconcile II.iii.257
    obtain v.ii.238
refer, appeal I.ii.63
reference, assignment I.iii.235
regard, respect, connexion I.i.149
    view II.j.39
relume, relight v.ii.13
remembrance, keepsake III.iii.290, III.iv.182
remorse, pity, compassion III.iii.466
repeal (v.), appeal to, restore to favour
    II.iii.336
reprobation, damnation v.ii.207
reserve (v.), keep III.iii.294
resolve, convince III.iii.180
respect, relevance I.iii.278
    regard, favour II.i.205, IV.ii.187
rest (v.), remain v.ii.332
restem, steer again I.iii.38
retire, return, turn back II.iii.358, III.iii.453
reverence, solemnity III.iii.459
revolt, mutinous act I.i.130
    infidelity III.iii.188
rheum (n.), cold III.iv.47
round (adj.), plain I.iii.91
rouse (n.), full cup of liquor II.iii.57
rout (n.), disturbance II.iii.196
rude, rough I.iii.82
ruffian (v.), behave violently, rage II.i.6
ruminate, speculate, think III.iii.132

S

sadly, gravely II.i.31
Sagittary, centaur (used as an inn sign)
    I.i.154, S.D. I.ii., I.iii.116
sail, ship(s) I.iii.38
salt (adj.), lecherous II.i.234, III.iii.402
salt rheum, running cold III.iv.47
sanctimony, holiness I.iii.347
sans, without I.iii.65
satisfy, answer, content v.ii.315

saucy, outrageous I.i.124
Save you, God save you, a form of
    greeting III.iv.164
's blood, By God's blood (an oath) I.i.4
scan, consider III.iii.245
scant (v.), neglect I.iii.263
    reduce IV.iii.92
scape (n.), escape I.iii.136
    (v.), escape v.i.113
scattering (adj.), random III.iii.151
scion, cutting from plant or shoot I.iii.327
score (n.), debt III.iv.175
    (v.), add up IV.i.127
scurvy, low I.ii.7, IV.ii.139, 191
'scuse, excuse IV.i.80
seamark, (literally) object placed in sea to
    guide sailors, (here) limit v.ii.266
seamy, with seams IV.ii.145
search (n.), search party I.i.154
second (v.), support IV.ii.232
sect, (misprint for *set*?) cutting from plant.
secure (adj.), unsuspected III.iii.198,
    IV.i.72
seel (v.), blind (by sewing up eyelids)
    I.iii.265, III.iii.210
segregation, dispersal II.i.9
seize upon, confiscate v.ii.363
self bounty, innate goodness III.iii.200
self-charity, regard for oneself II.iii.188
sennight, week II.i.76
sense (n.), meaning I.iii.12
    understanding, perception,
    knowledge I.i.127, I.iii.64, 70, II.i.70,
    III.iii.336, 372
    (i) physical sensation; (ii) reason II.iii.253
    the five senses IV.iii.95
    judgment, opinion v.ii.287
    to the sense, to the quick, to bursting
    point v.i.11
sentence, punishment I.iii.210
    moral maxim I.iii.214
sequent, consecutive II.i.40
sequester, sequestration, separation
    I.iii.339, III.iv.36
servitor, servant I.iii.41
session, sitting of a law court I.ii.86,
    III.iii.140
set (v.), plant I.iii.318
    (n.), round (of the clock) II.iii.116
set on, instigate II.iii.196, 362, v.i.185, 326
several, separate, different I.ii.45
shadowing, darkening IV.i.41
shambles, slaughterhouse IV.ii.65
shape (v.), imagine II.i.54, III.iii.148
shift away, get (someone) out of the way
    IV.i.79
shipped, in a ship II.i.46
shore (v.), sheared v.ii.204
show (n.), appearance II.iii.331
shrewd, ominous III.iii.427
shrift (n.), confessional III.iii.24
sibyl, prophetess III.iv.67

siege, rank I.ii 21
signior, (Italian) sir, gentleman I.i.75, etc.
Signiory, Venetian government I.ii.17
simple, foolish IV.ii.20
simpleness, innocence I.iii.243
sir, gentleman II.i.168
sirrah, form of address to inferiors III.iv.1
sith, since III.iii.378
skillet, saucepan I.iii.268
slipper (adj.), slippery, shifty, II.i.235
slubber, sully, spoil I.iii.224
snipe, fool I.iii.370
snorting, snoring I.i.87
so, so long as III.iii.345
So, all right, so let it be IV.i.123
So help me, I swear by . . . (an oath) III.iv.123
Soft you, just a moment! V.ii.335
solicit, pray V.ii.28
solicitation, courtship IV.ii.196
solicitor, advocate, spokesman III.iii.27
soon at night, towards evening III.iv.194
sooth, truth III.iii.52
sorry, wretched, painful III.iv.47
soul, manliness I.i.51
    heart I.i.104, I.iii.115, I.iii.195, III.iii.181
    nature, character III.iii.414
span (n.), handsbreadth II.iii.63
speculative, able to see I.iii.266
speed (v.), prosper IV.i.109
spend, say I.ii.47
    squander II.iii.181
spirit, feeling I.i.100
    inclination III.iv.59
spite, utmost injury I.ii.16
spleen, (literally) seat of ill-humour (hence)
    spiteful passion IV.i.89
splinter (v.), repair with a splint II.iii.304
spoil (v.), maim V.i.54
squire, fellow IV.ii.144
stamp (v.), coin II.i.236
stand in, face I.iii.71
stand in act, be operative I.i.147
start, startle, disturb I.i.98
startingly (adv.), abruptly III.iv.76
state, authority, rank I.iii.233
stay the meat, await the meal IV.ii.168
stead (v.), be of service to I.iii.333
steep (v.), submerge IV.ii.49
steep-down, precipitous V.ii.278
still, constantly, always I.iii.129, 147,
    II.i.103, III.iii.178
stillness, steadiness II.iii.177
stomach, appetite, capacity V.ii.75
stone (v.), turn to stone, harden V.ii.63
    (n.), thunderbolt V.ii.232
stop (n.), restraint II.iii.2
    pause, hesitation III.iii.120
    obstruction V.ii.262
store (v.), (i) fill up; (ii) populate IV.iii.85
stoup, drinking vessel II.iii.26
stoutly, wholeheartedly III.i.42
stowed, put, hidden I.ii.61

straight, at once I.i.133, I.iii.49, III.iii.87,
    IV.i.58
strain (v.), urge III.iii.250
strange, unknown II.iii.231
strangeness, reserve, unfriendliness III.iii.12
stranger, alien I.i.132
strike off, pay III.iv.175
stubborn, (i) fierce; (ii) difficult I.iii.225
stuff, essence I.iii.2
suborn, bribe or otherwise induce to commit
    perjury III.iv.150
succeed on, descend to V.ii.364
success, result, consequence III.iii.222
sudden, hasty II.i.264
    immediate IV.ii.187
sufferance, suffering, damage II.i.22
sufficiency, ability I.iii.222
sufficient, capable III.iv.89, IV.i.256
suggest, tempt II.iii.331
suit, petition I.i.8
    courtship IV.i.26
supervisor, onlooker III.iii.393
supply (v.), fill with a substitute III.iii.17
    sexually satisfy IV.i.28
sure (adv.), certainly III.iv.137
surety, certainty I.iii.375
surfeit (v.), enlarge II.i.49
swag-bellied, with a hanging belly
    II.iii.69
sweat (v.), exert III.iii.73
sweeting, sweetheart II.iii.238
swelling, inflated, full to overflowing
    II.iii.48
sympathy, agreement II.i.223

T

taint (v.), impair I.iii.267, IV.ii.160
    speak slightingly of II.i.260
take order for, arrange V.ii.72
take out, copy III.iii.295, III.iv.176,
    IV.i.147, 150, 152
take up, settle I.iii.172
task (v.), strain II.iii.36
teem, become pregnant IV.i.236
tell, strike (of bell or clock) II.ii.10
    count III.iii.169
    never tell me, I don't believe you! I.i.1
temper, degree of hardness and flexibility of
    steel V.ii.251
tenderly, easily I.iii.386
term, respect, regard I.i.36
terrible, terrifying I.i.79
test, testimony, evidence I.iii.108
theoric, theoretical knowledge I.i.21
thereunto, in addition II.i.138
thick-lips, negro (used contemptuously)
    I.i.63
thing, female sex organ III.iii.300
thrice-driven, three times sifted, i.e. softest
    I.iii.229
thyme, a kind of herb I.iii.318

tilt, thrust II.iii.169

timorous, frightening I.i.72

title, legal right to possession I.ii.30

toged, wearing togas I.i.22

top (v.), be on top in sexual intercourse
III.iii.394, v.ii.136

touch (v.), come near, affect closely II.iii.206,
IV.i.193
test III.iii.81

toy, trifle I.iii.264
idle fancy III.iii.156

trace (v.), follow after II.i.294

trade, profession, calling I.ii.1

trash, worthless object III.iii.157
worthless person II.i.294, v.i.85

traverse, quick march! I.iii.361

trespass, offence (archaic) III.iii.64

trick (n.), delusion IV.ii.128

trimmed, decked out I.i.47

triumph (n.), festivity II.ii.4
(v.), celebrate victory IV.i.119

trump (n.), trumpet III.iii.349

trumpet (v.), proclaim I.iii.246

tup, copulate with I.i.86

Turk, ruler of Turkey I.iii.21, 23, 28
heathen II.i.112

turn (v.), return IV.i.243
(i) play false; (ii) have sexual intercourse
IV.i.244–5

tush, nonsense (an oath) I.i.1

twiggen, covered with wicker work II.iii.134

'twixt, for *betwixt*, between II.i.3

U

unauthorized, illicit IV.i.2

unbitted, unbridled, unrestrained I.iii.326

unbonneted, on equal terms (literally, with
hat off) I.ii.22

unbookish, ignorant IV.i.102

undertaker, person to deal with IV.i.204

unfold, expose III.iii.243, IV.ii.140, v.i.21

unfolding, narrative, explanation I.iii.241

unhandsome, (i) unfair; (ii) inept III.iv.148

unhappy, bad, unsuitable II.iii.29

unhatched, unaccomplished III.iv.138

unhoused, unconfined I.ii.25

unkind, (i) unnatural; (ii) cruel IV.i.217

unlace, loosen, undo II.iii.180

unless, except for I.i.21

unlucky, unfortunate v.ii.338

unperfectness, imperfection II.iii.280

unproper, (i) not exclusive to a person;
(ii) defiled IV.i.69

unprovide, weaken IV.i.199

unswear, deny on oath IV.i.31

unwit (v.), drive mad II.iii.168

use (n.), habit IV.i.265
experience IV.iii.106

usurped, assumed I.iii.335

V

vantage, advantage, gain IV.iii.85

venial, excusable IV.i.9

venture (v.), risk IV.iii.77

Veronesa (n.), (ship) belonging to Verona
II.i.25

vessel, human body IV.ii.82

vexation, torment I.i.69

vicious, mistaken (as well as modern sense)
III.iii.145

virtue, power, ability I.iii.314, 315

virtuous, efficacious III.iv.108

visage, assumed appearance I.i.47

voice, approval, consent I.iii.223, 256

voluble, glib, persuasive II.i.232

voluntary, pertaining to the will IV.i.27

votarist, person under a religious vow
IV.ii.185

vouch (n.), testimony II.i.143
(v.), affirm I.iii.104, 107, 257

W

wage (v.), risk I.iii.31

want (v.), miss III.iii.340

warrant (n.), authority, justification I.ii.78,
III.iii.20, v.ii.60
(v.), swear III.iii.3.

wash, drench v.ii.278

watch (n.), division of the night I.i.119
(v.), stay awake II.iii.116, III.iii.284
(v.), prevent from sleeping (of a hawk)
III.iii.23
(v.), look out for IV.ii.230

wayward, capricious III.iii.291

web, weaving III.iv.66

well-painted, well-pretended IV.i.248

well said, well done II.i.162, IV.i.115, v.i.98

wheeling, wandering, restless I.i.132

whereon, at which point, whereupon
III.iii.84

whipster, contemptible fellow v.ii.242

whistle off, release hawk from fist III.iii.261

wholesome, healthy I.i.141
reasonable III.i.44

wight, person II.i.154

will, desire (often sexual desire) I.iii.341,
III.iii.232, 236, IV.ii.151
intention I.iii.378

wink (v.), close the eye IV.ii.76

wise, (i) prudent; (ii) sane IV.i.225

wit, sense, intelligence I.i.131, II.i.126, 129,
II.iii.347, 350, 351, III.iii.464, III.iv.17,
etc.

withal, with I.iii.94

witty, clever, wise II.i.128

womaned, accompanied by a woman
III.iv.191

wondrous, exceedingly (archaic) I.iii.161

works, fortifications III.ii.3

worser, worse I.i.92
would, I wish III.iii.244, 388, IV.i.264
wrangle (v.), dispute angrily III.iv.141
wretch, a term of affection III.iii.90
wrought, worked up V.ii.342

Y

yawn (v.), gape, split open V.ii.101

yerk, thrust I.ii.5
yoked, married IV.i.67

Z

zounds, by God's wounds (an oath) I.i.83,
        I.i.105, IV.i.37